# THE LAWS OF LIBRARY SCIENCE

# THE LAWS OF LIBRARY SCIENCE

**John D'Souza**

**CYBER TECH PUBLICATIONS**
4264/3, Ansari Road, Daryaganj, New Delhi-110002 (India)
Ph.: 011-23244078, 011-43559448 Fax: 011-23280028
E-Mail: cyberpublicationsdelhi@yahoo.com
Website: www.cybertechpublications.com

THE LAWS OF LIBRARY SCIENCE

**John D'Souza**



First Edition 2010



Asian Offset Printers

*Published by :*

**G.S. Rawat** for **Cyber Tech Publications**
4264/3, Ansari Road, Daryaganj, New Delhi-110002 (India)
Ph.: 011-23244078, 011-43559448 Fax: 011-23280028
E-Mail: cyberpublicationsdelhi@yahoo.com
Website: www.cybertechpublications.com

# Preface

Mr. Ranganathan's treatment of the subject is clear, logical and lucid. He has brought to his task extensive knowledge of the literature on the subject of libraries, personal acquaintance with the methods of management of libraries in Britain, a trained analytical intellect and a fervid but enlightened enthusiasm for the library movement. He has been the pioneer of the library movement in the Madras presidency and has been carrying on an energetic propaganda to spread it. He knows how to rouse and sustain the interest of the reader and has produced a very attractive and readable book. I have no doubt it will meet with wide appreciation and soon come to be recognised as a standard text-book of library science.

The five laws of library science are some of the most influential concepts in that field. Since they were published in 1931, these five laws "have remained a centerpiece of professional values...". These basic theories of library Science continue to directly affect the development of this discipline and the service of all libraries. S.R. Ranganathan's early education was of a mathematic background. This systematic way of thinking, he later applied to his work in library science, most notably his work on library classification and administration. From the middle of the nineteenth century, librarians in the west felt the need and started emphasizing the importance of enhanced services to library patrons. Formulation of the five laws of library science at long last, provided a solid and lasting foundation in this direction. The aim of this publication has been to identify and arrange together all these relevant materials on and about the life and works of Ranganthan and impact of Ranganathan's contribution on librarianship, comparative librarianship and other aspects of the library and information science

— *Author*

# CONTENTS

# 1

# Introduction

## FIRST LAW

It is wrong to conclude from my words that books are the only library materials that matter to me. My point is that libraries must acquire materials and make them accessible so they can be used. This law gives definition both to the concept of an open-stack library and to a library that is appointed with tools and furnishings that make the books it contains useful. Books are to be taken from locked back rooms and brought out to welcoming rooms with open shelves. Shelves need to be accessible to more than one user at a time. Libraries are to be located in the midst of their communities. Whatever be the library location, hours of operation, type of furniture and the way in which books are kept, it is the Library Staff that ultimately make or mar a library. A Modern Librarian who has faith in this law is happy only when the readers make the shelves constantly empty.

## SECOND LAW

This law reveals the fundamental issue of tension between the cost of materials and the basic right of all persons to have access t the materials they need. This makes acquisitions very important; each acquisition should call to mind a potential user. One must always be mindful that since no one individual can own all the 'books', the libraries must acquire a body of literature or research materials that will benefit each of its readers and researchers.

The collection must be appropriate to the Library's Mission. Librarians must know the materials, its uses, and how to use it. Reference service gains its legitimacy and its purpose from this law. Clearly, it is the business of librarians to know the reader, to know the books, and to actively help in the finding by every person of his or her book.

**Third Law**

This law addresses the fundamental issue of open access. Open access means that the collection can be examined with as much freedom as if it was the reader's private library. In addition, when a library user comes to the library, or gains access to the library's services, there are certain materials that will meet his or her needs. It is the library's job to ensure that the connection between the user and the materials are made, and that the connection is as speedy and practical as possible. There are many ways in which a library can connect its users to its resources:

Distribution of acquisition lists

New Book displays

Providing Research Guides

Newsletters

*Book Lists*

The use of a structured, well-thought out classification scheme is a necessity for connecting library users to materials, a. it ensures uniformity of treatment of various materials on similar topics. Also important is the accurate arrangement of materials, as misshelving a book can make it all but invisible to the user.

**Fourth Law**

Perhaps this law is not so self-evident as the others. None the less, it has been responsible for many reforms in library administration. A Library must examine every aspect of its policies, rules, procedures, and systems with the one simple criteria that saving the time of the reader is vital to the library's mission. Policies must formulate with the needs of the library's user in mind. For example, hours of operation must be set in order to ensure appropriate and convenient access, and the collection must be arranged in an inviting, clear, and obvious way so as not to waste the time of the users. Saving time of the user means providing efficient, thorough access to materials.

### Fifth Law

The 5th law tells us about the vital and lasting characteristics of the library as an institution and enjoins the need for a constant adjustment of our outlook in dealing with it. Libraries grow and change, and will always do so. Collections increase and change, technology changes and budgets change. Change comes along with growth, and in order to be healthy, that change and growth requires flexibility in the management of the collections, in the use of space, in the recruitment, retention and deployment of staff, and the nature of our programmes.

My laws are meant to be elemental, in order to capture essential meaning and to convey a deep understanding of libraries. As libraries change with time these laws are meant to endure. However, I would like to express how these Laws pertain to the present state of information management and access.

Limiting access to books has prevailed through time, and exists even today. The maintenance of special collections with limited access, storing materials off-site, restricting access to libraries based on membership or fees, and even by selecting materials that are contracted in such a way as to limit use, such as when print resources are eliminated in favour of an electronic version of the material that is only accessible to certain patrons with passwords, are all modern equivalents of chaining books to the shelves.

Another aspect of this first law that is still relevant is that libraries are about service or they are about nothing. In order to deliver and reap the rewards of services, libraries must identify the benefits that society can reasonably expect and then devise means of delivering those benefits. Service always has a purpose, and our careers of service still have purpose.

## Every Reader His or Her Book

Any library that limits access in any way must ensure that this restriction does not prevent adequate access to the collection by the people that the library was created to serve. Access policies also have implications for interlibrary loan, cooperative acquisitions, and consortia to which the library may belong. Libraries must also be concerned with programmes that provide for the preservation of materials in alternate formats, such as microfiche, CD-ROM, and other electronic formats. Librarians need to ask themselves:

*Which formats are appropriate?*

*Which format will be most useful for the user?*

*What additional hardware or software must be acquired to facilitate their usage?*

*Who will or won't have access?*

*What are the issues surrounding access to printing, passwords, etc.?*

Librarians must acknowledge that users of the libraries, themselves included, use and value different means of communications in the pursuit of knowledge, information and entertainment. Libraries must value all means of preserving and communicating the records and achievements of the human mind and heart.

## Every Book its Reader

In the digital age, getting the 'book' to its reader presents librarians with unique challenges, and the challenges presented by the emergence of electronic resources cannot be overstated! Libraries today must deal with electronic resources that are available 'within' the library but are neither owned nor shelved by the library. Libraries also have the additional challenge of providing access to 'cyber visitors' who use the library's web site for research. Technology, when intelligently applied, is a wonderful, life-enhancing thing. Technology exists to support the mission of librarians to assist in ready and free access to recorded knowledge and information, and to deliver library services effectively. However, technology must be useful, affordable, and cost-effective, and anything beyond that is on the path to dashed expectations and skewed priorities.

### Save the Time of the Reader

When a library subscribes to electronic resources, appropriate access to them must be provided. When electronic databases are made available to the public, public access terminals and printing resources must also be made available. Naturally, libraries must also make the best use of available IP and networking technology. If materials are stored off-site (which in essence breaks the first law), provision must be made for easy and timely retrieval of those items. Well-planned and executed library handbooks, stack guides, and library tours, or research instruction sessions also serve the goal of saving the time of the reader. The library must also provide adequate staffing of reference, information, and circulation desks, as well as telephone and chat reference. Ultimately, employing the best available technologies to provide quick access to materials saves the time of the reader.

### The Library is a Growing Organism

I have shown, both in my original writings and in the adaptations of those laws to the present, how libraries have changed over time. The most obvious change I've addressed here is the shift to electronic resources. This shift has had a major impact on library funding and budget management.

It is a common fallacy among many library administrators (professionals and non-librarians alike) who control library budgets that one way to save money is to merely cancel groups of subscriptions and then restart them in a year or so. As a living organism, libraries consume information, and any cessation in the flow of information starves the organism. Cutting a library off from its resources at any arbitrary point will surely make it ill, and perhaps may even kill it.

## RULES GOVERNING THE USE OF LIBRARY

***General:***

1. The Library will remain open from 8-00 a.m. to 8.00 p.m. on all working days except Tuesdays. On Tuesdays

& Sundays it will remain open from 11-00a.m. to 6-00 p.m.

2. The following persons are entitled to make use of the books etc., within the Library premises:
   a Members of the authorities of the University and members of Committees and various Bodies appointed by the University authorities;
   b. Teachers of the Karnatak University;
   c. The University employees;
   d. Graduates of this or any other statutory University and teachers recommended by the Dean or the Head of the University Department or the Principal of an affiliated/constituent college;
   e. Students of the University Departments holding identity cards;
   f. Students of the constituent/affiliated colleges and recognized institutions, recommended by the Heads of the Departments/Institutions;
   g. Other persons with the special permission of the Chairman of the Library
   h. Persons, enrolled for the external degree examinations conducted by the Karnatak University and ex-students of the University, can also become regular readers by paying a fee of Rs.125/-only, per term. Such readers will, however, not be eligible to borrow books from the Library.

**Advisory Board or the Librarian**

3. Identity Cards will be issued to postgraduate and research students by the Librarian on an application to be made in the prescribed from. The Identity Card will be valid for one academic year only and may be cancelled in the middle of the year by the Chairman of the Library Advisory Board on the recommendations of the Librarian in case of infringement of any of the Library Rules or for misconduct.

4. Every postgraduate/research student shall be required to show, while entering the Library the Identity Card to the Attendant at the Counter and write his/her name and the Identity Card number in the Register provided for the purpose. On demand by the Library staff, the student is required to show the Identity Card.

***Use of Books:***

5. Every person taking a book out of the Library and every reader using a book within the Library shall be responsible for its safe custody and return, undamaged in any manner, and in the event of its being lost or damaged (including pencil or ink markings) he shall either replace the book or pay the compensation as may be fixed by the Library Advisory Board.

6. A new book shall not, normally, be taken out of the Library during the first week after it has been classified and catalogued.

7. Every periodical publication shall be displayed till the receipt of the next number and shall not normally be taken out of the Library.

8. Manuscripts will be issued for reference purpose in the Library only with the special permission of the Chairman of the Library Advisory Board/Librarian.

9. Readers shall not write on, or damage, or turn down the leaves or make any mark on any book, manuscript or map belonging to the Library; nor shall they lay the paper on which they are writing on a book, manuscript or map etc. belonging to the Library.

10. Any reader noticing a defect in, or damage to any book or manuscript in the Library should bring it to the notice of the Librarian or the Assistant Librarian on duty.

11. No tracing, copying or mechanical reproduction of any book, map or manuscript shall be done without the express permission of the Librarian.

## DO DIGITAL LIBRARIES VIOLATE THE THIRD LAW?

An ideology of librarianship was created by Shiyali Ramamrita (SR) Ranganathan in his classic *The Five Laws of Library Science* (Bombay: Asia Pub. House, 1963). He formulated objectives and principles for the organization of, access to, and use of library materials. Given the changing information world, this is a good time to reconsider Ranganathan's five laws:

1. Books are for use.
2. Every reader, his book.
3. Every book, its reader.
4. Save the time of the reader.
5. A library is a growing organism.

These normative laws embrace standards of practice and are fundamental to what librarians and researchers do. They have points of similarity with the American Library Association's Library Bill of Rights, which might help explain why *The Five Laws* continue to have such consonance for American librarians. Now that researchers and librarians work in a digital environment, it is useful to see how they apply to "library" activities in the electronic world. To begin that examination we focus on the third law, "Every book, its reader," because of its particular relevance in the current proliferation of electronic resources.

The popularity of various "free" resources like Google and Yahoo has often drowned out the authoritative and authentic information that users would value if they could find it easily. We would not allow such third law "violations" in the print world. More important, we are not taking advantage of new ways to engage the principle of the third law.

### Maximum Connections

The third law concerns context rather than raw content. The mission of the librarian is to build a well-organized collection of resources in order to maximize the chance that users will find what they need. The third law is also subtle. "Every book, its reader" almost means that "resources look for people." Thus, the job of librarians is to help these resources find the people who want and need them the most. Library patrons, Ranganathan points out, often do not know enough about available resources to know what to request. Any organization of the electronic or physical library that focuses only on getting the readers what they ask for neglects two key components of good library practice: browsing and linking.

"The majority of readers do not know their requirements, and their interests take a definite shape only after seeing and handling a well-arranged collection of books," Ranganathan wrote. An example of how he applied the third law was the issue of open access to library stacks. We have all looked for a specific book and in the process discovered one we absolutely needed next to it or even on the opposite shelf. Ranganathan measured the great upsurge in circulation after the library went to open stacks. A significant number of books circulated that had never been requested before. They had been useless according to the first law, then they came back into use.

Ranganathan also writes about the importance of good catalogs, especially those with effective cross references. He advocates good marketing of library resources. He even suggests popularizing certain books as parts of edited series, so patrons learn that a book has "cousins" on other or related topics. In this way, Ranganathan suggested, new vistas are opened to users via books similar in style and approach to books they already know and like. Amazon.com implements a similar service with the "customers who bought this book also bought" feature to deliver relevant recommendations.

## A "Well-arranged" E-collection

Now, 70 years since Ranganathan formulated his laws, the challenge of creating a well-arranged collection of electronic library resources for patrons has made application of the third law problematic. With resources growing at an exponential rate, to maximize the ability of patrons to find what they want (even if they do not yet know it) is more difficult. Face-to-face coaching of information seekers is often impossible. Even such interactions do not necessarily make for more sophisticated users of the library. The 2003 OCLC Environmental Scannoted that "as users become more experienced and more discriminating, the shortcomings of current search solutions are surfacing.... All focus group participants felt that easier search methods are needed."

Because of today's confusing array of resources, new violations of the third law have emerged. Consider search engines. No one focused on creating a "well-arranged collection" of e-resources can ignore that users are going to Google for quick or even substantive information requests. Google gives marvelously fast access to massive amounts of information (and misinformation). It is almost everyone's favourite place for a quick search. In fact, one could say that Google usually passes the fourth law (save the time of the reader) with flying colours—except when the plethora of hits slows the reader down. With the advent of Google Print and particularly Google Scholar, more and more students and researchers will begin their work on Google.

While Google was not originally designed as a library resource, it is now so prevalent in libraries that we must test whether it measures up to the principles of librarianship. We must ask if Google meets the demands of Ranganathan's Third Law. Most information seekers using Google never go past the first page of results. Google's criteria for what goes on that first page are popularity and payment for placement. It is unlikely Google will change that. Library resources should match Google's ease of use but not its criteria for first page listing. Library tools must exhibit all the qualities of what Ranganathan calls a "well-arranged collection."

Such resources should have authority and carry attribution to the providers and authors who compiled the information. They should have citation formats so users can cite this information easily. They should provide excellent cross-referencing, not just within a single work but from work to work and to works from other providers. In a virtual library, the user wants the information to flow seamlessly, with no technical obstacles. The user should not be constrained to a selection of available information that is "book-bound," "publisher-bound," or even "subject-bound." At the same time, users must not be overwhelmed by a million meaningful but similar hits or blinded from seeing the one in a million entries they would find useful or enjoyable. Information should be organized for self-directed and learner-empowered inquiries. In such a schema, the best qualities of well-arranged collections contribute to the search.

### The Invisible Library

In Ranganathan's day, resources were hidden from the library user through closed stacks, poor displays, or a lack of services such as bookmobiles. Reference books are still often locked up in a "Reference Room" rather than available online for convenience.

Today, e-resources often remain hidden from the user. Our reliance on consumer-focused search engines leaves whole portions of the web inaccessible—the "invisible web," as Chris Sherman and Gary Price call it in their book *The Invisible Web* (CyberAge Bks., 2001). The larger the invisible web, the less likely resources will reach users. Google Print, OCLC's Open WorldCat, and similar initiatives provide ways for people to find these otherwise hidden resources.

In some libraries we see "The Invisible Library"—electronic resources hidden from users because they are not fully integrated into the many pathways by which readers look for information. Design choices by vendors or librarians have meant that in many libraries even electronic resources are organized as "closed stacks." Only those who already know how to search them will get to that information. Like circulating print reference books, electronic open stacks need to be freely accessible to searchers and browsers alike.

Some examples of electronic open stacks include adding proper MARC records to the catalogue; providing good integration with teachers' class pages from learning management systems; making good use of metasearch and link-resolving tools; and enabling contextual linking from library site pages and subject guides. Even diversions like a crossword solver or trivia quizzes linked into e-reference content can give the uninitiated exposure to electronic resources that they didn't know were in the library.

**Electronic Browsing**

Browsing allows the reader to match one unknown with another. The reader finds "what I really want even though I didn't know it," including all that is in the electronic library, even the most recent additions. Librarians must extend their work to facilitate browsing beyond the book stacks. While some of the joy of leafing through a good reference work is not possible online, new methods of browsing are feasible and nearly as much fun. Resources must be properly prepared, organized, and integrated. Some publishers (Alexander Street, Greenwood) are producing resources that can be traversed by time and geography. At least one publisher-neutral aggregator of reference sources (Xrefer) provides semantic, contextual, cross reference links across a librarian-customized collection of hundreds of reference works. [Coauthor Dove is the CEO of Xrefer.]

A librarian must use the opportunities inherent in the online environment to break out of the confines of the book. Posting flat content that's isolated into publisher-or book-specific silos won't work. Compelling online content needs interactivity and context. It must let the user find information in multiple ways and places. There should be no borders and barriers. If there are, passing or crossing them should be simple, even automatic. If searchers want to find all the people born in a particular country in the field of literature during a particular decade, help them do it quickly. Today's hyperlinked and networked users expect to find their information this way.

**The Semantic Web**

The computer screen is an excellent medium for dynamic and two-dimensional representations (or more, if you add colour, shapes, motion, or sound as indicators). An example of a multidimensional visual display of information is in what Xrefer is now calling its Concept Map. Intelligently built e-resources should help users discover things they didn't know they didn't know. A user browsing online should also be able to toggle between browse mode and search-and-read mode. Such self-directed learning is our goal.

Browsing and subsequent reading should show the reader the sources and their origin. While no library should be organized by provider, a user must be able to discern—and cite—the sources of information. A digital divide still exists. There are people for whom electronic networks are not yet accessible. There are information literacy barriers. Until they are eliminated, Ranganathan's "every reader, his book" and "every book, its reader" will remain unrealized.

Tim Berners-Lee, James Hendler, and Ora Lassila called for "The Semantic Web" (*Scientific American*, May 2001, p. 34–43) to enhance the web experience for everyone. This challenge will require web content creators to design new interfaces and pathways. In the electronic library, where we can assemble the best resources for our patrons, we have the chance now to apply the principles of the semantic web to their content, or select vendors that do.

The third law is violated when valuable resources that would truly delight the reader are effectively hidden away or crowded out by the noise and onslaught of irrelevant data. With increasing access to more resources and more ways to search for them, every book or information source can make its way to its appropriate user. As Ranganathan asserted, "It should be the business of...the librarian...to adopt all the recognized methods of attracting the public to the library, so that every potential reader may be converted into an actual one, thereby increasing the chances for the fulfilment of the Third Law."

Ranganathan's Third Law, inherently the most elusive of the five, is the most forceful. Getting authoritative information sources to potential users is the raison d'être of librarians and libraries.

## Abiding by the Third Law

By the Law :

- Implement as many pathways as you can for readers to get to any resource

- Focus on obtaining resources that enable semantic linking, not just at the title level but at the word and phrase level
- Establish subject gateways
- Market relevant portions of electronic resources via library homepages and email
- Empower teachers, professors, and subject experts to provide links to relevant material in the electronic library
- Provide personal reference support and advice anywhere and anytime with services like email and chat reference
- Pay attention to marketing: do everything that retailers do and more to catch the interest of those who would get a lot out of your electronic resources but might not know about them or how to use them
- Meet the users where they already are—online!

Against the Law:

- Fail to install MARC records for your electronic resources
- Spend all of your budget on print reference resources that can be used only ten hours a day and are limited to use in the reference room, when that same resource could be available 24/7 and remotely
- Organize online resources by publisher or brand name, forcing users to know the specific trade names of bundled resources in order to access them
- Allow vendors to charge fees in proportion to usage or based on number of simultaneous users. These usage restrictions pit the mission of librarianship against the constraints of the budget
- Assume that your entire patron base has access to your electronic resources just because you have purchased and installed them
- Fail to think through what barriers there might be for different sectors of your users

## THE FIVE LAWS IN INFORMATION SOCIETY AND VIRTUAL LIBRARIES ERA

The Delhi Library Association is to be commanded for being a vibrant association with a vision. It is a model for other professional organizations. Thus it is a great honour and a privilege to be invited to deliver S.R. Ranganathan Memorial Lecture instituted by this Association. In all my professional life I have endeavoured to spread the message and zeal of Ranganathan. This is a great and unique opportunity. I am grateful to the DLA Executive Committee, especially the President, Sh. Girja Kumar, and Secretary, Professor C.P. Vashisth for bestowing this honour on me.

### Origin of the Laws

Ranganathan was highly impressed and influenced by the library services to each and every citizen of the U.K. given by its library system. I But despite the devoted teachers with best minds having wide and varied experience, Ranganathan found library science teaching a bundle of tricks in the School of Librarianship and Mhives, University College, London during 1924-1925. His inquisitive and analytical mind inured on philosophy and mathematics could not submit itself to what he considered unworthy practices and rules that were taught to be remembered by the rule of the thumb-take it as such or leave it. After a great deal of pondering and further experience of library work, he realized the lack of normative principles to guide and explain the myriads of library practices then prevailing.

The prescription lay in formulation of normative principles to cure the hodgcpodge situation. He realized that library is a social institution providing service to the society. By the late 19th century the scientific method had already been successfully applied to what later became social sciences.. Professor Pierce Butler (1886-1953) and his colleagues at Library School of the University of Chicago had already advocated the use of scientific methods to library management. Having diagnosed the malady, Ranganathan set out to discover and formulate the normative laws governing libraries. This, a stupendous task, required lot of intensive experience, insight, vision and a catalyst of intuition. Intuition helps the large number of empirical precepts to boil down to a few fundamental laws. Ranganathan with perseverance and keeping the problem in the subconscious mind analytically observed all the practical details to distil them into laws. This dramatic story of the origin and formulation of laws has been told and retold by Ranganathan.

Thereafter, Ranganathan set out to elucidate and deduce their general implications. Conformity of the deductions with the existing practices confirmed their validity. Subsequently these were fully developed and published in a book in 1931 with the title: The Five Laws of Library Science (Chennai: Madras Library Association, xxxii, 458p.) The book was an instant success despite the doubts of some sceptics on the scientific nature of our work.

The second edition was brought out in 1957 when he had gained immense experience of teaching and observation of documentation work in R & D centres in India, Europe and USA. The second edition also contained a chapter on the nature of science and scientific methods to convince others that library service lay in this domain. It reached more hands than the earlier edition. There was even a unfulfilled demand for an American edition of the book in American English. Nevertheless, it got him deservedly famous. To quote Pauline Cochrane "If Dr. Ranganathan had done nothing more than publish the Five Laws of Library Science, he would have to be seriously considered for the Library Hall of Fame".

The Laws have stood the test of time as these became more and more acceptable as the time passed by. The popularity continued even after Ranganathan's death as evident from comments on them in different languages of the world, *e.g.*, in Chinese. To say that they are mere slogans is to be ignorant of the nature and structure of scientific laws.

These laws have not been dictated from above. These are not statements of opinions or mere ideals of a missionary. These are shared definitions of ideal conduct. These laws have been precipitated and sifted from actual practices in all categories of libraries. Ranganathan had an uncanny gift to do this. Peter Achinstein, a philosopher of science, lays down the Following lingual characteristics of a stated laws:

- Laws are simple, precise, and few in number.
- Laws are essentially general in nature.
- Their subject is general.
- Syntactically they are general, as they generally begin with "All", "Every", or "No".
- A law expresses a generality which can be used to express other regularities.

Simplicity does not mean shallowness, but it is in unraveling the complex structure of universe in that discipline, and stating that in simple linear equations. Simplicity lies in the smallness of numbers of parameters and their interrelations.

How strikingly and easily the Five Laws qualify Achinstein test is too obvious. From philosophical and epistemological standpoints they fully hold the status of the laws. These are quite simple in appearance as the basic laws always are and should be. These laws are not anything invented or imposed but have been discovered and formulated. Struck by their simplicity many votaries wondered as to why these laws could not be formulated earlier!

Their acceptance as normative laws has been acknowledged by numerous library scientists and practitioners. With time not only these have attracted more adheres and advocates, but they continue to be valid in changing library environment. Laws inhere modernity and have self renewing power of applications.

The laws are subject to the Quarnic principle of ijihad-a principle of reinterpretation. In his life time Ranganathan had shown them to be equally applicable to documentation work. In the succeeding era of intensive and pro-active service of micro-documents by information canters his disciples and others have demonstrated the validity of laws by simply changing the parameter "book" to 'information". The laws have logico-deductive structure. They evince to hold latently, or as obvious corollaries, every practice current or future. They attest the dictum that a true theory is a repertoire of practice. The laws have proved fountainhead of his path breaking and voluminous work. They further attest Francis Bacon's conviction in the Novum Organum that "axioms rightly discovered... will draw after them trains and troops of work".

They have prognostic value and portend towards the future trends as elucidated by FW Lancaster. These laws provided fundamental statements of goals that information services should strive for, and they are as relevant today as they were... years ago."" The Five laws hold the reins of every bit of theory applicable to information services. It requires a moderately inventive mind to deduce from them) new principles from time to time. All the /ultra-modern services of information centres could be deduced from or validated by the Five Laws. Automated libraries have witnessed their applications more tangibly. But every invention is grounded in social milieu of its time. Is not the information society environment with virtual libraries radically different one?

**Information Society**

Ushered by the information revolution, the information society has heralded a new era in human civilization. It has brought in wide and far reaching changes: new modes and technology of Communication, new life and work styles and new modes of education. It has been facilitated by democracy and free flow of information. Not only the outlook seems different, there is a clear shift in economic and social values. Information Technology (IT) has emerged as the most powerful agent of social change and economic transformation. The IT has made constantly swelling volume of knowledge ever accessible to the masses. New forms of telecommunications spread cornucolpia of information round the world in a split second and diffuse it with amazing' speed. The Internet has brought more knowledge in circulation than ever before.

Information society is witnessing the power of information and knowledge' at its best. Today the information is most valuable and sought after commodity and a resource. It is prime mover of the society. Production, distribution and consumption of information has multiplied to astronomical figures. Knowledge is now an international public good and its benefits extend to all those who can access it irrespective of political boundaries.

Investment in its generation gives much higher returns than in production of industrial goods. Recent economic theories indicate that growth of knowledge can generate endless potential for economy. Knowledge growth is brought out by Institutions of higher education and research through R & D. Libraries help generate more knowledge by disseminating it. Investments in Knowledge creation and dissemination is becoming an engine of economic growth, sophisticated and systematic theoretical knowledge aides advances in every social sphere.

Economy, social mores and politics have been affected visibly. Social laws, values and attitudes are changing. Fast flow of information is radically changining social relations and have brought in new educational technology, especially for distance learning. The governments world over are acquiring new roles while jettisoning some old jobs. The MNCs are acquiring para governmental roles. Free and fast flow of information, easy and inexpensive means of transportation, fall of dividing lines have shrunk the world into a global village where everybody and place is connected and wired. Political structure need redesigning. This in turn has resulted in the emergence of world economy, cosmopolitan culture and international movements. New techniques in genetics and molecular biology have transformed the quality of life throwing both formidable geographical, cultural, ethical and legal issues. In fact a whole range of political issues have cropped up. Feminine, human rights, green peace movements, even international terrorism, and rampant cyber crimes are product of the information revolution. Today's wars are info-wars in many senses of the term. Social and cultural mobility brought in by globalization has been well stated by S.T.Hettige.

Today, the market forces plays significant part in the distribution of life chances in society. Almost unrestricted flow of information, media images and cultural goods into the country has facilitated the spread of—new life styles and consumption patterns. As. result consumption based life styles and social identities today openly complete with conventional life styles and identities based on social positions occupied by individuals. In the new environments, the dress, hairstyles, personal possessions, consumer tastes, hobbies etc. may be even more important than the actual occupational roles individuals occupy.

This shift requires the enactment of new cyber laws on the part of the governments and legislators.

Knowledge society is an ever learning society. Alvin Toffler has aptly said that the illiterates of the 21st century will not be those who cannot read and write, but those who cannot learn, unlearn and relearn. Eric Hoffer has emphasized the same value with a warning: "In a time of drastic change, it is the learners who survive; the learned find themselves fully equipped to live in a world that no longer exists". Its citizens have to constantly acquire new set of skills. Full literacy is the minimum basic requirement. Spread of participatory democracy moves in tandem with the knowledge and information revolution.

Alvin Toffler in a long drawn empirical and analytical study of the social and economic trends distils the following characteristics of the information society:

a. Knowledge creation and transfer leads to creation of wealth.

b. Industrial production has become cyclic, customized and de- massified with the use of IT.

c. Knowledge is a superior substitute for the conventional factors of production, such as land, labour, raw materials and capital.

d. Electronic information, being eminently fluid, has become a fine medium of exchange.

e. Managers, researchers and information professionals are the new heroes of the information society.

f. Producer and the consumer fuse into a "prosumer".

g. This global and wired society allows local production with global technology.

## New Features and Roles of Library and Information Centres

Libraries and information canters are the warehouses of the most valuable goods of the information society. Information production is in astronomical quantities leading to information overload in many cases. See how the internet is taking everybody in its fold. Its 195 million users in 1999 will grow to 300 million by 2005. Every third house in advance countries owns a PC. There are 800 million web pages; and 5,50, 000 books published every year.

Organic and inorganic materials have different physical and chemical properties under extremely high or low pressure or temperature. Systems, be they social or biological, have to be managed differently in abnormal environs. Is not this phenomena applicable to information, which is a pattern of mass-energy? Electronic information and libraries have the following distinct features:

a. Highly compact storage

b. Ease of reproduction. multiplication and manipulation

c. Contents can be easily detached from its container / media. and Put into other media without trace of the previous.

d. Ease of transmission. Communication and storage.

e. Hypertext and non-linear format allows a text to be fragmented and organized in a new mode.

f. Seamless integration of print and electronic media; and then of Audio, video, text and animation in multimedia.

g. Sophisticated and multi prong searches through keywords, freetext, Boolean operators, class numbers, thesauri and their permutations and combinations.

h. Wall less libraries leading to the vision of multimedia global virtual library (MGVL) inaugurating an era of "death of distance".

i. Remote and wireless access transcends barriers of time and place.

j. Convergence of technologies: see the cell phone is getting more multifunctional and powerful than the PC.

k. Cost of technologies is decreasing while its power is increasing.

Power and nature of new media have a visible impact on the shape, wares, functioning and services of libraries. We are called upon to organize CDs and websites just as books and other documents. Traditional acquisition policies and methods are no more practical. Library and information use pattern has changed in face of information networks, wall-less libraries, powerful library systems, OPACs and convergence of technology. This technology is not static or stable. Metamorphic changes are still in the offing. Apex outcome of the new environment is virtual library.

**Virtual Library**

A library is a growing social institution, as described by the 5th Law. The major stages in its evolution are:

- *Pre-paper Library:* of clay tablets, papyrus, tree leaves, parchment, etc., etc.
- *Traditional Library:* of manuscripts, incunabula and printed books and documents on paper
- *Hybrid Library:* Individual and stand alone library of print, micro and electronic documents served mostly through automation.
- *Virtual Library:* Networked digital library configured in the cyber space from the collection of scattered physical libraries.

At the outset it may be made clear that it has nothing to do with virtual reality, nor it is antithetical to the traditional or physical library. This library is a vision of technology with great potential for the future. Even the term has been challenged. 18 It is a computer based telecommunication linked practical library which provides services as any other library. As the name suggests it does not exist as any single housed collection, but is a medium to access information scattered in various physical collections.

It has to be configured by an individual searcher, thus making an ultimate multimedia experience. Though a collaborative effort, it has to be configured and structured individually. Being a hypermedia, it provides much more services which a paper based library cannot. Therefore, it is rightly seen that "decades from now... the physical library will be less visible to the public than the virtual library..." Digital and virtual libraries hold a special promise for the developing countries. Their priorities include poverty alleviation, unemployment, public health, safe drinking water, disaster management, environment protection and human rights. Information and awareness on these issues can now more easily be given than ever before Digital technology provides the system developers a golden opportunity to develop a non-commercial mechanism to build and disseminate information for social development..

Ranganathan's laws were sufficient and quite valid in the pre-virtual libraries days. But system behave differently in extreme environment or in paradigm shift. Ranganathan himself had visualized that normative laws are valid till the boundary conditions laid down by social needs remain the same. Kuronen and Pekkarinen have given the example that Newtonian physics is valid with small masses and velocity. In the space travel era these are subsumed by the theory of relativity. Take a social example, huge information with fast communication have changed the face of national and international money markets.

"The amount of money transacted in international money market is at least hundred times greater than that in real economy". A similar situation occurs when the information-which is instant power-flows globally and is delivered or accessed at the speed of light. The five laws though still valid do not seem sufficient. Two Finnish authors with arguments have proposed two new laws in their various writings, these are:

***6th Law:*** Every reader his library

***7th Law:*** Every writer his contribution to the library.

Here, the reader means a searcher, and library means the virtual Variety.

Information is for use. It signifies availability of information and removal of barriers in its use. Information being a prime mover of the information society is the most valuable commodity and an asset. Information and knowledge industry employs more than the 65%, of the labour force in advance economies.

It has devised methods and policies for the free flow of information overcoming the barrier of time and space. Information marketing and Knowledge Management square well with this law.

The super highway of information at the moment is the highest manifestation of the 1st law. Inter and international digital divide is a matter of serious concern for all of us. Next comes the formulation of information policies-which India still does not have to our great national disadvantage and embarrassment. We do not have any policy to harness, utilize and control our greatest asset. As a nation we are somewhat flouting this Law. Libraries need to playa role in the development of national information infrastructure.

Information is for all. Virtual library is an individual oriented library. It ensures accessibility of information. Information is a social commodity which needs a producer and consumer. Different channels of information TV, DTH TV Cable TV, cell phones, networks especially the Internet, intranets, LAN ensure information for all.

In face of information overload, it is mandatory to customize information to suit individual need Information literacy programmes, IF LA's UAP are a step in this direction. E-books, navigation systems, and digitization programmes support this law.

This law recommends users studies and education programmes. Search engines, subject gateways, e-mails, bulletin boards ensure information for all. Virtual library provides simultaneous access to, numerous documents through intelligent agents. IT has come as a great boon for physically or mentally challenged, and geographically isolated.

Every byte of information its user. Second and third laws are based on democracy and service. Third Law, which supplements the first two laws, ensures usability of information. Information is effective when it is used. There are two users of information: a) Computers, b) Human Beings. With use it multiplies and produces knowledge which in turn produces wealth.

In the market it-is a commodity strictly governed by the demand-supply law. No information will be generated for which there is no demand.-All the present research on user studies is to ensure the generation of that information for which there are likely anticipated users. Marketing of information products and services is in fulfilment of this law.

Save the time of the netizens is to ensurc timely information Time is the most scarce, exhaustible and unreplenishable resource. All the information storage and communication technology is geared to save time. As the information grows exponentially, so quickly it becomes obsolete.

So timely supply of information makes a difference in this competitive world. To save the time of the staff the policies are outsourcing, becoming a member of a network, consortia or a bibliographic utility like OCLC.

OPACs offer a single interface to numerous databases with seamless integration of print and electronic sources save time of the user. CCF, MARC, Metadata and various Markup Languages help standardization. Technology convergence is a great time saver. New tools and techniques are required to organize electronic knowledge for its timely delivery.

Library is a trinity of users, staff and collection. This law has a holistic approach. Information is growing. Information from the very beginning has the property of growing, multiplying and improving qualitatively. The information revolution, we are witnessing, is the highest manifestation of this law. Knowledge grows as the society grows and vice versa.

Growth of knowledge and social change are intertwined- and cannot be seen separately. Growth is diversity in time. In that way it is linked with the 4th law. FW Lancaster's famous thesis of paperless libraries ensues from this law not only new information and subjects are emerging, new media and communication services too are growing. Content Management (CM) is the technique developed to combat with ever changing information on the web and intranets. The virtual library is at the apex of this growth.

## A Look at Ranganathan's Laws and it's Applications and Derivations

In 1931, S.R. Ranganathan published his *Five Laws of Library Science*, which reflect how the library and librarian, and the public relate to each other. The five laws are as follows: books are for use, books are for all, every book its reader, save the time of the reader, and libraries are growing organisms. These five laws have been a foundation on which librarians practice librarianship (Finks 1981, Rubin 2004).

## THE LAWS

The nice thing about the five laws is that they are straight forward. Books are for use means exactly that. The importance of this law, however, is that Ranganathan felt that there was no point in storing and preserving books if no one would be able to use them as a result. In addition, the set up of the library should be such that a person can easily gain access to the books (Finks 1981, Rubin 2004).

Books are for all or every person his or her book means everyone, regardless of race, gender, social status, etc., must have equal access to all materials.

As well as, equal usage, librarians should develop collections that reflect the needs of the community and equal service and the users should be respectful of the library and materials, the rules of the library, and the other users (Finks 1981, Rubin 2004).

Every book its reader refers to the book finding the person who wants or requires it. This means that through cataloging, open stacks, and organized shelving, the book can easily get to a patron, because a book is useless if no one can find it to use.

Open stacks are especially important because this can allow a user to browse the collection and find materials that can be useful, but would have been missed in closed shelves. In addition, promoting certain books with displays, story hours, and other means is an important aspect to this law (Finks 1981, Rubin 2004).

Save the time of the reader is something everyone can identify with. This allows the user to access the materials with out a long, drawn out process.

Signs, guides, user education, indexes, and bibliographies that are easy to use and understand will make the library easier to use and understand. Librarians with expertise in reference, cataloging, and other areas can achieve the same thing (Finks 1981, Rubin 2004). There is no point in having a library if it is so complex to use that no one can find anything or they give up trying to find it.

The library is a growing organism refers to changes in the size of the collection, users, staff, and space. It also refers to other changes that may take place in the library and it is important for a library to grow and change in a good way, rather than remain exactly the same (Finks 1981, Rubin 2004).

While it can appear that each of these laws in a way repeats the other laws, I feel that to remove on law would reduce the overall clarity of the laws and would weaken the remaining laws, because while cataloging for example can help find books for use, and all patrons books and all books patrons and save the time of the patron and allow the library to grow, each is a different aspect or way to look at librarianship.

Perhaps the cataloging system is set up in such a way that it applies to the first four laws, but the growth of the library through additional books can be done with the system because there is no way to easily make space, in terms of cataloging, between the old books.

This would either prevent growth or throw off the other laws, such as save the user's time, because you don't change the system of cataloging, but if you did change the system to allow volume growth, your library will grow due to the change both because of a new system and the ability to add more books.

## Application of the Laws for Digital Items

Since Ranganathan came up with his laws there have been many changes in technology and the formats information can come in.

Ranganathan's laws refer specifically to books or at least to paper printed materials, but today there are audio-books, electronic materials, the internet, CDs, DVDs, Video cassettes, microforms, etc., but especially digital information.

Do the laws apply to these too? Yes and no. While it may not be implemented in every case it certainly can be. There are libraries today which don't even follow the laws with just there books, even though it is possible.

There are still closed collections and with copyright laws and electronic access use some materials are limited to only the users of that library, while with printed materials they can be provided via interlibrary loans.

However, there are many open access materials as well. An empty search for free access items at The University of Hawai'i at Mânoa Library's e-resources reveals that 7,619 out of 50,318 (also found through an empty search) databases, journal, and books are free access.

Internet sites such as Bartleby.com include free access to Columbia Encyclopedia, 6th edition, American Heritage Dictionary, 4th edition, as well as thesauri, quotations and other reference materials.

There are also ways organize the information so it can be found. Again, for the UHM library you can search for their electronic items or browse them alphabetically.

They are also accessible through the UHM Library online catalogue, so if you are doing a search for a topic in the catalogue you don't have to do a separate search in the E-resources page. The previous examples are relevant to the first four laws and the fifth law could arguably be considered the easiest or most relevant law to digital collections.

The library is growing through digital resources in jobs, organization, implementation, as well as space. In essence, you could have an infinite collection in digital format compared to a physical collection; you are only limited by they size of a monitor and the size of the storage, which has continuously for a set amount of memory gotten smaller in size or for a given size increased in memory.

With the growth of the internet more information has become available, and if we look at the essence of Ranganathan's laws, and this appears to be supported by Lee Finks (1981) and Michael Gorman and his new laws (1995), the laws are about the books or the library, but the information contained within, so the laws should apply to all formats, digital or not.

# 2

# Gorman's Laws

While Gorman believes that Ranganathan's laws are still valid, he has reinterpreted the laws to reflect a more current context. His laws are "libraries serve humanity", "respect all forms by which knowledge is communicated", "Use technology intelligently to enhance service", "protect free access to knowledge", and "Honour the past and create the future" (1995). The laws libraries serve humanity, respect all forms by which knowledge is communicated, I feel are the very essence of what Ranganathan's laws are conveying and protect free access to knowledge is exactly what he was saying.

Use technology intelligently to enhance service is a means by which to carry out Ranganathan's laws, and honour the past and create the future is an extension to his laws. Gorman's laws are a valuable supplement or extension to Ranganathan's laws and should be used to help carry out and understand Ranganathan's laws in a modern context. These ten laws are an excellent basis for librarianship, and in accordance with Ranganathan's fifth law they help a library to be a growing organism, and to continue to grow we still need these, but we need to look at them in a broader sense and reinterpret them to fit a specific new context and continue into the future with the original and revised concepts.

## RANGANATHAN'S RELEVANT RULES

Some things are timeless: the golden rule, family traditions, and even the more materialistic simple black dress or string of pearls. These classic items are often passed over for a shinier new toy or the latest trend. However, they are timeless because we can always return to and trust them. They ground us. For librarians, Ranganathan's five laws of library science are timeless objectives that put our profession's goals in perspective. If we ever lose sight of why or how we're doing our job, Ranganathan's laws provide guidance and structure. So take yourself back to library school—where you probably first heard of Ranganathan—and explore why his laws are timeless for librarianship and how they help libraries stay relevant.

Shiyali Ramainrita (S. R.) Ranganathan (1892–1972) was an Indian mathematician and library science scholar. In 1931 he published his *Five Laws of Library Science,* which were meant to be essential principles to define a library's function and purpose. The five laws state:

1. Books are for use
2. Every reader, his/her book
3. Every book, its reader
4. Save the time of the reader
5. The Library is a growing organism

## A CLOSER LOOK

Books are for use:

In other words, library materials and services should be accessible to users. This law might seem trivial in our day and age, but it harkens back to times when books were often chained to bookshelves and locked in rooms away from the patrons who wanted to use them. Fortunately, we're seeing less and less of this type of restriction to access. However, the digital age does have new repercussions for this first law. One way libraries are making their materials more accessible is by providing free online access to resources where and when the users need them. This means that more and more, our users can access materials when they want and from the location of their choice. An extension of this law is that libraries ensure that their users at multi-campus locations have access to the same resources as at the main location.

A caveat to keep in mind is that electronic access is not always the only way to go for better access. While it seems like most users today prefer online access, it's a careful balancing act. Eliminating free access to print resources in lieu of complete online access for only those users with a login and password can be viewed as a modern-day equivalent to breaking this first rule, and librarians should take their patrons' habits and desires into thoughtful consideration.

One way that libraries have exemplified this law is interlibrary loan (ILL) service. While librarians tend to overlook this service because we're so familiar with it, it is quite powerful. Often explaining the ILL concept to patrons produces that wow-factor that is sometimes hard to come by. At Penn State, I often hear our student Lion Ambassadors mention ILL to prospective families on campus tours—so you know the concept resonates with them. Recently my sister asked me for "the skinny" on ILL so she could inform a parental support group about the service to help them locate more resources about raising children with autism. ILL is a true manifestation of the adage that there's strength in numbers, and by building networks of information resources, libraries are truly indivisible. Collaborating is something we do well and we should capitalize on it to pass this great service on to our patrons.

While it's easy to think of examples of making materials accessible to patrons, we can also look at this law from a service standpoint. Librarians have strong commitments to service and finding out what kinds of services our patrons want is another way we continue to stay relevant in today's world. For example, we realize that learning doesn't stop after the library's doors close at night, so when possible, libraries increase their hours—often staying open all night. Serving patrons via shared 24/7 virtual reference services is another way libraries are making their services accessible, even if they don't have the budget to keep the physical library open later.

## Every Reader, His or Her Book

No patron can own all the materials they need. Unlike some who think that libraries are being marginalized because anyone who needs a book just buys it, patrons cannot own *all* the resources they need, nor do they want to. This is especially true in an academic environment where textbooks and research materials can be cost-prohibitive to faculty and especially students. Also, research interests and discoveries change frequently. Libraries are in the business of targeting collections for their user populations and building collections around their users.

We talk to our users, attend faculty meetings, and scour book reviews to find out what kinds of materials our patrons are interested in—we'll even buy a book based on a user's recommendation or request. Starbucks and Barnes and Noble do their own research about their clientele in general, but librarians take it a step further. Librarians take into consideration format issues so that the most appropriate form for the patrons using it is available. We also consider preservation issues and do our best to ensure long-term access to the material. Not only do we do this, but we make sure that we provide materials that are credible and reliable. We're happy to help and we take pride in finding a reader his or her book.

The second law speaks mainly to the areas of acquisitions and collection development. However, it also speaks to the very basic materials that libraries supply but librarians tend to forget about, such as photocopiers, staplers, pencils, computers, and reserve items.

By providing the basics, we serve patrons throughout the continuum of their quest for knowledge and the research process. First, they can receive assistance and direction for finding resources from librarians and then obtain the actual resources. Often patrons use library printers to print the assignment and our staplers to drive the final staple into the corner of a research paper before turning it in. From beginning to end, the library is there.

Another service that gains its relevance from Ranganathan's second law is reference services. Librarians know their patrons and collections and provide expertise you will not find anywhere else. Reference questions are more complex than in the past because users often do preliminary research online first. When someone does ask a reference question, they have most likely done some searching on their own and are stumped by the time they come to the library. Through our expertise, we know what kinds of materials best help our users and we know how and when to use them. This is how we ensure that every reader has his or her book.

## Every Book, Its Reader

This is the complementary reverse of the second law and supports the first law as well—it is all about providing pathways. Although the first and third laws sound similar, they actually support each other.

The third law serves to remind us to build more connections for our users so that they can find all the materials that we have made free and accessible. Classification systems are one way to do this. When used intelligently, technology helps to increase connections exponentially through tools like course management systems and Web 2.0 technologies that promote conversations about our materials and services. Technology must be accessible, intuitive, affordable, and simple if it is to be useful to patrons.

Instruction is another often-overlooked way librarians make connections. As librarians, we can provide almost anything patrons need to make the information relevant: hour-long sessions that are expertly tailored to students' needs, one-on-one research assistance, or open sessions on a variety of topics. Instruction entails both connecting the user to available resources and educating them about what we as librarians can do for them. If patrons leave with nothing else but the knowledge that the library can help them, we have done our job and we have taken this third law to heart.

In a similar vein comes outreach. Reaching out to the community and networking is perhaps the quintessential representation of the third law. Through programming that supports information literacy, making contact with groups such as adult learners or immigrant populations, and providing orientation sessions and tours to new users, we are constantly making new pathways to the library.

## Save the Time of the Reader

This law is self explanatory—everyone likes to save time—but how are libraries providing *efficient* access to materials and services? Not only do we staff service desks with trained employees, but our virtual presence through e-mail and chat reference has grown. Of course, these services save users' time by getting them to the information they need more quickly. Virtual and phone reference allows users to stay in their location and not have to worry about physically visiting the library. Soon reference services accessible by handheld wireless devices will make this service even more convenient. It is no surprise that technology has helped librarians to apply this law. Online catalogs, link resolvers, metasearching, and Z39.50 technology make finding online full-text content much easier.

While there are still some kinks to be smoothed out, just try going back to the old ways of searching. Similarly, tools like the Google Library Links programme help our patrons save time by allowing them to use an interface they are familiar with to find quality resources that are owned by their local library. At Penn State, we have seen evidence that Ranganathan's fourth rule is much appreciated by patrons. An "I Want It" button in our online catalogue is a feature that allows patrons to easily place a hold or recall a book that is not available at their current Penn State location or campus. This feature lets them pick up the item at any other Penn State location, including a branch library that might be closer to their lab or dorm.

At a large university like Penn State, this feature can save quite a bit of time for users and the feature gets used heavily. Finally, taking advantage of Web 2.0 technologies like RSS feeds can save users' time by allowing them to get updates for content that they regularly like to see without having to visit a number of sites to get that content. Everyone likes to save time and the fourth law reminds us to do it for our patrons.

## The Library is a Growing Organism

Libraries are growing by broadening and deepening their collections. Public, school, and academic librarians are planning new outreach initiatives and offering new services such as roving and remote reference services. We are also expanding and reworking our physical spaces by building beautiful new libraries, moving to an information commons model of service, and remodeling spaces to make them more inviting. Ranganathan's fifth law leaves us with this logical conclusion that libraries are, and always should be, changing.

Even though repercussions of today's digital age may seem to cloud what Ranganathan's five laws mean for libraries, his laws are still relevant. No matter which of Ranganathan's laws a new service falls under, libraries always provide services that people value and that remain timeless. Two things that patrons always appreciate are personal attention and a smiling face—those never go out of style. Libraries provide empowerment. Knowledge is power and libraries provide the materials necessary for gaining that knowledge. Libraries provide a place for discovery and serendipity. Perhaps browsing a new-books display leads a researcher to a new area of interest, or a young student discovers a new career path by consulting the career section of the library. The idea that libraries are life-changing places not only provides a great feeling to librarians but to patrons as well—and that is especially timeless.

## REFLECTIONS ON THE EVOLUTION OF ACADEMIC LIBRARIES IN THE 21ST CENTURY

As The ALA Glossary of Library and Information Science states, a library is "a collection of materials organized to provide physical, bibliographic, and intellectual access to a target group, with a staff that is trained to provide services and programmes related to the information needs of the target group." A library is not worthy of the name if it is not organized and administered according to sound principles of library and information science. Without such organizing principles, collections of information resources of any substantial size cannot be used effectively or efficiently.

Without such organizing principles, you don't have an effective library-you have the Internet. Information retrieval becomes an arduous process of hit and miss, of trial and error, with no assurance that the search-engine-of-the-day has really turned up all relevant sites. But organizing and administering information resources is becoming increasingly challenging due to the explosion in recent years of new publications, both in paper and electronic formats. In reality, no academic library is capable any longer of meeting all the needs of its users, if that was ever possible. Even the great research libraries log thousands of interlibrary loan and document delivery requests every year. In short, truly effective academic libraries are more reliant than ever on highly skilled and well trained professionals who are sensitive to the needs of library constituents. The primary mission of the library faculty and staff as we enter the 21st Century should be to support educational goals and priorities through whatever media, means, and services are most appropriate, and to accomplish this mission the library faculty and staff must be an integral part of institutional planning and decision making.

I believe that those of us who try to carry out this academic library mission will find that while the surface veneer of our work will continue to change in dramatic and often stressful ways, we will also continue to be guided most wisely by the values and principles that have been the library's bedrock for decades. Consider S.R. Ranganathan's five laws of library science, which he published in 1931:

1. Books Are For Use.
2. Every Reader His/Her Book.
3. Every Book Its Reader.
4. Save The Time Of The Reader.
5. The Library Is A Growing Organism.

Maurice Line underscored the validity of these laws by turning them on their heads to describe what he believed to be the reality of too many libraries:

1. Books Are For Collecting.
2. Some Readers Their Books.
3. Some Books Their Readers.

4. Waste The Time of the Reader.

5. The Library Is A Growing Mausoleum.

The laws of Ranganathan and Line assert in their own ways that the academic library should be measured by the extent to which it selects resources on the basis of user needs, organizes the resources so they may be identified and accessed efficiently, promotes and exposes resources to potential users, engages its users in an ongoing dialogue regarding evolving user needs, and responds to social and technological trends affecting higher education. Not only does that describe the ideal academic library of today, but I believe adherence to Ranganathan's laws will continue to provide the best guide to achieving the ideal library in the 21st Century. The balance of this paper will expand on that assertion.

Consider the first law, Books Are For Use. This means there should be no unnecessary barriers or constraints on the use of information resources. The ideal academic library seeks the best balance between preservation concerns and the need for patrons to use materials efficiently and effectively. Rare or irreplaceable materials require greater emphasis on preservation than on user convenience, but so far as our general collections are concerned the ideal academic library tailors its loan and related service policies to maximize the opportunities for students and faculty to use materials. A new but very important aspect of eliminating barriers and constraints on access is the negotiation of favourable license terms for electronic databases.

Many of the standard contracts which vendors present us contain restrictions that go beyond a copyright owner's statutory rights and infringe upon fair use. In response, we should insist upon license terms that protect fair use without affecting the vendor's right to a fair profit or its competitiveness in the marketplace. I am encouraged that a number of experts have published sample license terms that are intended to accomplish just that task. I hope that as academic libraries in the early 21st Century assert their rights and reject such dangerous requirements as indemnification of vendors against lawsuits, we will find standardized language in license agreements that is more realistic and less one-sided. Another constraint on access involves the authentication of eligible users of electronic resources. As we rely more and more on electronic databases, both for users on campus and for remote students enrolled in distance learning programmes, we must perfect authentication techniques such as web access management programmes.

The academic library will continue to be a vanguard in the protection of free access to knowledge. First, consider that the people in the future will only know about us that which we preserve. Allowing the records of the past to disappear is a form of censorship. We must beware of being too selective about what we collect and preserve. The universe of academic libraries must preserve all records of all societies and communities and make those records available to all. This will be a major challenge in the future since we can expect the trend toward managing and controlling information as a commodity will continue. Libraries must be responsible for ensuring information is archived and doesn't simply disappear because a commercial vendor goes out of business. And libraries must strive to make information as accessible as possible, so that in the Information Economy about which we hear so much, there is not an unnecessary chasm between haves and have-nots.

A related issue of information preservation is that of data permanence. The May 1999 issue of *American Libraries* records some facts that should give pause to anyone who thinks the paperless society will be within reach in the first decade of the 21st Century:

- Magnetic media such as floppy disks have a data life span of five years or less. According to data-preservation scientist J.W.C. Van Bogart, even in extreme circumstances high quality paper lasts 10 times longer than the best magnetic media used for commercial and scientific data storage.
- Optical media, such as CD-ROM and DVD-ROM, are proving to be far less durable than originally expected. The longest warranty in the industry for CD-ROM products only guarantees for 25 years, in spite of the

claims that CD disks are good for more than a century. DVD's can be expected to have a shorter life span since increased data density has been proven to be associated with shorter life spans. In contrast, the life span of acid paper, which libraries have tried to avoid collecting for decades, is 50 to 100 years.

- As of the end of 1999, Kodak still stated on its web site, "Digital storage media impose a strict discipline that human-readable records do not: their rapid evolution creates a continual progression of technology that cannot safely be ignored for too long." In other words, according to Van Bogart, libraries seeking to use digital media for long-term data and information storage could be faced every 10-20 years with either

  (a) copying such data to the latest formats, or

  (b) purchasing the latest programme for uploading data on obsolete formats to the latest medium.

Even given the obvious advantages of electronic media for remote access and searching for specific information, will we be able to justify this new kind of "planned obsolescence" to our funding authorities?

The academic library in the first five years of the 21st Century will need to make tough decisions about what resources will need to be archived for the long term, and in what format. I suggest to you that paper will continue to be one of our most important long term data storage formats.

Let us now reflect on the second law, Every Reader His/Her Book. Here Ranganathan is telling us we are obliged to help find the resources that meet a user's need, and that may include going beyond the resources that are easily at hand. As I said earlier, no academic library is able to collect comprehensively.

We must engage our constituents in the development of our collection development policy and ensure that when class assignments are made there will be adequate information resources to support them. We should try to stay abreast of the research needs of the faculty and support those needs as much as possible through materials purchases and subscriptions, and also through fast, accurate, and (to the user at least) free document delivery systems.

The ideal academic library, particularly one that is a member of a state-supported university system, will help build an infrastructure of policies and procedures that facilitate resource sharing among the system's libraries.

The library should take full advantage of the dialogues that are possible with library advisory committees, through focus groups and surveys, suggestion boxes and e-mail addresses, informal communication of all kinds, and by the library faculty and staff being fully engaged in the academic community. The dominant ethic of librarianship is service to the individual, community, and society as a whole.

This is especially true for publicly supported academic institutions. This requires attention to quality and living up to-and even surpassing-the expectations of library users. I would add that it also requires a commitment to human diversity and multiculturalism, which should be reflected in collection development policies and respected in our patron services.

The third law is Every Book Its Reader. In the ideal academic library, the librarians seek to match information materials with their potential users.

New acquisitions which could be helpful to someone's ongoing research should be brought to that individual's attention. We should be as concerned with the exposure and promotion of our resources as we arc with their accessibility. Over the course of the next five years, and indeed into the foreseeable future, this goal will not only be more difficult but also more urgent due to the remarkable proliferation of paper and electronic publications.

As Richard Dougherty wrote: "There is a striking contradiction between our professional imperative of providing free and easy access to information and the rising tide of information that is rapidly engulfing us... we need to face the reality that more and more people haven't the time, the expertise, or the psychological make-up to find the information that best serves their needs."

Through such means as electronic and printed bibliographies, current awareness services, and liaison programmes with academic departments, librarians should be the matchmakers that bring materials to the people who could use them.

Law number 4 is Save The Time Of The Reader. Information services must satisfy needs as efficiently as possible. Clearly this relates back to my earlier comment about the difference between a library and an unorganized collection of materials.

An important way in which an academic library will save the time of the reader is by bringing greater bibliographic order to the Internet and World Wide Web.

As marvelous as these are, they leave much to be desired as efficient and orderly means of archiving and retrieving information. I enjoyed Will Manley's humorous take on the Internet, to wit: "If we were to go about acquiring the Internet like any other resource we would probably try to read a review of it.

What would the objective reviewer say? 'The Internet is a vast informational network with millions of entries on a myriad of diverse subjects.

It is loosely and unreliably indexed and is awkward to use because of the increasingly slow response time. While some of the entries are well researched by reliable authors, many others are poorly written by people with no literary or academic credentials who have a pronounced proclivity to punctuate their points with the repeated use of the words cool and suck.'" In summary, says Manley, "the Internet is the global village's vanity press. It has no editorial board and no editorial principles."

Given the vastness of the Internet and its resources, we cannot rely on existing Internet search engines to help us find all of the best information available to meet our needs. A 1999 study sponsored by the NEC Research Institute of 11 search engines revealed that none of the 11 indexed more than 16 percent of the World Wide Web.

I think over the course of the next several years we will need to re-double our efforts to save the time of our users by identifying those reliable Internet sites that are likely to be of the greatest utility and facilitating access to those sites.

This can be done through subject bibliographies that are printed as well as mounted on the library's web page with links to the sites. It can be done through creative proposals like Dan Hazen's selective scanning.

In this scheme, digitizing front matter like tables of contents could result in quicker and cheaper cataloging, and in the enhancement of the information that cataloguers can provide users trying to make informed choices of which materials to examine in depth.

It can also be done by helping users learn advanced searching skills and evaluate critically the results of their searches. And it certainly should be done through working as partners with commercial vendors and campus computer centres to design, test, and implement improved search capabilities, user interfaces, and ergonomic hardware.

In the future we must certainly continue to use technology intelligently to enhance our services. We must reject the false dichotomy of having to pick between two sides; in reality, we do not have to choose between being a Luddite or a technocrat. I agree with Michael Gorman's view, "electronic methods are best for...giving access to data and small, discrete packets of textual, numeric, and visual information (such as those found in many reference works).

Each of the other media has areas in which it is the best. In particular, print on paper is and will be the preeminent medium for the communication of cumulative knowledge by means of sustained reading."

Finally, law number 5 states that The Library Is A Growing Organism. While all of Ranganathan's laws, as I interpret them, imply the need to be prepared for change, this fifth law reinforces that need explicitly.

We will need to continue to adapt to new social conditions, technological developments, and changing needs of the clientele. The number of challenges we face can seem daunting at times, but change is the norm in the library world and we must not delude ourselves into hoping that we are ever going to reach a steady-state plateau.

A clear implication of this law is that the ideal academic library will make a major ongoing investment in the continuing development of faculty and staff knowledge and skills.

We must take advantage of workshops and seminars offered on and off campus-some of which are now offered electronically. We must attend professional conferences, engage in informal networking with peers, and learn from the literatures of our own and other appropriate disciplines.

The academic library of the future will use all kinds of carriers of knowledge and information, with each new means of communication enhancing and supplementing the strengths of all previous means.

To quote Michael Gorman again, "There is no reason to cling to print on paper, images on film, or grooves on discs in cases when it can be demonstrated clearly that technology offers a cost-beneficial alternative.

What is the point, however, in replacing print on paper, etc., when new technology is less effective, more costly, or has other disadvantages? The best approach to the future of libraries lies in this utilitarianism."

The academic library in a publicly supported university will find itself increasingly called upon to serve the citizens of the region and to engage in cooperative ventures with other post secondary institutions in the state.

For example, GALILEO is the paradigmatic example of the benefits of libraries working cooperatively and with the state to establish an electronic network that brings enormous information resources to all citizens of the state, at a fraction of the full cost that the individual libraries would have paid for those resources.

In the future, I think such collaborative efforts will become ever more important means of maximizing access to information and controlling costs. Within such initiatives, an individual academic library must be prepared to demonstrate leadership, contribute whatever strengths of personnel and collections it may have, and continue to keep its primary users' unique set of priorities in mind as it works with other libraries for the good of the entire state.

Another intriguing challenge to academic libraries is the growing tendency of superstores like Barnes & Noble or Borders to usurp the academic library as the favoured location for students to study.

Renee Feinberg, a reference librarian at Brooklyn College, has reported on her interviews with college students she encounters at B&N superstores, and not surprisingly to those of us who have enjoyed patronizing these stores, the students indicate a preference for B&N over their campus libraries because of the more comfortable and congenial settings, good coffee, the buzz of conversation, and in some cases even the more convenient hours of operation.

Perhaps most disturbing, however, is the recurring statement that B&N has better and more accessible monograph holdings, especially of recently published materials.

This is worth bearing in mind when we hear the stories of how our X Generation students are plugged into technology to the point of ignoring printed resources.

The truth may fall somewhere in between these two extremes. As Feinberg states: "Students want their books. If libraries choose to weaken their book collections in favour of increased electronic information, they will lose patrons who would support them as they argue for protection of collections."

What libraries can learn from these bookstores, as Leonard Kniffel wrote, is to return to the niceties we appear to have abandoned: tasteful signs, cozy spots, comfort, elegance, and the human touch. We in academic libraries should concede nothing to Barnes & Noble in terms of comfort, convenience, and service, and we certainly should not bow to B&N's holdings of scholarly books.

## CONCLUSION

As academic libraries evolve to meet new challenges, they must retain the best of the past and a sense of the history of libraries and of scholarly communication. With a sense of history, and a knowledge of enduring values and the continuity of our mission, there must also be the acceptance of the challenge of innovation. If the library ever ceases to be a growing organism, then it really will become Maurice Line's growing mausoleum.

# 3

# The Role and Purpose of the Public Library

## INTRODUCTION

This chapter is a general statement on the role and purpose of the public library. The key issues are developed in greater detail in the book.

## DEFINING THE PUBLIC LIBRARY

Public libraries are a worldwide phenomenon. They occur in a variety of societies, in differing cultures and at different stages of development. Although the varied contexts in which they operate inevitably result in differences in the services they provide, and the way those services are delivered, they normally have characteristics in common, which can be defined as follows: A public library is an organisation established, supported and funded by the community, either through local, regional or national government or through some other form of community organisation. It provides access to knowledge, information and works of the imagination through a range of resources and services and is equally available to all members of the community regardless of race, nationality, age, gender, religion, language, disability, economic and employment status and educational attainment.

## THE PURPOSES OF THE PUBLIC LIBRARY

The primary purposes of the public library are to provide resources and services in a variety of media to meet the needs of individuals and groups for education, information and personal development including recreation and leisure.

**Education**

Supporting both individual and self conducted education as well as formal education at all levels "(Manifesto) The need for an agency available to all, which provides access to knowledge in printed and other formats to support formal and informal education, has been the reason for the foundation and maintenance of most public libraries and remains a core purpose for the public library.

Throughout their lives people require education either at formal institutions *e.g.* school, colleges and universities or in a less formal context related to their employment and daily life. Learning does not end with the completion of formal education but is, for most people, a lifelong activity. In an increasingly complex society people will need to acquire new skills at various stages of their life. The public library has an important role in assisting this process.

The public library should provide material in the appropriate media to support formal and informal learning processes. It should also help the user to make use of these learning resources effectively as well as providing facilities, which enable people to study. The ability to access information and make effective use of it is vital to successful education and where possible public libraries should cooperate with other educational organisations in teaching the use of information resources. Where adequate library facilities exist to support formal education the public library should complement them rather than duplicating library provision available elsewhere.

The public library should also actively support literacy campaigns, as literacy is the key to education and knowledge and to the use of libraries and information services. Newly literate people need easy access to appropriate reading materials to maintain and develop their skills.

In some countries the need for educational development is seen to be paramount and the focus of public libraries is to support formal education. There are, however, a variety of ways in which public libraries can support both formal and informal education. How this is achieved will depend on the local context and the level of available resources

- o In Mexico public library services have been deliberately developed to support formal education with special emphasis on secondary education.
- o In Singapore the stated mission for the public library service is "to continuously expand this nation's capacity to learn through a national network of libraries and information resource centres providing services and learning opportunities to support the advancement of Singapore."
- o In South Africa, where many people have inadequate living space and no electricity to enable them to study, public libraries give a high priority to providing the basic facilities, light, tables and chairs.
- o In many countries libraries are provided which fulfil the function of both public and school library. In Trafford, England three smaller libraries have been integrated into existing facilities. One branch library has been combined with a school library and two located with leisure facilities.
- o In Bulawayo, Zimbabwe a weekly mobile library service visits thirty-seven primary schools greatly increasing access to the library service for children in the city.
- o In Amazonas State, Venezuela, where there are no school libraries, rural libraries concentrate on providing support for school students and teachers.
- o In Barcelona province, Spain some library services give support to distance learning students from the Open University in Catalonia.

**Information**

The public library is the local centre of information, making all kinds of knowledge and information readily available to its users." (Manifesto)

It is a basic human right to be able to have access to and an understanding of information, and there is now more information available than ever before in the world's history. As a public service open to all, the public library has a key role in collecting, organising and exploiting information, as well as providing access to a wide range of information sources. The public library has a particular responsibility to collect local information and make it readily available.

It also acts as a memory of the past by collecting, conserving and providing access to material relating to the history of the community and of individuals. In providing a wide range of information the public library assists the community in informed debate and decision making on key issues. In collecting and providing information the public library should, wherever possible, cooperate with other agencies to make the best use of available resources.

The rapid growth in the volume of available information and the continuing technological changes, which have radically affected the way information is accessed, have already made a significant effect on public libraries and their services. Information is very important to the development of the individual and of society and information technology gives considerable power to those able to access and use it.

Despite its rapid growth it is not available to the majority of the world's population and the gap between the information rich and the information poor continues to widen. A vital role for the public library is to bridge that gap by making information technology easily accessible as well as providing information in traditional formats.

Public libraries should recognise and exploit the opportunities provided by the exciting developments in information and communications technology. They have the opportunity to become the electronic gateway to the information world.

- Sabah State Library, Malaysia provides electronic corners in its libraries. These are one-stop sources of information and entertainment, which can access the

Internet, and a wide variety of CD-Roms. Public seminars on how to use the Internet are also organised by the library.

- o The Rural Audio Libraries of Mali use cassettes to distribute information on hygiene, health, animal husbandry and other topics relevant to people's daily life. These reach 146 villages and collective listening sessions are organised.
- o Some public libraries in South Africa provide space for information kiosks and telecentres
- o Open access Internet points have been established in public libraries in Estonia.
- o Rural multi-purpose community telecentres have been established in five African countries (Benin, Mali, Mozambique, Tanzania and Uganda) to provide access to modern information and communication tools.
- o The public library in Sunderland, England is developing ' electronic village halls '. Five have been opened based in library buildings, a further education college, a community business centre, and around a community and voluntary network. They provide free access to PC's and the Internet, a wide range of software for adults and children and trained staff available to help users.

## Personal Development

The opportunity to develop personal creativity and pursue new interests is important to human development. To achieve this people need access to knowledge and works of the imagination. The public library can provide access, in a variety of different media, to a rich and varied store of knowledge and creative achievement which individuals cannot acquire on their own behalf. Providing access to major collections of the world's literature and knowledge, including the community's own literature, has been a unique contribution of the public library and is still a vitally important function. Access to works of the imagination and knowledge is an important contribution to personal education and meaningful recreational activity.

The public library can also make a fundamental contribution to daily survival by being directly involved in providing information to developing communities *e.g.* basic life skills, adult basic education, Aids awareness programmes. In communities with a high illiteracy rate the public library should interpret and translate information where necessary and provide basic user education.

## Children and Young People

*Creating and strengthening reading habits in children from an early age.*" (Manifesto)

The public library should attempt to meet the needs of all groups in the community regardless of age and physical, economic or social circumstances. However it has a special responsibility to meet the needs of children and young people. If children can be inspired, by the excitement of knowledge and works of the imagination at an early age, they are likely to benefit from these vital elements of personal development throughout their lives, both enriching them and enhancing their contribution to society. Children can also encourage parents and other adults to make use of the library. It is also important that young people who experience problems in learning to read should have access to a library to provide them with appropriate material.

## Public Libraries and Cultural Development

An important role of the public library is providing a focus for cultural and artistic development in the community. This can be achieved by working in partnership with appropriate local and regional organisations, by providing space for cultural activity, organising cultural programmes and by ensuring that cultural interests are represented in the library's materials. The library's contribution should reflect the variety of cultures represented in the community. It should provide materials in the languages spoken and read in the local community.

## An Agency for Change

In carrying out its role in these key areas the public library is acting as an agency for social and personal development and can be a positive agency for change in the community. By providing a wide range of materials to support education and making information accessible to all the public library can bring economic and social benefits to individuals and to the community.

It contributes to the creation of a well-informed society and helps to empower people in the enrichment and development of their lives and that of the community in which they live.

## Freedom of Information

The public library should be able to represent all ranges of human experience and opinion, free from the risk of censorship. In some countries a Freedom of Information Act will help to ensure these rights are maintained. Librarians and governing bodies should uphold these basic human rights and resist pressure from individuals and groups to limit the material available in the public library.

## Access for All

A fundamental principle of the public library is that its services must be available to all and not directed to one group in the community to the exclusion of others. Provision should be made to ensure services are equally available to minority groups who for some reason are not able to use the mainstream services, for example linguistic minorities, people with physical disabilities or those living in remote communities who are unable to reach library buildings.

The development of services, the design of libraries and their opening hours should all be planned with the concept of universal access as a basic principle.

The development of collections should also be based on the principle of access for all and include access to formats appropriate to specific client groups *e.g.* Braille and talking books for blind people. Information and communications technology should be used to allow access to the library's collections and those of other information sources both from within the library or from remote sites.

## Local Needs

Public libraries are locally based services for the benefit of the local community and should provide community information services. The services and collections they provide should be based on local needs which should be assessed regularly. Without this discipline the public library will get out of touch with those it is there to serve and will, as a result, not be used to its full potential. Librarians should, therefore, be aware of the changes in society arising from such factors as demographic change, variations in the age structure, levels of education, patterns of employment and the emergence of other educational and cultural providers.

## Local Culture

The public library should be a key agency in the local community for the collection, preservation and promotion of local culture. This can be achieved in a variety of ways *e.g.* the maintenance of local history collections, exhibitions, storytelling, publishing of items of local interest and developing interactive programmes on local themes. Where the oral tradition is an important method of communication the public library should encourage its development.

- In the services offered by the Rural Libraries and Resources Development Programme in Zimbabwe the incorporation of drama, song and dance as part of information transfer is juxtaposed to reading, lending and literacy support
- Village Reading Rooms in Botswana act as centres for storing Setswana literature and promoting the Setswana language and for the promotion of culture where discussion groups, traditional songs, dances and meetings are organised
- Rural libraries in Cajamarca, Peru are involved in the reinstatement and revitalisation of the Andean indigenous language base. A project was set up to publish material on the local culture and the resulting Rural Encyclopaedia provides an alternative to school, empowers people and promotes self-education.

## The Cultural Roots of the Public Library

It is important to the long-term success of the library that it should be based on the culture of the country or area in which it operates. It is less likely to succeed if the form and structure of the public library are introduced from a country or area with a very different cultural background.

## Libraries without Walls

In developing policies to fulfil the role and purpose of the public library the emphasis should be on the services it provides. In meeting the needs of its community the public library will provide a range of services, some of which, for example large collections of printed material, can be most effectively delivered from a library building. However there will be many circumstances where it is more effective to provide the service beyond the walls of the library. Examples will vary in different societies but the principle of planning library development from a service rather than building perspective is important in all public library policy development. The provision of services using information and communications technology also presents exciting opportunities to take library and information services direct to the home and the workplace.

A variety of forms of transport are used to deliver services to sparsely populated areas. The provision of library and information services to people unable to visit a library due to physical disability or lack of transport, for example, ensures that access to these services is available to all at their home or workplace regardless of their circumstances.

## Library Buildings

Library buildings play an important part in public library provision. They should be designed to reflect the functions of the library service and be sufficiently flexible to accommodate new and changing services. They should be located close to other community activities *e.g.* shops and cultural centres. Wherever possible the library should also be available for community use, for example for meetings and exhibitions and in larger buildings for theatrical, musical, audiovisual and media performances. A well-used public library will make a significant contribution to the vitality of an urban area and be an important learning and social centre and meeting place, particularly in scattered rural areas. Librarians should, therefore, ensure that library buildings are used and managed effectively to make the best use of the facilities for the benefit of the whole community.

The public library has an important role as a public space and meeting place, particularly in communities where there are few places for people to meet. It is sometimes known as the drawing room of the community.

### Resources

To fulfil its roles satisfactorily the public library must have adequate resources not just when it is established but also on a continuing basis to enable it to sustain and develop services that meet the needs of the local community. This means it should provide materials in all formats, updated regularly to meet the changing needs of groups and individuals, including newly-published and replacement materials. It should also provide adequate levels of staff with appropriate training and sufficient funds to support whatever methods of service delivery are needed for it to meet its vital role in the community.

### The Legal and Financial Framework

Public libraries are a community agency providing access at local level to a range of knowledge and information for the benefit of the individual and society as a whole. In order to maintain the level of service required to fulfil their functions public libraries should be supported by legislation and sustained funding.

### The Public Library and Government

There are many different models of the relationship between public libraries and government. Equally the laws that govern their activities and funding arrangements are varied and complex. In different countries, provinces, regions, states or municipalities are either in whole or in part responsible for library services. As public libraries are a locally based service local government is often the most appropriate place in the government structure for them. However in some countries public libraries are provided at regional or state level and the national library sometimes has responsibility for providing the public library service. There are instances of two or more levels of government cooperating in the provision of the service.

- The Estonian Public Libraries Act (1998) details the responsibilities of each level of government. It states that the public library is established by the local government body, and that the county or city library is responsible for the coordination of library service, inter-library loans and book mobiles. The local authority is responsible for employees' wages but the funding of library materials is shared between the local authority and the state.

### *Alternative Structures*

In some countries, although the local authority has nominal responsibility for the public library, it does not have the required funds and non-governmental organisations or private foundations undertake the practical operation of the public library services. However to ensure sustained development and its role in the information network the public library should be closely related to and funded by the appropriate level of government. The eventual aim should be to bring public libraries into the formal government structure operating under national legislation and with appropriate levels of funding.

Argentina has 1600 popular libraries provided by non-governmental organisations or organised communities and regulated by national legislation.

## National Information Policies

In order to make the most effective use of available library and information resources, and take full advantage of the opportunities offered by the development of electronic information sources, many countries are developing national information policies. Public libraries should be a key element in such policies and public librarians should ensure they are full involved in their development.

## Public Library Legislation

Public libraries should be based on legislation, which assures their continuance and their place in the government structure. Public library legislation takes various forms. In some countries or regions the legislation is specific to public libraries whereas in others it is part of wider legislation which includes different types of libraries. Public library legislation is also varied in its provisions. It can be simple, allowing the establishment of public libraries but leaving standards of service to the level of government directly responsible for the library, or more complex with specific detail on what services should be provided and to what standard. Because governmental structures vary so much in different countries the form and detail of public library legislation is also likely to vary significantly. However legislation governing public libraries should state which level of government is responsible for their provision and how they should be funded. It should also place them in the framework of libraries in the country or region as a whole.

- Mexico and Venezuela have specific public library legislation whereas in Colombia and Brazil legislation on information services includes references to public libraries
- The Finnish Library Act (1998) stipulates that the public library should be provided by the municipality, either independently or in cooperation with other public libraries, that public libraries should cooperate with other types of library and that the municipality should evaluate the library and information services that it provides.
- The Constitution of the Republic of South Africa 1996 provides the constitutional framework for the provision of library and information services in South Africa. It lists ' libraries other than national libraries' as an area of exclusive provincial legislative competence. It is therefore a provincial responsibility to develop the legislative framework in which library and information services can be provided.

- In Armenia local authorities have responsibility for the financing and maintenance of public libraries. The Law on Local Self-Government (1996) defines their obligations for maintaining and developing public libraries.

## Related Legislation

Public libraries are subject to a range of legislation apart from the specific legislation relating to them. This can include legislation on financial management, health and safety and staff conditions and there will be many other examples. Library managers should be aware of all legislation affecting the operation of the public library.

They should also be aware of global trade negotiations which can result in policies and agreements, which could have a serious impact on public libraries. In such cases librarians should take every opportunity to bring the effect of such policies on public libraries to the notice of the public and politicians.

## Copyright

Copyright legislation is of particular importance to public libraries, particularly that relating to electronic publications. It is constantly subject to amendment and review and librarians should keep up-to-date with the legislation in relation to all media. Librarians should promote and support copyright legislation which achieves an equitable balance between the rights of creators and the needs of users.

In the Czech Republic the library association, SKIP, acting on its own initiative participated in the preparation of copyright legislation. After discussions with the Ministry of Culture and the Cultural Committee of the Czech parliament, changes beneficial to libraries were introduced.

## Public Lending Right

In some countries public lending right legislation has been introduced which provides a payment to authors and others involved in the creation of a book, related to its provision in and loan from public libraries. It is important that funds for payment of public lending right should not be taken from funds libraries have for the purchase of materials. However public lending right, if separately funded, does provide support for authors without affecting public libraries' budgets. In some schemes it can also provide useful statistics on the loans of books by specific authors. Librarians should participate in the development of public lending right schemes to ensure they are not financed from library budgets.

**Funding**

Adequate levels of funding are crucial to the success of a public library in fulfilling its roles. Without suitable levels of funding over the long-term it is impossible to develop policies for service provision and make the most effective use of available resources.

This can be seen in number of examples: a new library building without adequate funds to maintain it, collections of new books with no money for their replacement and computer systems without funds to maintain and update them. Funding is required not only when a public library is established but should be sustained on an assured and regular basis.

**Priorities**

A public library and its services is a long-term investment on behalf of the community and should be funded appropriately. It is recognised that even in the wealthiest of societies it may not be possible to provide appropriate levels of funding for every service requirement.

It is vitally important, therefore, that service development should be conducted on a planned basis with clear priorities. This process is necessary whatever level of funding is available to the library service. To determine strategic planning and the maintenance of agreed priorities, written policy statements should be developed for services. They should be reviewed at regular intervals and revised where necessary.

**Partnership**

No public library, however large and well funded, can meet all the needs of its users on its own. Partnerships with other organisations, networking and providing access to other sources of information are essential if the public library is to satisfy the information needs of its users.

## Sources of Funding

There are a number of sources of funding used to finance public libraries but the proportions of funding from each source will vary depending on local factors in each country.

The primary sources are:

- o taxation at local, regional or central level
- o block grants from central, regional or local level

Secondary sources of income may include:

- o donations from funding bodies or private individuals
- o revenue from commercial activities *e.g.* publishing, book sales, sale of works of art and handicrafts
- o revenue from user fees *e.g.* fines
- o sponsorship from external organisations
- o lottery funds for specific initiatives.

## Charging the User

The IFLA/UNESCO Public Library Manifesto states "The public library shall in principle be free of charge ". Charging users for services and membership should not be used as a source of revenue for public libraries, as it makes the ability to pay a criterion in determining who can use a public library. This reduces access and therefore breaches the fundamental principle that the public library should be available to all. It is recognised that in some countries with very limited financial resources for public services a policy of 'cost-sharing' has been introduced, as a result of which subscriptions for use of the library are levied. This practice denies access to those unable to pay and should be seen as an interim situation and not as a permanent feature of public library funding.

It is common in some countries to ask users to pay a fee or fine when keeping an item after it is due for return to the library. This is sometimes necessary to ensure that items are kept in circulation and not retained for a long time by one user.

The fine should not be set at a level that would deter anyone from using the library.

**External Funding**

Librarians should be imaginative in seeking external sources of funding for the public library. However, they should not accept funding from any source, if by so doing the fundamental status of a public library as an agency available to all is compromised. Commercial organisations, for example may offer funding with conditions, which might prejudice the universal nature of the services provided by the public library.

**The Governance of the Public Library**

Public libraries should be governed by a properly established body made up largely of representatives of the local community including those elected either to the local council or to the library board. Library committees and boards should have rules of procedure and their proceedings should be open to the general public.

They should meet on a regular basis and publish agenda, minutes, annual reports and financial statements. Normally the governing body will be responsible for matters of policy rather than the day-to-day operation of the library. In all cases the chief librarian should have direct access to the meetings of the governing body of the library and work closely with it. Policy documents should be made available to the public and, where possible, steps should be taken to involve local citizens in the development of the public library.

Public librarians must be fully accountable both to their governing bodies and local citizens for their actions by providing reports, holding public meetings and through consultation. They must also maintain the highest professional standards in carrying out their duties and in advising the governing body. Although the final decisions on policy will be taken by the governing body and the librarian, ways should be sought to involve the local citizens who are the actual or potential library users.

The concept of a 'Library Charter', which identifies and publicises the level of service the public library provides has been developed in some countries. This establishes a 'contract' between the public library and the users. Library Charters have more credibility if they are developed in consultation with users.

## The Administration of the Public Library

Public libraries should be well managed and administered. The administration of a public library should be directed towards improving the quality of service to the users and not an end in itself. It should be efficient and accountable. To get best results the administrative and management staff of a large public library service should be multi-disciplinary involving staff with specialist skills *e.g.* librarians, accountants, public relations officers and system managers. It may also be necessary to draw on the expertise of staff of the parent authority or other related organisation in certain areas *e.g.* lawyers, payroll and pensions staff.

## Publicity and Promotion

Public libraries operate in an increasingly complex society, which makes many calls on people's time and attention. It is important; therefore that libraries publicise their presence and the range of services they provide. Publicity ranges from simple techniques, like signs on library buildings, which state what they are and leaflets advertising opening hours and services, to more sophisticated methods like marketing programmes and the use of web sites to promote the library's services and activities.

## Meeting the Needs of the Users

To be successful in fulfilling its goals the public library service must be fully accessible to all its potential users. Any limitation of access whether deliberate or accidental will reduce the ability of the public library to fully achieve its primary role of meeting the library and information needs of the community it serves. The following are important elements in delivering an effective public library service:

- Identifying potential users
- Analysing users' needs

- Developing services to groups and individuals
- Introducing customer care policies
- Promoting user education
- Cooperating and sharing resources
- Developing electronic networks
- Ensuring access to services
- Providing library buildings

**Identifying Potential Users**

The public library has to aim to serve all citizens and groups. An individual is never too young or too old to use a library.

The potential target groups of the public library include:

- People at all ages and at all stages of life.
  - o Children
  - o Young adults
  - o Adults
- Individuals and groups of people with special needs
  - o People from different cultures and ethnic groups inc. indigenous people.
  - o People with disabilities *e.g.* blind and partially sighted, hearing impaired
  - o Housebound people
  - o Institutionally confined *e.g.* in hospitals, prisons
- Institutions within the wider community network
  - o Educational, cultural and voluntary organisations and groups in the community
  - o The business community
  - o The governing body of the parent organisation *e.g.* local authority

As resources are limited in even the wealthiest society it is not always possible to serve all users to the same level. The library must establish priorities based on an analysis of user needs and related to their access to alternative services.

## Analysing Needs within the Community

It is important to establish who uses and who does not use the library service. It is also necessary to collect and analyse data which identifies those needs of individuals and groups within the community which can be met by the public library.

## Services to Users

The public library must provide services based on an analysis of the library and information needs of the local community. In planning services clear priorities must be established and a strategy developed for service provision in the medium to long term. Services should be developed for identified target groups and only provided if such groups exist in the local community.

The services of the library should not be subject to any form of ideological, political, religious or commercial pressure. Services must be able to adjust and develop to reflect changes in society *e.g.* variations in family structures, employment patterns, demographic changes, cultural diversity and methods of communication. They should take account of traditional cultures as well as new technologies *e.g.* support for oral methods of communication as well as making use of information and communication technology. In some countries the services which the public library must provide are defined in library legislation.

***Service Provision:*** Public libraries provide a range of services, both within the library and in the community, to satisfy their users' needs. The library should facilitate access to its services for all, including those who have difficulty reading print. The following services, which should be easily accessible to the user in a variety of formats and media, should be provided.

- o Loan of books and other media
- o Provision of books and other materials for use in the library
- o Information services using print and electronic media

- o Readers' advisory services including reservation services
- o Community information services
- o User education including support for literacy programmes
- o Programming and events

This is not an exhaustive list but an indication of some of the key services of the public library. The range and depth of provision will depend on the size of the library and the community it serves. Every library should aim to be an active participant in one or more networks, which will give the user access to a wide range of material however small the access point. Service provision should not be confined to the library building but also taken direct to the user where access to the library is not possible. In providing services both within the library and beyond use should be made of information and communications technology as well as the printed word. A list of some of the resources the library should provide.

***Services to Children:*** By providing a wide range of materials and activities, public libraries provide an opportunity for children to experience the enjoyment of reading and the excitement of discovering knowledge and works of the imagination. Children and their parents should be taught how to make the best use of a library and how to develop skills in the use of printed and electronic media.

Public libraries have a special responsibility to support the process of learning to read, and to promote books and other media for children. The library must provide special events for children like story telling and activities related to the library's services and resources. Children should be encouraged to use the library from an early age as this will make them more likely to remain users in future years. In multi-lingual countries books and audiovisual materials for children should be available in their mother tongue.

- o In France public libraries in many regions are cooperating with Health Services for Children to organise programmes for parents and their children while they are waiting for medical consultation. These are aimed at children from birth to three years old, to encourage parents to read aloud to their children and to visit the public library.

- o In Bucharest, Rumania the city library is offering summer programmes, run by volunteers, aimed at children from eleven to fourteen whose parents are at work.

***Services for Young Adults:*** Young people between childhood and adulthood develop as individual members of society with their own culture. Public libraries must understand their needs and provide services to meet them. Materials, including access to electronic information resources, should be provided which reflect their interests and culture. In some cases this will mean acquiring materials, which are not traditionally part of a library's resources, which represent youth culture in a variety of media *e.g.* popular novels, book and television series, music, video tapes, teenage magazines, posters. To ensure it reflects their interests it is important to enlist the help of young people in selecting this material. In larger libraries this material with appropriate furniture can form a special section of the library. This will help them to feel the library is for them and help to overcome a feeling of alienation from the library, which is not unusual among this age group. Relevant programmes and talks to young adults should also be provided.

- o In Hamburg, Germany young adults help to select and buy media stock for the young adults library. They select media reflecting their own cultural background and have organised and gained sponsorship for their own Internet cafe.

***Services for Adults:*** Adults have a number of different requirements of an information and library service related to the variety of situations they will encounter. These requirements should be analysed and services developed on the outcome of that analysis. They should include support for

- o Lifelong learning
- o Leisure time interests
- o Information needs

- o Community activities
- o Cultural activity.

Services meeting these needs should also be available to children and young adults.

***Lifelong Learning:*** The public library supports lifelong learning, working with schools and other educational institutions to help students of all ages with their formal education. The challenge of providing educational support provides an opportunity for public libraries to interact and network with teachers and others involved in education. It should also provide a range of materials on a variety of topics, which will allow people to follow their interests and education on an informal basis. The public library should also provide materials to support literacy and the development of basic life skills. In addition the library must provide study facilities to students who have inadequate or no access to these facilities in their homes.

The development in distance learning and its increasing reliance on the Internet is having an impact on the public library. Distant learners, studying at home, are likely make use of their local library as their primary source for material. Public libraries play an increasingly important role within the educational network and should provide space and access to materials to meet this demand.

- o South Dublin County Library Service, Ireland provides self-learning facilities for adults, including computer-based learning and audio and video based language learning materials. The aim is to provide a neutral and supportive environment in which individuals can learn at their own pace.

***Leisure Time Interests:*** People need information to support their leisure time interests and meeting this need by a range of resources in a variety of formats is another key role of the public library. Public libraries must be aware of the cultural, social and economic changes in the community and develop services which are sufficiently flexible to adjust to these changes. The public library should also help to preserve the culture, history and traditions of the local community and make them readily available. The public library, by organising activities and exploiting its resources, should encourage artistic and cultural development in people of all ages. The library is also an important social centre for individuals and groups to meet both formally and informally. This is of special importance in communities where other meeting places are not available.

***Information Services:*** The rapid development of information technology has brought a vast amount of information within reach of all those with access to electronic media. Information provision has always been a key role of the public library and the ways in which information can be collected, accessed and presented have changed radically in recent years. The public library has a number of roles in providing information

- o Providing access to information at all levels
- o Collecting information about the local community and making it readily accessible, often in cooperation with other organisations
- o Training people of all ages in the use of information and the associated technology
- o Acting as a gateway to the information world by making it accessible to all, thus helping to bridge the gap between "the information rich" and "the information poor".

The dramatic development of the Internet has been largely unstructured and uncontrolled. The vast amount of information that can be accessed via the Internet is of variable quality and accuracy and a key role of the librarian is to guide users to accurate information sources which will meet their requirements.

***Services to Community Groups:*** The public library should be at the centre of the community if it is to play a full part in its activities. It should therefore work with other groups and organisations in the community. This will include departments of government and local government, the business community and voluntary organisations. An analysis of the information needs of these bodies should be conducted, and services provided to meet these needs. Not only will this help the organisations involved it will also demonstrate in a practical way the value of the public library to people in the community who are likely to have some influence on the future of the library service. Many public libraries, for example, provide an information service to local government politicians and staff, giving a practical demonstration of the value of the public library.

- o Essex County Library, England creates web sites for voluntary organisations. It makes a small charge, below the commercial level.

***Services to Special User Groups:*** Potential users who, for whatever reason, are unable to use the regular services of the library have a right to equal access to library services. The library should therefore establish ways of making library material and services accessible to these users. These will include

- o Special transport *e.g.* mobile libraries, book-boats and other forms of transport to serve those living in isolated areas
- o Services taken to the home of those people who are housebound
- o Services for those confined in institutions *e.g.* prisons and hospitals
- o Special equipment and reading materials for those with physical disabilities *e.g.* hearing impaired and visually impaired people
- o Special materials for people with learning difficulties *e.g.* easy-to-read materials and cassettes
- o Services for immigrants and new citizens to help them to find their way within a different society and to provide access to media of their native culture
- o Electronic communication *e.g.* Internet catalogues

Services for people with special needs can be enhanced by the use of new technology *e.g.* speech synthesizers for the visually impaired, online access catalogues for those in isolated areas or unable to leave their home, connections to remote sites for distance learning. Innovative schemes should be developed to exploit the new technology to make the public library's services available to as many people as possible.

Services for ethnic groups in the community and for indigenous peoples should be developed in consultation with the group concerned. They are likely to include

- o The employment of staff from the group in the library
- o Collections including the native literature of the group and reflecting the oral tradition and non-written knowledge of the people
- o The application of special conditions, developed in conjunction with local people, to culturally sensitive material.

Library services can also be provided in a variety of places in the community where people congregate

- o Library services are provided at Metro stations in Santiago, Chile.
- o Beach libraries are provided in Catalonia, Spain and in Portugal during the summer months
- o Many forms of transport are used to deliver library services. Book mobiles are common in many countries. There are book boats in Norway and Indonesia, where bicycles and pedicabs are also used, donkeys in Peru which transport laptop computers as well as books, camels in Kenya and donkey-carts in Zimbabwe.
- o In parts of South Africa library services are supplied to informal settlements or squatter areas with no infrastructure. This is done in a variety of ways *e.g.* from car boots, steel cabinets in clinics, cargo containers, under a tree or by individuals or shops to other members of the community. Block loans are provided to schools and old people's homes and storytelling and school project information is available at after-care centres for children unable to go the library.

***Reading Promotion, Information and Literacy:*** Reading and writing and the ability to use numbers are basic prerequisites to being an integrated and active member of society. Reading and writing are also the basic techniques needed for making use of new communication systems. The public library should support activities, which will enable people to make the best use of modern technology. It should support other institutions, which are combating illiteracy and promoting media competence. It can achieve this by

- o promoting reading
- o providing appropriate materials for those with poor literacy skills
- o working with other agencies in the community involved in combating illiteracy
- o participating in campaigns to combat illiteracy and improve numeracy
- o organising events to promote an interest in reading, literature and media culture
- o promoting and providing training in the use of computer technology
- o promoting awareness of new developments in the media market
- o helping people to find the information they need in the appropriate format
- o cooperating with teachers, parents and other contact persons to help new citizens acquire the necessary educational skills which will help them to manage their lives in the new context.

  Public libraries provide a range of creative literature and can use promotional techniques to bring its variety and range to the attention of its users. It can also organise interactive programmes which enable users to exchange views about books they have read.
- o An interactive programme developed in Wandsworth, England uses multimedia software to encourage readers to experiment with their reading and engage in dialogue about books they have read.

- o Offaly and Limerick County Libraries, Ireland, in partnership with literacy students, tutors, local literacy organisers and the National Adult Literacy Agency, are active agents in literacy provision. They make a wide range of books and other materials available to adult literacy students and their tutors and generally promote a reading culture.

### Customer Care

The policies and procedures of the library should be based on the needs and convenience of the users and not for the convenience of the organisation and its staff. Quality services can only be delivered if the library is sensitive to the needs of its users and shapes its services to meet those needs. Satisfied users are the best advocates of the library service.

The public library should have a positive policy of customer care. This means ensuring that in all policy planning, design of libraries and of systems, preparation of operational procedures and drafting of information and publicity material a positive effect on the user should be a prime objective. The following actions should be elements in a customer care policy

- The image projected by all libraries must be neutral and objective
- Staff should be courteous, friendly, respectful and helpful at all times
- There should be a regular programme of staff training in customer care
- Jargon should be avoided in all forms of communication, verbal and written
- Staff should have a friendly and informative telephone manner
- Methods of communication with the users must be provided, *e.g.* billboard, bulletins, web-site
- Library services should be properly planned, adequately prepared and reliable

- The design of the library should be as convenient and inviting as possible
- Opening hours should be convenient for the users
- Open public access catalogues should be available on the Internet so that the user can access services from home and outside opening hours
- There should be efficient renewal and reservation services
- Services should be delivered beyond the library building when users' needs require it
- Users should receive a response in the shortest possible time. Letters and other forms of communication should be answered promptly and courteously
- Equipment should be provided to make library use convenient *e.g.* drop-in boxes for returning materials out of hours; self-service issue and return equipment in the library; answering machines for communicating with the library out of hours
- Where resources allow good quality electronic equipment should be provided in the library including special equipment for the partially sighted and hearing impaired.

***User Participation:*** Customers should be involved in service development:

- o by asking them through surveys what services they use and require
- o by analysing and responding to users' complaints
- o by ensuring the input received from users is considered in the development of policy and procedures
- o by providing feedback to users about the effects of their input on service development
- o by providing suggestion boxes and a complaints procedure.

## User Education

The public library should help its users develop skills which will enable them to make the most effective use of the library's resources and services. Library staff must act as information navigators to help users of all ages make the most effective use of information and communications technology.

Programmes of user education should be developed and the library should make every effort to bridge the gap between the information rich and the information poor. As the new technologies become more commonly available the role of the public library both in providing access to these technologies and in helping people learn how to make best use of them is of vital importance.

Guided tours of the library should take place regularly to introduce people to the library building and services and how to use its tools *e.g.* catalogues and technical equipment. These guided tours have to be carefully planned according to the needs of those taking part. Tours for groups should be organised in cooperation with the institution from which they come.

## Cooperation and Resource Sharing

Overall service to the community is enhanced when libraries develop links for exchanging information, ideas, services and expertise. Such cooperation results in less duplication of service, a combining of resources for maximum effect, and an overall improvement in community services. In addition, individual community members may in some cases be of great assistance in helping the library to carry out special tasks or projects.

***Formal Links:*** The library should establish formal links with other organisations in the local community, *e.g.* schools, cultural institutions such as museums, galleries and archives, literacy programmes, chambers of commerce or boards of trade, in order to coordinate the resources and efforts of each partner and thereby jointly improve services to the community.

***Relations with Schools:*** One of the most important institutional relationships for a public library is that with the local schools and the education system in the service area. Types of linkages and/or forms of cooperation include

- o Sharing resources
- o Sharing staff training
- o Cooperative collection development
- o Cooperative programming
- o Coordination of electronic services and networks
- o Cooperation in the development of learning tools
- o Class visits to the public library
- o Joint reading and literacy promotion
- o Web-awareness for children programme
- o Sharing of telecommunications and network infrastructures
- o Jointly arranged authors' visits.

***Resource Sharing:*** Each library collection is in some degree unique. No collection can contain all the materials that the members of its public require. Libraries therefore can greatly enhance services to their users by providing them with access to the collections of other libraries.

The library should also make its collection available for loan to other libraries through participation in a resource sharing network *e.g.* in a union catalogue or in a local network of information providers, such as schools, colleges and universities.

***Bibliographic Records:*** The library should classify and catalogue its resources according to accepted international or national bibliographic standards. This facilitates their inclusion in wider networks.

***Borrowing from Other Libraries:*** In order to meet the information needs of users the library should borrow materials from other libraries both within the same organisation and beyond. The library should establish interlending policies which address such issues as

- o lending materials to other public libraries
- o the type of materials it is prepared to lend or not to lend
- o the length of time for which materials will be lent

- o when it will request materials from other libraries
- o methods of shipment
- o how the costs of the service will be met
- o action to be taken if materials are lost or damaged.

## Electronic Networks

Public libraries are instruments of equal opportunity and democracy and provide a safety net against alienation and social exclusion from technological advance-a route to universal access and opportunity. The public library is a great equaliser and must reinforce this role by becoming the electronic doorway to information in the digital age.

It should enable all citizens to have access to the information, which will enable them to manage their lives at the local level, to acquire essential information about the democratic process and to participate in an increasingly global society.

The library should provide access to the resources of the library and to those of other libraries and information services through the creation, maintenance and/or participation in effective electronic networks at the local, regional, national and increasingly international levels.

- It is planned to introduce a virtual public library in Denmark. It will be possible to gain access to the catalogues of all public libraries plus the biggest research and special libraries. People will be able to order an item from anywhere in the country and collect it at their local library.

***User Access:*** The library should provide free public access to the Internet/World Wide Web to enable all citizens, regardless of economic means, to have access to information available in electronic form. It should have at least one public access work station with Internet access and a printer that is not shared with staff.

***Remote Access:*** The library should exploit information and communications technology to enable the public to gain access to as many of its electronic resources and services as possible from their home, school or workplace.

If possible they should be made accessible 24 hours a day, seven days a week. Making the library catalogue available on the Internet increases its accessibility for the public and for other libraries. The quality of service is enhanced when the library forms partnerships with the library and information world beyond the local community.

***Staff Access:*** Library staff should have access to the Internet/World Wide Web to enable them to provide better reference and readers' advisory service to users. Staff should have regular training in using the Internet

***Electronic Partnerships:*** Public libraries must form part of information networks and contribute to national information policies if they are to fulfil their role as major information providers. The library should participate in local and/or regional initiatives such as community networks, programmes to develop technologically advanced communities, and electronic networks linking two or more separate agencies, where available.

***Information Navigator:*** The public library's role is becoming one of mediator, of being the public's electronic doorway to digital information and of helping citizens cross the "digital divide" to a better future. The librarian's role is increasingly one of "information navigator" ensuring that the user gets accurate and reliable information

**Access to Services**

Physical accessibility is one of the major keys to the successful delivery of public library services. Services of high quality are of no value to those who are unable to access them. Access to services should be structured in a way that maximises convenience to users and potential users.

***Location of Service Outlets:*** Public library service outlets should be located for the maximum convenience of residents of the community. If possible they should be near the centre of transport networks and close to areas of community activity *e.g.* shops, commercial centres, cultural centres.

The outlet should be highly visible and easily reached by foot, public transport, where available, or by private vehicle. In well developed urban and suburban areas a public library should be available within a journey by private vehicle of about 15 minutes

***Opening Hours:*** In order to provide the best possible access to the library service, the library must be open at times of maximum convenience to the residents of the community.

## Library Buildings

In general when planning a library, the librarian and governing body should consider the following elements:

- The function of the library
- The size of the library
- Designated spaces
- Design features
- Accessible shelving
- Sign-posting
- The ambience of the library
- Electronic and audiovisual equipment
- Safety
- Parking

***The Function of the Library:*** The library should have adequate space to implement the full range of library services that are consistent with the library's strategic plan and that meet local, area or national standards/guidelines.

***The Size of the Library:*** The amount of floor-space required by a public library depends on the unique needs of the individual community as determined through a community needs assessment and the level of resources available. There is no universal consensus on the space required for a public library. Aids to measurement, based on standards developed in North America are included in an appendix and may be of use in the planning process.

***Designated Spaces:*** The library should include space for services to adults, children and young adults and for family use. It should aim to provide a range of materials to meet the needs of all groups and individuals in the community. The range of functions provided and the space available for each will depend on the size of the library. In planning a new library the following should be considered for inclusion:

- *The Library Collection Including*: books, periodicals, special collections, sound recordings and video cassettes and other non-print and digital resources
- *Reader Seating Space*: for adults, children and young adults to use for leisure reading, serious study, group work and one-one tutoring. Quiet rooms should be provided.
- *Outreach Services*: space should be provided to house special collections and preparation areas for outreach services
- *Staff Facilities Including*: work space including desks or PC work stations, rest space for eating and relaxing during breaks and meeting rooms where staff can meet with colleagues and supervisors in private.
- *Meeting Room Space*: for large and small community groups. It should have separate access to the washrooms and to the exterior to enable meetings to be held while the library is closed.
- *Technology Including*: public access work stations, printers, CD-ROM stations, copiers, microfilm/fiche readers, public typewriters and facilities for listening to recorded sound.
- Special equipment including: atlas cases, newspaper racks, self-service book circulation, dictionaries, wall mounted display racks, display stands, filing cabinets, map cases etc.
- Circulation space: sufficient space should be provided for ease of circulation by both public and staff. This can be 10%-15% of public areas and 20%-25% in staff areas.
- Building services: space must be allowed for the mechanical services of the library *e.g.* elevators, heating, ventilation, maintenance, storage of cleaning materials etc.

***Design Features:*** The library should guarantee easy access for all users and in particular persons with physical disabilities. The following features should be included in the planning of a new library:

- o The exterior of the library should be well lit and identified with signs clearly visible from the street
- o The entrance of the library should be clearly visible and located on that part of the building that most users approach.
- o The library should focus on eliminating barriers to use
- o There should be no design features that limit the ability of an individual or groups to use any part of the library
- o Care should be taken to avoid steps as much as possible in both interior and exterior design
- o Lighting levels should comply with those stated in international or national standards
- o Libraries that occupy two or more floors should provide elevators that are close to the library entrance and that easily accommodate wheelchairs and child strollers
- o Baskets or carts can be provided for users in larger libraries
- o The library should provide facilities for the return of library materials when the library is closed. After-hours deposit boxes should be theft and waterproof
- o A library should undertake an "accessibility" audit on a regular basis to confirm that there are no barriers to easy use
- o Wherever possible, local, national or international standards on making public buildings accessible to the disabled should be followed.

***Accessible Shelving:*** Materials should be displayed in open shelves and arranged at a height within easy reach for users. All shelving should be adjustable and preferably on lockable wheels so that it can easily be moved. The furniture in the children's section should be appropriately sized. Shelves should be of accessible height and width for persons using a wheelchair.

***Sign-Posting:*** The library's exterior signs not only identify the particular function of the building but is the library's most basic form of publicity. Signs should therefore be carefully planned to communicate an appropriate image of the library. Internal areas of the library and parts of the collection should be clearly identified by signs of a professional standard so that users can easily find them *e.g.* the library catalogue, magazines, reference services, the children's area, washrooms, Internet stations, copy machines etc. Signs should also be posted in Braille where necessary. Where appropriate signs should be provided in languages used by ethnic groups in the community. Talking kiosks could also be considered to help all users find their way in the library. Directional signs should be erected in nearby streets and town centres to guide the public to the library.

***The Ambience of the Library:*** The library should provide a physical setting for the library service that is inviting to the public and that provides:

- o adequate space to store and display the library collection
- o adequate, comfortable and attractive space for the public to make proper and convenient use of the library's services
- o sufficient space for the library staff to carry out their duties in an efficient and comfortable setting
- o adequate space and flexibility for the future.

The climate of the library should be maintained at a comfortable temperature, using efficient heating and air conditioning. Humidity control helps to protect the stock as well as increasing the comfort of the library.

Larger libraries may include a cafe open either throughout the opening hours of the library or for special occasions. Such facilities are sometimes contracted out to a commercial provider.

***Electronic and AV Equipment:*** As a major function of the public library is to bridge the gap between the information rich and the information poor, it has also to provide access to the necessary electronic, computer and audiovisual equipment. This will include personal computers with Internet access, public access catalogues (OPAC's), microform readers, tape recorders, slide projectors and equipment for the visually and physically handicapped. Wiring should be up-to-date and easily accessible for alterations at a later date. It should also be inspected regularly.

***Safety:*** Every effort should be made to ensure that the library is safe for the public and the staff. Smoke and fire alarms should be provided and security protection for staff and resources. The location of fire extinguishers and emergency exits should be clearly marked. Staff should be trained in first aid and first aid supplies made readily available. Evacuation drills should be carried out regularly. The Library Manager in cooperation with the emergency services should prepare a disaster plan to be put into action in the event of a serious incident *e.g.* fire

***Parking:*** Where users travel to the library in private vehicles there should be sufficient safe and well-lit parking either at or close to the library with appropriately identified spaces for persons with disabilities. If bicycles are a common mode of transport cycle racks should be provided outside the library.

## COLLECTION DEVELOPMENT

The public library should provide equality of access to a range of resources that meets the needs of its users for education, information, leisure and personal development. The library should provide access to the heritage of its society and develop diverse cultural resources and experiences. Constant interaction and consultation with the local community will help to ensure this objective is achieved.

### Collection Management Policy

Each public library system requires a written Collection Management Policy, endorsed by the governing body of the library service. The aim of the policy should be to ensure a consistent approach to the maintenance and development of the library collections and access to resources.

It is imperative that collections continue to be developed on an ongoing basis to ensure people have a constant choice of new materials and to meet the demands of new services and of increased use.

In the light of today's technological advances, the policy must reflect not only a library's own collections but also strategies for accessing information available throughout the world.

The policy should be based upon library standards developed by professional staff with regard to the needs and interests of the community, and reflecting the diversity of society.

The policy should define the purpose, scope and content of the collection, as well as access to external resources.

***Content of the Policy:*** The policy may proceed from statements of universal applicability that are relevant to all library services, through more general statements that are relevant to particular countries, or regions, to statements that are specific to particular library services.

The universal and general statements should form the basis of the policy and could include the following elements

- o Universal:
  - Article XIX of the Declaration of Human Rights
  - IFLA statement on freedom of access to information
  - Statements on Intellectual freedom, free access to library collections
  - Freedom of Information
  - Consideration of the International Copyright Convention
- o General:
  - Purpose of the collection management policy and its relation to the corporate plan of the library service
  - Long and short term objectives

- Access strategies
- History of the collection and/or library service
- Identification of relevant legislation

o Specific:

- Analysis of community needs
- Priorities of the library service
- Parameters of the collection, including special collections and collections for special needs, such as multi-cultural material, literacy and resources for people with disabilities
- Selection and discard principles and methods
- Budget allocation
- Responsibility within the organisation for collection development, selection and discard
- Access to electronic resources including online access to periodicals, databases and other information sources
- The role of the library as an electronic gateway to information
- Cooperative relationships with other libraries and organisations
- Preservation and conservation policies
- Auditing requirements-accessioning, recording, control, discard, sale or disposal
- Financial accountability
- Donations policy
- Complaints procedure
- A resource management plan assessing the current and future needs of the collections.
- Review and assessment of the policy

This is not an exhaustive list but an indication of some of the issues which may be included.

## Range of Resources

The public library should provide a wide range of materials in a variety of formats and in sufficient quantity to meet the needs and interests of the community.

The culture of the local community and society must be reflected in the resource collection. Public libraries must keep abreast of new formats and new methods of accessing information.

All information should be as readily available as possible irrespective of format. The development of local information sources and resources is vital.

***Collections:*** The following categories of library materials may be represented in a typical public library, although this list is not exhaustive

- o Fiction and non-fiction for adults, young adults and children
- o Periodicals
- o Local, regional and national newspapers
- o Community information
- o Government information, including information by and about local administrations
- o Business information
- o Local history resources
- o Genealogical resources
- o Resources in the primary language of the community
- o Resources in minority languages in the community
- o Resources in other languages
- o Music scores
- o Computer games
- o Toys
- o Games and puzzles
- o Study materials including textbooks

***Formats:*** The following formats may be included in a public library collection although this list is not exhaustive and new formats are continually appearing

- o Books, both hard and soft covers
- o Pamphlets and ephemera
- o Newspapers and periodicals inc. cuttings files
- o Digital information through the Internet
- o Online databases
- o CD-ROM databases
- o Software programmes
- o Microforms
- o Tapes and CDs
- o Digital Versatile Disks (DVD's)
- o Videocassettes
- o Laser discs
- o Large print materials
- o Braille materials
- o Audio books
- o Electronic books
- o Posters

## Collection Development

Collections complement services and should not be seen as an end in themselves, unless their specified primary purpose is the preservation and conservation of resources for future generations. Large collections are not synonymous with good collections, particularly in the new digital world. The relevance of the collection to the needs of the local community is more important than the size of the collection.

Collection size is determined by many factors, including space, financial resources, catchment population of the library, proximity to other libraries, regional role of the collections, access to electronic resources, assessment of local needs, acquisition and discard rates, and policy of stock exchanges with other libraries.

***Criteria for Collections:*** The main criteria for collections should be

- o a range of resources which cater for all members of the community
- o resources in formats which enable all members of the community to make use of the library service
- o inflow of new titles
- o inflow of new books
- o a wide range of fiction categories and of subject coverage
- o provision of non-print resources
- o access to external resources such as libraries of other institutions, electronic data bases, local societies, government departments or the community's knowledge of oral cultures
- o discard of old, worn and out-dated books, non-print resources and information sources

### Collection Maintenance Principles

Public libraries of any size will contain materials in a variety of formats. Collection maintenance applies equally to all materials whatever their format. Materials on open access should be in good physical condition and contain current information. A smaller, high quality stock will result in more usage than a large stock with a high proportion of old, worn and out-dated books, in which newer titles can be lost among mediocre stock. Using out-dated reference material can result in the user being given inaccurate information.

Materials in electronic formats complement book collections and will replace them in certain areas. Reference works and periodicals on the Internet and on CD's are viable alternatives to printed formats.

***Acquisition and Discards:*** The library collection is a dynamic resource that requires a constant inflow of new material and outflow of old material to ensure that it remains relevant to the community and at an acceptable level of accuracy. Acquisition rates are more significant than collection size. The acquisition rate is often determined largely by the size of the resource budget. However it can also be affected by other factors *e.g.* the number of books published in local languages, the population served, the multicultural and linguistic diversity, age distribution of the population, access to on line information and special needs such as people with disabilities or older persons. The size and quality of the stock should reflect the needs of the community.

***Reserve Stocks:*** It may be necessary to maintain a collection of books not on open access. This should only contain books, which have a current or future use and which cannot be replaced or found in any other format. This may include special subject collections, which are used on a regular if limited basis and out-of-print fiction. Books, which contain out-dated information or are in poor condition and can be replaced, should be discarded and not held in a reserve stock. In some cases it is efficient to maintain a cooperative reserve with other libraries. The maintenance of a reserve stock should be a regular and on-going activity. The availability of a wide range of information on the Internet and electronic data bases reduces the need for public libraries to keep extensive reserve stocks.

***Interlending:*** No library or library service can be self-sufficient in stock, and an efficient and effective inter-library loan system should be an essential part of every public library service. Within a library service with several outlets a regular programme of exchange of stock between libraries makes maximum use of the stock and provides users with a greater variety of titles from which to choose.

## Standards for Book Collections

The following proposed standards relate to book collections. Local and financial circumstances could lead to variations in these proposed standards. Where resources are severely limited these may be regarded as target figures and medium and long-term strategies should be developed to work towards achieving these standards in the future.

- As a general guide an established book collection should be between 1.5 to 2.5 books per capita.
- The minimum stock level for the smallest service point should not be less than 2500 books.

In the smallest collections materials for children, adult fiction and adult non-fiction may be provided in equal proportions. In larger collections the percentage of non-fiction titles will tend to increase.

These ratios can vary according to the needs of the local community and the role of the public library. Relevant collections to serve the needs of young adults should be developed. Where the library has a strong educational role this is likely to be reflected in the composition of the stock.

Where reliable population figures are not available alternative methods of developing standards are needed. The estimated size of the community served, the size of the library, and the number of current and anticipated users can be used as a basis for developing standards for the size of the collection. Comparisons with a number of existing libraries serving communities of a similar size and make-up can be used to determine a target figure for the size of the collection and the resources needed to maintain it.

## Standards for Electronic Information Facilities

The development of standards for the provision of electronic information facilities is at an early stage. Current standards include the following:

- A standard of one computer access point per 5, 000 population has been used in Canada
- A recently developed standard in England recommends that the total number of work stations, including those for online catalogues, which are available for public use, should not be less than 0.7 per 1000 population
- In Queensland, Australia it is recommended that the following be provided
    - o For populations up to 50, 000-I Personal Computer (PC) per 5, 000 population

- o For populations over 50, 000-1PC per 5, 000 population for 50, 000 population and 1 PC per each additional 10, 000 population.
- o These standards recommend that at least half the public PC's should have access to the Internet and all should have access to a printer.

## Collection Development Programme for New Libraries

An assessment is required of the population demographics in the catchment areas of proposed new library developments to determine the initial mix of collections. The development of local and regional standards should be undertaken to take account of variations in the catchment population to be served by the new library.

***Establishment Phase:*** A basic collection should be established in new libraries to serve the needs of the general population within the catchment area. A sufficient range and depth of resources to meet general needs should be the aim at this stage rather than comprehensive coverage.

The inter-library loan system should be at its peak utilisation during this phase to supplement the developing collections. Ideally a new library should be established with a minimum base stock of 1.0 books per capita. Where this is not achievable a modest growth plan should be implemented to establish this minimum base stock over a period three years. Access to electronic information sources should also be included in this phase of development.

***Consolidation Phase:*** The objective under this phase is to achieve growth in the bookstock size, range and depth. Special conditions of the population are taken into account and collections developed to meet the more in-depth needs of the population served. The book discard factor comes into play and the collection growth rate decreases as discards begin to offset acquisitions. A growth to 2.0 books per capita would be a modest target over a three year period.

***Steadystate Phase:*** The collections meet the needs of the community in depth, range and quantity. The quality of collections is maintained by acquisition rates matching discard rates. New formats are accommodated within the collections as they become available and access is provided to the widest possible range of resources through the use of technology.

***Content Creation:*** The service becomes a content creator and a preserver of local community resources. Content creation includes publication of information booklets and the development of web content by providing access to information about the library or held by the library in printed formats. This positions the library as an electronic gateway by the creation of links to useful web pages.

## Acquisition and Discard Rates

For general bookstock in an established library service the following acquisition rates may be applied:

| Population | Books per Capita per annum | Books per 1000 Population per annum |
|---|---|---|
| Below 25 000 | 0.25 | 250 |
| 25 000 - 50 000 | 0.225 | 225 |
| 50 000 + | 0.20 | 200 |

The following examples suggest the size of stock for communities of different sizes.

***Scenario 1:*** Established library service serving 100 000 population

Median book stock of 200, 000 volumes

Annual acquisition rate of 20, 000 volumes

***Scenario 2:*** Established library service serving 50 000 population

Median book stock of 100, 000 volumes

Annual acquisition rate of 11, 250 volumes

***Scenario 3:*** Established library service serving 20, 000 population

Median book stock of 40, 000 volumes

Annual acquisition rate of 5, 000 volumes

***Small Libraries and Mobile Libraries:*** The general acquisition rates would be inadequate to meet the needs of small libraries and mobile libraries where stock numbers are limited. All libraries require a certain minimum stock in order to provide a sufficient range of books from which users may make their selection.

The acquisition rate of 250 books per 1000 population may not be relevant in the smallest service points where physical limitations may reduce stock levels to below the minimum recommended level of 2500 volumes. In these cases the acquisition rates, renewal rates or exchange rates should be based upon the collection size rather than the population served, and be in the order of 100% or more per annum. An efficient inter-library loan system is essential in these situations (See IFLA Mobile Library Guidelines).

***Special Collections:*** General acquisition and discard rates may not be relevant to some parts of the collection or to particular special collections or where special circumstances prevail. In these cases the collection policy must reflect the special needs. Particular examples of these exceptions are

- o Indigenous resources-the public library has a role in maintaining and promoting collections of resources related to the culture of indigenous people and ensuring access to them
- o Local history resources-material relating to the history of the locality should be actively collected, preserved and made available
- o Libraries in communities with a high proportion of particular groups *e.g.* children, retired people, young adults, indigenous peoples, ethnic minorities or unemployed people should reflect the needs of these groups in their collections and services
- o Reference collections-older reference material may need to be retained to provide historical data for research.

## HUMAN RESOURCES

Staff are a vitally important resource in the operation of a library. Staff expenses normally represent a high proportion of a library's budget. In order to provide the best possible service to the community it is necessary to maintain well trained and highly motivated staff to make effective use of the resources of the library to meet the demands of the community. Staff should be available in sufficient numbers to carry out these responsibilities. The management of library staff is itself an important task. All staff should have a clear understanding of the policy of the library service, well defined duties and responsibilities, properly regulated conditions of employment and salaries which are competitive with other similar jobs.

## The Skills of Library Staff

The public library is a service aimed at all members of the community who will have varied and changing needs. Public library staff will require a range of skills and qualities, including inter-personal skills, social awareness, teamwork and leadership and competence in the practices and procedure of the organisation. The fundamental qualities and skills required of public library staff can be defined as:

- The ability to communicate positively with people
- The ability to understand the needs of users
- The ability to cooperate with individuals and groups in the community
- Knowledge and understanding of cultural diversity
- Knowledge of the material which forms the library's collection and how to access it
- An understanding of and sympathy with the principles of public service
- The ability to work with others in providing an effective library service
- Organising skills with the flexibility to identify and implement changes
- Imagination, vision and openness to new ideas and practice
- Readiness to change methods of working to meet new situations
- Knowledge of information and communications technology

## Staff Categories

The following categories of staff are found in public libraries:

- qualified librarians
- library assistants
- specialist staff
- support staff

In some countries there is an additional category of library technician with an intermediate level of qualifications.

Staff in all categories may be appointed on either a full-time or part-time basis.

***Qualified Librarians:*** Qualified librarians are professional staff who have undertaken a course of study in librarianship and information studies to degree or postgraduate level. A librarian designs, plans, organises, implements, manages and evaluates library and information services and systems to meet the needs of the users of library and information services in the community.

This will include collection development, the organisation and exploitation of resources, the provision of advice and assistance to users in finding and using information and the development of systems which will facilitate access to the library's resources. Qualified librarians will have regular contact with members of the community that they serve. In order to fulfil its functions staff with expertise in specific areas *e.g.* children's libraries, information officers and reference librarians should form part of the professional team. The following is a list of some of the duties of the qualified librarian. This list is not exhaustive nor is it likely that the qualified librarian will undertake all these activities simultaneously.

o Analysing the resource and information needs of the community

o Formulating and implementing policies for service development

o Planning services to the public and participating in their delivery

- o Answering reference and information enquiries using appropriate material
- o Assisting users in the use of library resources and information
- o Developing services to meet the needs of special groups *e.g.* children
- o Creating and maintaining data bases to meet the needs of the library and its users
- o Designing library and information services and systems to meet the needs of the public
- o Developing acquisition policies and systems for library resources
- o Managing and administering library and information systems
- o Cataloguing and classification of library materials
- o Promoting library services
- o Evaluating library services and systems and measuring their performance
- o Selecting, evaluating, managing and training staff
- o Budgeting
- o Strategic planning
- o Keeping up-to-date with current developments in librarianship and information services, particularly electronic information resources.

***Library Assistants:*** The duties of the library assistant include routine circulation functions and operational library tasks such as shelving, shelf-checking, processing library materials, data entry, filing, secretarial support and basic level reader enquiry work. Library assistants are the staff the public will come into contact with most frequently. It is essential, therefore, that they should have a high level of interpersonal and communication skills.

***Specialist Staff:*** Large public library services may employ specialist staff to carry out specific functions *e.g.* computer system managers, administrative, financial, training and marketing staff. Specialist staff may have a qualification in their specialism rather than in librarianship.

***Support Staff:*** Support staff include caretakers, cleaners, drivers and security staff. They carry out important functions which contribute to the smooth operation of the library service. They should be regarded as an integral part of the library's staff.

## Ethical Standards

Public library staff have a responsibility to maintain high ethical standards in their dealings with the public, other members of staff and external organisations. All members of the public should be dealt with on an equal basis and every effort must be made to ensure that information provided is as full and accurate as possible. Librarians must be sure not to allow their personal attitudes and opinions to determine which members of the public are served and what materials are selected and displayed. The public must have confidence in the impartiality of the library staff if the library is to meet the needs of all members of the community. Library associations in some countries have developed codes of ethics, which can be used as models to introduce similar codes elsewhere.

## The Duties of Library Staff

The operation of a library should be a team effort with a close working relationship between all members of staff. It is important, however, that staff are used primarily for tasks related to their skills and qualifications. It is a wasteful use of scarce resources, for example for qualified librarians to regularly carry out routine circulation functions. For the same reason it is not necessary to have a qualified librarian in every library regardless of size or circulation rate. Small libraries open for limited hours do not require the continuous presence of a qualified librarian. They should however be under the supervision of a member of the qualified staff. All staff should have a written contract at the time of their appointment, which clearly states their duties and responsibilities. These should not be changed without consulting the member of staff involved.

## Staffing Levels

The number of staff required in each library service will be affected by a number of factors *e.g.* the number of library buildings, the size and layout of library buildings, the number of departments within each building, services provided beyond the library and requirements for specialist staff. The level of available resources is also a critical factor. Allowing for these and other local differences the following basic staffing level (excluding support staff) is recommended:

- One full-time equivalent member of staff for 2 500 population
- One-third of staff (excluding support staff) should be qualified librarians.

These are basic recommended levels, which will be affected by local circumstances. Where reliable population figures are not available staffing levels can be related to the size of the library, the range of its functions and the number of users. Another method of developing an appropriate staffing level for a library service is to carry out benchmarking with libraries of comparative size and similar characteristics.

## Education of Librarians

Qualified librarians will have undertaken a degree or postgraduate course in librarianship and information studies at a school of librarianship. To ensure that they remain in touch with the latest developments librarians should maintain a process of continuing professional development on a formal and informal basis. It is important that public librarians maintain close links with the school of librarianship in their country and are fully aware of course content. Whenever possible they should participate in the work of the school *e.g.* by contributing lectures, assisting in interviewing of prospective students and other appropriate forms of cooperation.

## Training

Training is a vital element of the activities of a public library. There must be a planned and continuous programme of training for staff at all levels which should include both full-time and part-time staff. The rapid developments in information technology make the need for regular training even more essential, and the importance of networking and access to other information sources should be included in training programmes.

In budgeting for the implementation of new systems, an element should be included for training. In large library services a post of Training Officer should be created to plan and implement the training programme. To ensure funds are available for training a set percentage of the budget should be earmarked for this function.

- It is recommended that 0.5%-1 % of the total library budget should be earmarked for training purposes.

This level of funding for training should be maintained at times of budget reductions as the need for a well-trained staff is very important in such circumstances.

***Monitoring:*** An effective and economical method of training is to introduce a system of monitoring. New staff work with a more experienced colleague who provides guidance and training. The mentor should be able to advise the new member of staff about issues relating to their work and employment. A check list of the training provided by the mentor should be maintained to ensure that it is carried out effectively.

***Contacts:*** In addition to in-service training staff should be given the opportunity to attend short courses and conferences relevant to their ability to do their work. They should be encouraged to be active members of the relevant library association as this creates links with other library staff and provides opportunities for an exchange of ideas and experience. It may also be possible to arrange staff exchanges with staff in other libraries either in the same country or in a similar library in another country, which can be a valuable experience for all those involved.

### Career Development

In order to motivate and retain skilled staff opportunities for career development should be available at all levels. If possible there should be separate career ladders for staff in different categories but when this cannot be achieved opportunities for career progress should be available to all staff. A scheme of performance appraisal should be in place that provides staff with an evaluation of current performance and guidance in improving and developing their skills. It also presents an opportunity to review career progression.

## Working Conditions

All library staff should have satisfactory working conditions and the conditions of employment should be clearly stated in the contract given to the new member of staff when they are employed. Salaries should be at a level appropriate to the level of work being undertaken and competitive with other similar jobs in the community.

***Health and Safety:*** The health and safety of staff must receive priority treatment and policies and procedures be put in place to reduce risks. Consideration should be given to

- o good working conditions for staff
- o ergonomically designed furniture and equipment
- o availability of technical aids for employees with special needs and disabilities
- o the drawing up of evacuation plans and their testing on a regular basis
- o identified health and safety risks being rectified at the earliest opportunity
- o ensuring that all equipment and cabling conforms with recognised safety standards
- o the establishment of a staff health and safety committee
- o appointment and training of staff as first aid officers and fire wardens
- o provision of safety devices for staff, particularly when staff work at nights or away from the library
- o providing advanced driver training for staff who drive library vehicles
- o protective clothing when required
- o limiting the weight of cartons and loads on book trolleys.

Public libraries are often open for long hours including evening and weekend working. In creating work schedules for staff every effort should be made to ensure their working hours provide them with adequate time off at appropriate times for social activity. It is vital that good labour relations are maintained and fostered with staff.

***Anti-Social Behaviour:*** In any building freely accessible to the public, staff will occasionally encounter users who behave in an unpleasant and antisocial manner. Staff should be trained in how to deal with such situations and have alarm systems which can alert other staff. Senior staff should be immediately available to assist staff and full records of such occurrences should be kept.

### Volunteers

Where a library uses volunteer help from individuals in the community to assist library staff a written policy should be in place defining the tasks of these volunteers and their relationship to the library operation and staff. Volunteers should not be used as a substitute for paid staff.

# 4

# Electronic Age Libraries

The thesis of this paper is that the advent of electronic sources of information and their ever increasing volume and variety will require a major redefinition and integration of the role of archives, museums and research libraries. It is my view that the distinctions between all of these apparently different types of institutions eventually will make little sense, though we can anticipate continuing turf battles between the professional groups that manage them as we get to this point. Moreover, some of the functions typical of these institutions will be performed—are already being performed—by other players in the information generation and dissemination game, especially publishers, networks, data archives, and various kinds of information brokers.

New kinds of functional re-alignments between the agencies involved with electronic information sources, a new approach to understanding the kind of market in which they operate, are needed. Until the fact of these re-alignments is accepted and understood, until the integration of the roles and functions of libraries and archives especially is accepted we will not be able properly to come to grips with the information needs of historians.

These and other scholars need access to more information in electronic form than is currently available through commercial and non-commercial services of various kinds. Problems created by new kinds of information and the possibilities of new kinds of information access and manipulation for scholarly purposes will not be solved. The key issues are the impact of new electronic technologies on the custodial, keeping, archival role of "collecting" institutions such as museums, libraries and archives and the increasing availability of information sources in electronic form.

## The Traditional Collecting Institutions

In the past the distinctions between libraries, museums and archives rested on the formats of the typical artifacts that were in their care. Specialised techniques were required to manage these different formats. Libraries and librarianship have been centred on the acquisition of printed books and journals, or surrogates of them such as microfilm. To manage the collections that they created, librarians have developed special techniques for cataloguing, classification and physical arrangement of these materials. In addition extensive and often complicated systems of bibliographic control, backed up by interlibrary lending procedures, have been devised to provide "intellectual" and physical access to what has not been acquired.

Modern librarianship has tended to stress the importance of the library as an access mechanism because of the volume, complexity and cost of the information sources which fall with in the purview of libraries but which no one library, no matter how great a research collection it aspires to acquire, can hope to obtain. Though librarians talk of information storage and retrieval as their *raison d'être,* they usually do not tell an enquirer what he or she might want to know: they provide texts or locations for texts that might be useful in a particular case. They perform their professional functions by identifying and retrieving whole or parts of recorded texts that are held in their own collections or in the collections of other libraries to which they have access. The texts are printed and written collections of manuscripts and personal papers, for example. They may also be images derived from collections of documentary photographs, maps, prints or pictures.

The research library in particular has a clear archival function. It preserves texts over time against possible future uses. The size and comprehensiveness of its collections set it apart from other kinds of libraries and provide the basic criteria for its usefulness to many kinds of scholars. Such libraries are literally documentary archives.

In another sense they are also museums of printed or written artifacts, though this notion seems more appropriate to the rare and other special materials that they contain in an original format. The parts of their collections in print-surrogate form, such as microfilm, would not normally be seen to have the kind of artifactual value that typically attaches to museum objects. Nevertheless, most research libraries functioning to this extent as museums, segregate certain items in their collections for special treatment, including exhibition or display.

These items are usually books and manuscripts whose texts, illustrations and binding are important examples of the book arts. They may also be considered rare, valuable or "curious" for other reasons, as might be the case of books with a foredge paintings or a collection of miniature books. The texts of these items are of secondary-or of no-interest. It is their artifactual importance as "codicological" printed or manuscript objects that counts. Another major category of these special materials are those whose physical characteristics provide important evidence for the scholarship centred on the texts—the province of analytical bibliographers and others concerned with establishing the authenticity of texts and patterns of textual transmission, for example. While these texts, like any texts, are readily reproducible in microfilm or electronically, for example, there are scholarly needs for access to the physical documents as such.

In general, however, the major functionality required of the library is to be able to retrieve the texts in its own or other collections so that the texts can be read or consulted. Except in the instances outlined above the form in which the text is made available, apart from convenience of consultation, is not an issue. Original book or journal or microfilm or electronic versions are equally acceptable. In libraries collections of images, such as photographs or print and picture collections, are usually not permanently exhibited but form part of the stored collections of the library and are retrieved and consulted in the same way as other texts.

The objects collected by museums theoretically have no limit. There are natural history, science and technology, and ethnographic museums; there are museums of musical instruments, costumes, furniture and household equipment, maritime and railway museums. Aquaria and botanical gardens are "living" museums; national and regional art galleries are museums.

Museums are identified by their commitment to the collection, storage and educative display of physical, three dimensional, objects which are in some way representative of the classes of objects, the genera and species, to which they belong. The major use to which the museum puts the objects in its collection is exhibition. They are typically "viewed." Nowadays touring "blockbuster" exhibitions or special temporary exhibitions for which items are borrowed are important aspects of the work of many museums, especially art galleries.

Most museums have an important research function. This typically involves identifying acquiring and processing the objects that fall within a particular museum's ambit. It also underpins the museum's display activities and informs the labelling of items and the special guides to collections or catalogues produced for exhibitions. Depending on the nature of the material, this research function is usually carried out by a permanent staff of specialist personnel such as ethnographers, palaeontologists, archaeologists, art historians and so on. In terms of their permanent collections whether in storage or on permanent display, museums may be considered in a general way to be archives or libraries of objects or specimens. They preserve objects as evidence of the past.

Traditionally, archives collect the records that government and other organisations create as part of their day to day operation. Special techniques have been required to appraise what is often the vast bulk of these records in which individual items are of relatively little pre determinable value—although, subsequently, identification of such items may well be crucial for the research of a particular investigator—to determine what will be retained and for how long. However, as Bearman observes, unlike the case of library bibliographic material, "when we accession, transfer, arrange, weed, document and inventory archival material we change their character as well as enhance their evidential and informational value. The fact of processing, exhibiting, citing, publishing and otherwise managing records becomes a significant fact in their meaning as records, which is not true of library materials" (Bearman 1992: 10)—but may well be true of museum objects?

The anchor of modern archival science is the principle of provenance or "respect des fonds," the identification of the agency creating the records essentially in terms of its institutional relationships and the maintenance of the integrity of the body of records as originally created (Gavrel 1990). This is not dissimilar to the extension that librarians have had to make to what once seemed the relatively simple idea of the author of a book or article which has now become "primary responsibility" for a "work." Because of the nature of the activities of government and other organisations, traditionally archives have contained much library-like material as well as many museum-like objects—maps, printed documents, photographs, motion pictures, sound recordings, architectural models and so on. Unlike libraries and museums, these items are acquired as part of the records that document a particular activity, function or responsibility of the creating body.

***An Undifferentiated Past:*** It is clear that modern libraries, museums and archives are different mainly because of the nature of the materials for which they have primary responsibility and because of the ways in which they provide for the educative and research uses of these materials. The emergence of their specialised functions can be traced in modern times from the previously undifferentiated collections of books and objects of seventeenth and eighteenth century rulers, aristocrats and scholars. In England at the time of the great intellectual movement that began with Bacon and was fuelled by the Puritan rebellion, many scholars and divines speculated about how knowledge of God's creation might be more effectively advanced and disseminated than in the past.

For the circle of reformers that surrounded Samuel Hartlib, for example, the advancement of learning required the creation of a centrally located complex of new kinds of institutions. These would undertake, when appropriate, the systematic collection of antiquities, items of natural history and books and manuscripts. In this complex of institutions would be found scientific colleges and societies, herbaria, laboratories, workshops and specialised information bureaux called Offices of Publick Addresse which would function in association with new kinds of professionalised library services (Webster 1975; Rayward 1994a).

The cabinets of curiosities, so much a feature of the households of gentlemen of the period, reflected not only an interest in what was rare, valuable and out of the ordinary but, as Hudson (1988: 21) has pointed out, also an acute, eager interest in the natural world. There was little of the division between the sciences and humanistic disciplines so widespread today. All learning was seen as having a fundamental unity, ultimately deriving from religion. "Curiosity" and "antiquarian" were terms widely in use then with strongly positive connotations. They have acquired in recent times a more restricted, in the latter case indeed a pejorative meaning, that they did not have in this earlier period. What was important was the acquisition of whatever artifacts—books or objects—that were appropriate to the broad, multi-disciplinary intellectual interests of these individuals. No real distinction of library and museum, nor at another level, of personal from government papers was contemplated.

Thus towards the end of the seventeenth century, the Ashmolean Museum at Oxford, reflecting John Tradescant's Closet of Curiosities in which it had originated, consisted among other things of collections related to natural history and antiquities, a library, and a chemical laboratory (Hudson 1988: 21). Some seventy years, later Sir Hans Sloane's great collection "contained specimens of plants, animals, birds, fossils, minerals, as well as antiquities, works of art, coins, books and ethnographical materials" (Hudson 1975: 18). It is only today that the final separation of the library from other parts of the British Museum, set up by Act of Parliament in 1753 and for which Sloane's collection was a principal base, is occurring, though the natural history collections were removed to South Kensington in 1857. It should also be noted that the other foundation collections for the Museum were the extensive manuscript collections of Sir Robert Cotton and the Earl of Oxford, Robert Harley, which contained large and important collections of State papers and other archives, along with the library of George III which came to the Museum in 1827 (Miller 1974).

An interesting expression of the early complementary relationship of library and museum was the Charleston Library Society. Created in South Carolina in 1748, its collections contained scientific instruments as well as books, and it lent both to its members. In 1773 it initiated an appeal for natural history specimens and in a few years it had amassed "an extensive collection of Beasts, Birds, Reptiles, Fishes, Warlike Arms, Dresses and other Curiosities." This became the nucleus of the collections of what was described in the mid Nineteenth Century as "one of the best museums in the United States" (Hudson 1975: 32-33).

The point being made here is simple and perhaps obvious. It is that the functional differentiation of libraries, museums and archives as reflected in different institutional practices, physical locations, and the specialist work of professional cadres of personnel is a relatively recent phenomenon. This functional differentiation was a response to the exigencies of managing different kinds of collections as these have grown in size and have had to respond to the needs and interests of an ever enlarging body of actual and prospective users. It does not reflect the needs of the individual scholar or even the member of the educated public interested in some aspect of learning or life. For the individual the ideal is still the personal cabinet of curiosities that contains whatever is needed for a particular purpose or to respond to a particular interest, irrespective of the nature of the artifacts involved—books, objects, data, personal papers, government files.

How to regain this functional integrity has been an implicit theme in speculations over the recent centuries about how to mobilise the growing knowledge that is potentially available in the service of society if only a firm enough grip could be taken on it. Hartlib's Office of Publick Addresse, Leibniz's Encyclopedia, Otlet's Office of Documentation and Palais Mondial, Wells's World Brain all imply distress at, or explicitly lament, the problems of complexity and dispersion created by the ever-escalating growth of knowledge. Each represents a special suggestion for a single institutional framework within which the world of learning might be encompassed and better managed (Rayward 1994a).

***"Information-as-Thing"* and its *Electronic Representation:*** This point reflects the argument of an important recent paper by Michael Buckland. Buckland suggests that the institutional arrangements of libraries, museums, archives and the like are concerned with "information-as-thing," things which are informative, which constitute evidence which "could change one's knowledge, one's beliefs, concerning some matter" (Buckland 1991: 353). He seeks to reintroduce into the analysis of information and information systems the extended notion of "document" formulated by Paul Otlet at the turn of the century in Europe and accepted by the English and European "documentalists" (Rayward 1991), a notion that reaches across institutional distinctions.

***Buckland Observes That:*** information storage and retrieval systems can only deal directly with "information-as-thing," but the things that can be stored for retrieval in actual or virtual collections vary in significant ways. Historic buildings, films, printed books, and coded data impose different constraints on the tasks associated with information retrieval systems: selection, collection, storage, representation, identification, location, and physical access. Put simply a museum, an archive, [a] library of printed books, an online bibliographic database, and a corporate management information system of numeric data can all be regarded as species of information retrieval system. But differences in their physical attributes affect how the stored items can be handled (Buckland 1991: 359).

Increasingly "information-as-thing," as text, image, object, datum, specimen, record group or file, is represented or representable electronically or indeed may only be available in that form. In so far as these electronic representations are adequate for a particular purpose, the physical distinctions between the different formats or media of record disappear. That is to say, digitisation eliminates physical distinctions between types of records and thus, presumably, the need for institutional distinctions in the management of the systems within which these records are handled.

Modern telecommunications systems now make it of little concern to the individual researcher where the record he or she wishes to access is held—library, archive, museum, commercial database vendor, or any personal or institutional location on the Internet—provided only that what is wanted is available electronically. In effect he or she can at will create ever-changing virtual "cabinets of curiosities" in which any kind of digitised document—text, image or object—can be introduced and used. The kind of almost science fiction like speculations of Paul Otlet are now realisable practically (Rayward 1994b). Nevertheless, the information retrieval functions outlined by Buckland remain of the greatest importance, though they may be distributed institutionally in new and different ways that require urgent attention

The fundamental question is: *what is to be collected, by whom, and under what circumstances of preservation, availability and access.* This is not a new question. Modern libraries, archives and museums represent historically determined, institutionalised answers to it. Now, however, answers to such a question are no longer certain. In so far as the media of the past continue to be centrally involved there is little problem—books for libraries, objects for museums and government and organisational records for archives. But the electronic versions of these media create problems as to who has responsibility for identifying and collecting them preserving them physically, and maintaining systems of access to them. The new kinds of electronic information sources in their turn present even more pressing problems of this kind because there is no real precedent for dealing with them.

***Problems of "Electronification":*** Traditionally the library has served as a major intermediary between the publisher of bibliographic and substantive information and the scholar. An important function of the library has been to provide access to bibliographic services and to the journal and other literature represented in these services. As the publication of what were formerly printed materials—books and journals particularly—increasingly takes an electronic dimension, publishers and the brokers of online database services are exploring new ways of packaging and marketing this material. It is now possible for individuals quite independently of libraries to search bibliographic databases and to acquire copies of articles and reports and so on from databases held by commercial organisations. These organisations have entered "the document supply" business and their new services are intended to circumvent what they would consider to be the slow cumbersomeness and inefficiency of traditional libraries. These bibliographic and document supply services, however configured and labelled, are performing important "library" functions, clearly recognisable though not usually acknowledged as such.

The question they pose is the extent to which the services are essentially based on what is currently available and commercially practicable to supply at the moment. The complement to this question is the extent to which older, out of date, less used parts of these electronic files will be effectively and permanently "archived." This issue has hardly become a problem yet because most of the files now being dealt with cover a relatively short period of time. But in two or five or ten or fifty years one may assume that the commercial organisations responsible at the moment for these services, given the rapidly increasing size of most of the files and assuming that the pace of technological change will continue unabated, are unlikely to want to preserve the files permanently in an always currently accessible database. Presumably the responsibility for the preservation and the provision of access to these files after their current commercial exploitability has passed will at some point be given over to what have hitherto been called libraries or data archives.

It may well be that libraries will enter the life cycle of formally published material of this kind, the knowledge food chain, if you will, at a later point than in the past. Less concerned with current availability than now because of the way in which commercial organisations have taken over this aspect of their work, they will become essentially archives of databases that no longer have current commercial viability. Critical in this electronic archival process will be the extent to which the files will have to be "remastered" or converted for preservation and access as system software and hardware change.

Museum collections have been undergoing similar processes of digital representation and transformation. In some cases, the traditional "viewing" function that they have performed has been amplified by new kinds of information systems. In these systems electronic representation of objects allows for manipulation, a more intimate, detailed, muitidimensional inspection than is possible conventionally. It also can provide a variety of explanatory and or analytic contexts for them. Museum information systems involve the enormously complex business of contextualising and indexing and retrieving images. The systems use a variety of library related or language-based techniques and graphical expert system techniques. In 1988 it was suggested that there were "almost 250 automated projects of various types... including databases for institutional collections, typological corpora and inventories of monuments" (Cawkwell 1992: 308). Multimedia or hypermedia applications—from museum tours to recreations of eighteenth century Montreal to the exploration of Piero della Francesca's fresco Legend of the True Cross (Trant 1993; Bearman 1991)—pose special problems of storage and access beyond the occasion of initial development and use as working databases. They are important electronic information sources about which typical "library" decisions about collection, physical preservation and the maintenance of access systems have to be made. Similar decisions have to be made for the various manifestations of expert systems used in architecture, engineering, city planning, astronomy and medicine, for example. They represent the status of specialist knowledge at a given time.

Apart from current use, they too have important archival value in documenting the development and history of the aspects of science and scholarship to which they relate. If they are routinely updated as new information comes to hand or if they go through various stages of development, unless "copies" of earlier versions—"editions?"—are kept and "archived" there will be an incomplete record of these developments. Forms of publication of new knowledge, as these systems evolve distributable products on CD-ROM or other media, for example, they become less problematic as materials available for integration into library collections, though even so they will still present the typical preservation problems of system obsolescence and impermanent and changing storage media that are inherent in "electronification."

A similar "edition" problem is presented by various "reference" databases that are constantly updated without new versions of the database being created. The information involved handled in this way knows theoretically no limit. It can be cartographic, economic, social and demographic, meteorological, and company and business related, for example. These databases are electronic versions of directories, handbooks and other reference sources.

They are regularly updated in traditional libraries by new editions and supplements, one function of which is to allow changes in the information presented over time to be tracked. Such changes may be critically important information for particular purposes. Of course loose-leaf services present this same problem in the paper environment. Unless libraries implement some sampling procedure for these databases important "historical," developmental, time-series information will be lost.

Certain new forms of electronic "information-as-thing" that have now to be brought within the set of functions that libraries, archives and museums entail, present these problems in a particularly striking way. Like the databases mentioned above, electronic journals and hypertext systems contain text that may be regarded as unstable, as shifting in meaning as it accumulates commentaries, revisions and interpolations.

The hypertext document, it has been observed somewhat hyperbolically, "functions as an elastic palimpsest allowing access to and reworking of layered texts." For Davenport and Cronin "Hypertext may transform the practice and culture of science by opening up texts for comment and verification in ways which previously have been impossible "(Davenport and Cronin 1990:).

As texts shift and change and merge not only are general questions raised about the responsibility of the author and the integrity and authority of the document, practical issues of what parts or states of the text will be kept and how changes in it will be monitored and recorded become pressing. Perhaps this is an area to which archival appraisal techniques, which focus centrally on the evidential value and uses of records and are concerned as much with disposal as retention, may well be brought to bear.

The electronic office which utilises an enormous range of software and hardware has dramatically affected the work of archivists. It epitomises some of the major problems that are created by electronic information sources that originate in new processes of communication based on telecommunications and electronic networks. As Gavrel points out, "sophisticated systems provide access to a variety of software and hardware, as well as gateways to exterior information systems.

In most cases, these systems do not have record management capabilities and documents can be destroyed voluntarily or involuntarily by the creators at any point in time. Naming conventions for documents are not standardised within organisations and the choice of document names is left to the creators of the documents... The knowledge of file classification systems within a particular organisation is limited and documents are often given acronyms which may have meaning at the time of the creation of the document but usually not several weeks later and certainly have no meaning to others in the organisation. Most creators manage their documents within their own personal filing systems without reference to any corporate system or link to existing hard copy records within the organisation" (Gavrel 1990: 18)

Gavrel notes that while hitherto few documents related to policy development, programme management an other organisational activities have been maintained in electronic form, with the development and use of more and more Local Area Networks this can be expected to change.

She also points out that many of the sources of information "do not reside inside the organisation but are accessed by communication links or gateways outside the organisation" (Gavrel, 19). Not only, then, do the records have to be appraised and account taken of the particular problems of inter organisational databases, but "it may also be necessary, to ensure that the archival record is complete, to preserve certain software and access records of the system.

If certain records only existed for seconds on the screen, it may be important for the archivist to select, along with the records, the access logs for the system which identify by whom and when the system was accessed. The value of these logs will not be in the records themselves but in providing proof that certain systems were accessed at a particular time and by whom. In a similar vein, it will become important to retain certain software particularly if decision-making processes are a fundamental part of the software" (Gavrel, 22)

## The Centrality of the Archival Function

It can be expected that archival records in electronic form make possible the use of indexing techniques that have been developed for more general applications. The principle of provenance or *respect Des fonds is* essentially inadequate for all but the few users of archives who are interested in the nature of the organisation that the record arrangements reflect. Most users are interested in general problems or topics on which they are seeking information. Captured electronically, it should be possible instantly to recreate or change information about provenance to reflect shifting organisational alignments of functions and offices if this is required.

The records themselves can be copied and manipulated in any way that available software allows; their original order should he automatically regeneratable. It should be possible to search them for personal, corporate or geographic names and by subjects either in full text mode or on text surrogates to the degree that these have been provided. Effectively the archive and the library become identical as bodies of text, though record volume in the archive, its "legal, fiscal and operational need for evidence" (Bearman 1992), and the complexity and variability of record structures may remain a problem for the design of the data content of archival documentation and for information retrieval techniques.

Equally appropriate for the application of archival techniques is the ever changing list servers and electronic noticeboards available through the Internet. Who is to assume responsibility for the appraisal of these "record groups" and the development of a permanent archive from them? This is an important conundrum given the near universality and the informality of access that is possible to them. Are there to be special libraries or computer-based archives into which these "records" will go. Certainly contemporary data archives pay no attention to them.

How are the bulletin boards and list servers to be monitored, weeded, sampled, acquired, processed and stored? Is it sufficient to leave this to chance in the same way that in the past libraries have left the collection of ephemeral materials that document social movements or other phenomena to chance, relying for what they obtain not on their own collecting activities to ensure continuous contemporary coverage but on later bequests and donations? Is someone cumulating a special interest file related to an issue or subject now being explored nationally or internationally through these Internet functions? In what form might this file come to a library?

This raises the more general problem of casually created files that might be of later value, what might be called a personal archive. In the past this took the form of drafts, sketches, notebooks, files of correspondence, all involving the creation of paper records whose preservation was often purely accidental. Libraries and archives have collected these "personal papers" as an important part of their archival function. These personal records are now increasingly kept electronically on hard disks or down loaded onto floppy disks. Particularly important is correspondence through electronic mail. Electronic mail can provide automatically a record of what can be frequent, regular, sometimes almost daily interactions between individuals or groups of scholars and others sharing common interests. Informal electronic mail networks have become a vital a part of academic life.

They approximate nothing so much as the correspondence networks that were so important a feature of the Republic of Letters of the late seventeenth and early eighteenth centuries, a "virtual" institution effectively displaced by the growth of our modern pattern of scientific communication involving journals, newsletters and the like. The messages in the e-mail system will be as important for historians in the future as the messages that flowed as written correspondence in the networks of the Republic of Letters have been for contemporary historians. How are we to approach the problems of identifying, collecting, weeding and preserving them?

These electronic personal records are presumably no more effectively maintained than similar paper records in the past. Weeding personal electronic files or not is more or less related to the same qualities of personality that govern the management of personal files on paper. It could be that, as the costs of disks have fallen and their capacity increased, more documents or records are casually being kept in electronic format than was the case in the past because nothing much has to be done with the disk unlike paper records which have physical bulk and space requirements. On the other hand it is easier to erase electronic records than to destroy their paper counterparts, though their informative or evidential value for the scholar is certainly as great.

Managing access to the contents of these electronic files constitutes a far greater problem for libraries and archives than managing access to the contents of paper documents. The disks that contain the electronic files, like their paper counterparts, will be found in drawers and boxes and attics at long periods after their creation, perhaps at long periods after the death of their authors. In principle of the greatest value for biographers, historians, literary critics and others, just as their paper counterparts were, they cannot be appraised visually as paper record can. They require software and hardware that so far has quickly been superseded and become obsolete. Thus with the passage of time these electronic records may not easily be converted from one format to another if at all. All of the problems mentioned above in relation to the electronic office characterise such files.

As industry standards become more widespread and inter convertibility easier, some of these technical difficulties will lessen. Nevertheless, how to acquire these files and from whom and how to manage them—above all how to read them—will constitute, are currently constituting, important challenges for the librarian and archivist. Close access to museums of computer hardware and software supported by historical "research" collections of system documentation will be needed. These will be the tools by which technical specialists, who will function in effect as system cryptographers, will in the future decode the mysteries of "found" electronic files.

Recently Orlikowski and Yates have studied database of about 2000 e-mail messages that were generated by a group of programmers from around the United States who were working to create a standard LISP programming language from the many dialect forms in which it existed. The messages, as well as being sent to all sites for the project, were automatically archived.

The research of the two investigators is interesting not only inherently but because of the way in which it indicates the kinds of unexpected, generally unanticipatable uses to which historical, documentary, archival evidence may be put. Orlikowski and Yates used the archive, not to reveal anything about the task at hand, not to explore the manifest content of the records, but to "show how members of an ad hoc group attempting to accomplish a particular task imported existing genres of communication into their electronic interactions, then modified them to reflect the social context, the particular capabilities of the medium, and the specific nature and timing of the project" (Orlikowski and Yates 1993: 30). Where is the archive now? Where are the messages that the researchers indicated were not included—what they called the "backdoor" communications between individuals? The archive was transcribed by the researchers who thus created another manifestation of it. Where will one or other body of records be in ten years time? Will individual project workers have maintained their copies of the e-mail correspondence? How can we ensure that if located in ten years time the archive in electronic form can still be read? Whose responsibilities are the practical answers to these questions?

It is becoming possible to replace paper materials with electronic versions which can be manipulated in various ways not possible in the original versions. As new kinds of high volume scanning techniques and new kinds cheap, high density storage media emerge, it will be possible to capture electronically the text, the information content, of printed materials ever more quickly and cost effectively. Preservation and space problems that bedevil libraries attempting to manage huge paper collections might well then be obviated by electronic storage.

The "electronic" archive, representing runs of journals or large bodies of special materials—texts in the Short Title Catalogues, for example, or the correspondence and other papers of important historical or literary figures—may replace microfilm as the way to build up research collections. Such archives will become increasingly easy to create; they are readily duplicated and are certainly saleable.

It may be that for libraries, for example, the increasing volume of information available in electronic form may not only require them to re-define their archival function as discussed in this paper, it may also change their relationship to their traditional materials. If paper is largely replaceable for every day library use by text in electronic form then libraries will begin to view paper sources differently. Perhaps some of the paper-based sources will be for current casual use to be replaced by electronic forms for preservation and storage.

The analogy here is the cumulation on microfilm of the issues of newspapers and journals that are then discarded when the microfilm copy becomes available. Other sources may have artistic or evidential or rarity or exemplary value that electronic versions of text cannot replicate. These will tend to be relatively few in number, if past experience is anything go. What is fundamentally important about them is their physicality as books and manuscripts and they become functionally little different form traditional museum objects.

Thus libraries, because of the emphasis they place on the artifactual value of materials that are retained in that format will begin to resemble museums. The question may well become: why would one wish to retain materials in printed form except for what they represent as atifacts if their texts can be cost effectively transferred to electronic systems which provide better storage and access capabilities?

**Preserving Access to Digital Information in Libraries, Museums, Archives**

In Australia there have been sustained attempts to find practical answers to the last question above. In 1985 the Australian Council of Libraries and Information Services (ACLIS) created a Task Force on the Preservation of Australian Electronic Information, observing that "the preservation of Australian information in electronic format will be the responsibility of Australian libraries, archives and possibly museums" (ACLIS 1992: 4). The rather limited approach adopted by the ACLIS task force and the slow development of is work were subsumed in a much more comprehensive and far-reaching initiative.

In March 1992, sponsored by the National Library of Australia, a national conference, "Towards Federation 2001: Linking Australians with their Heritage," was held in Canberra. Its purpose was to explore how to provide cooperatively across the range of national heritage and other interested organizations improved access to the Australian documentary heritage. One of its resolutions was "that the Australian Archives, the Australian Council of Library and Information Services (ACLIS), the National Preservation Office and the National Film and Sound Archive establish a working party to develop guidelines for the management of material in electronic format "(Towards Federation 2001, 1992: p.).

The working party, now known simply as PADI (Preserving Access to Digital Information), comprises as well as the organizations listed above representatives of the Mathematical and Information Sciences Division of the CSIRO (Commonwealth Scientific Industrial and Research Organization), the Commonwealth Government's Department of Communications and the Arts, and the National Museum of Australia. The involvement of the archive sectors-and other sectors as well we can surmise-"was identified as critical since the issues were seen to be basically the same regardless of the nature of the organization" (PADI AVCC Report: n.p.).

PADI "major goal" is "providing mechanisms that will help ensure that digital information is managed with appropriate consideration of preservation and future access. The Medium Term Plan, only available in digital form through the World Wide Web, lists six objectives for the working party:

1. To facilitate the development of national strategies.
2. To develop and maintain a Web site for information and promotion purposes.
3. To establish a forum to exchange views.
4. To develop preservation and access guidelines and strategies.
5. To impact on preservation aspects of national digital information initiatives.
6. To actively identify and promote relevant activities. (PADI Medium Term Programme, n. p.)

The Working Party has developed a range of strategies by which it hopes to meet its objectives and each strategy is targeted at major players in the game. "While collecting institution, governments and the records management industry will remain the key players in PADI 's activities, attempts will be made to involve universities, the information technology industry, publishers and creators of digital information, and commercial business sectors."(PADI Medium Term Programme, 1996, n. p.). With funding from the Australian Vice Chancellor's Committee (AVCC), in 1996 PADI commissioned a survey of

242 cultural bodies grouped as archives, galleries, libraries, museums others "to determine policies and procedures associated with the acquisition, production and preservation of Australian digital information." A Website has also been established.

PADI represents a coordinated, sophisticated but practical attack on the problems thrown up for the historian and other scholars by "electronification." of information. Implicit in its work is a recognition that the boundaries between collecting organizations such as libraries, archives and museums are now necessarily blurred as has been argued in this chapter. It is clear that the active involvement of representatives of all of these kinds of organizations is necessary in the search for solutions that will allow appropriately managed preservation of electronic information for the future.

## Conclusion

It is clear that the availability of increasing volumes of information in electronic form and the emergence of new kinds of electronic information sources are presenting critical professional challenges for librarians and other "information professionals." How they meet these challenges will determine how the institutions under their care respond to the needs of historians and other scholars for the sources needed for them to fulfil their scholarly roles and responsibilities. Being able to respond to these challenges effectively will largely depend on how well these "information professionals" are able to transcend the limitations that their highly developed professional "cultures" impose upon them.

These professional cultures have defined themselves to some extent in opposition to each other and those influenced by them necessarily tend to see the world differently. Libraries, archives and museums are agencies that represent institutionalized organizational practices that the different professional cultures have evolved and sanctioned. The key element around which the cultural differences have crystallized has been the different kinds of artifacts for which historically the different professional groups have assumed responsibility.

At least for the foreseeable future each of the professional groups will still have to continue to deal—perhaps preponderantly—with their "traditional" materials. Thus there is no reason to suggest that differences between them will cease to exist and that we must envisage their physical consolidation. Nevertheless, the argument of this paper is that "electronification" can only be dealt with adequately by questioning and rising above traditional modes of territorial demarcation between these groups. To the extent that they are dealing with the same kinds of "thing"—electronic records—we must begin to explore the idea of functional integration between the agencies—libraries, archives and museums—that are responsible for collecting and managing the public's access to them.

# 5

# The Law of Indigenous Librarianship

Several publications describe the historical development of tribal libraries. Instead of reviewing similar ground, this article will instead present a snapshot of library services today in tribal communities. Tribal communities are populated by independent sovereign nations of indigenous peoples residing within the contemporary boundaries of the United States. There are 550 federally recognized tribes, and it is impossible and erroneous to generalize about tribal libraries. They may have separate or combined archives, community libraries, school libraries, tribal college libraries, technology centres, cultural centres or museums, and literacy programmes. One or more of the programmes may be combined into a delivery outlet or may be provided in tandem in a multipurpose tribal information centre, social service centre, or health clinic.

The variations in organization may be due to tradition and/or to the local economic situations. In terms of governance, tribal librarians may report to another tribal agency, such as the tribal education office, to a head of information technology, or directly to the tribal council. Just as their organization structures and missions vary, so do their services. Tribal library patrons are Native peoples across the lifespan: library personnel are just as likely to work with preschoolers in reading readiness programmes as they are to plan and coordinate oral history projects that document elders' lives. They develop collections that reflect indigenous lifeways across generations.

While tribal library organization and services vary, they do share the same needs for stable funding, education and training for personnel, and access to new materials and technologies. This article provides a summary of some current initiatives in tribal college, tribal school, and tribal community libraries. Instead of reporting on a single case study, the emphasis is on describing statewide, regional, national, and even international efforts to further indigenous library services.

## Support for Tribal Libraries

Tribal library budgets are determined within the tribal community, whether it is tribal council/governance, tribal school board, or tribal college coordinating board.

Regardless of the source, tribal libraries are notoriously under funded. The needs of tribal libraries are great yet tribal librarians often operate in isolation. Even electronic communication may be difficult due to unreliable Internet access and little technical support.

The challenges of great geographic distances, insufficient financial support, lack of reliable communication systems, and the overtaxed lives of tribal librarians makes national coordination very difficult.

There are some efforts to support gatherings of indigenous librarians internationally. The first International Indigenous Librarians Forum was held in Auckland, Aotearoa/New Zealand, in November 1999 and the second in Jokkmokk, Sweden, in September 2001. A third Forum is scheduled for November 2003 in Santa Fe, New Mexico, USA. Forums are organized by representatives of the indigenous library organizations in the respective countries and include workshops, formal presentations, and directed deliberations. While these events provide opportunities for local indigenous information specialists to meet with others, they have largely been open only to those with the financial means to attend.

International efforts need to investigate other mechanisms to be more broadly inclusive of indigenous information specialists residing outside of developed countries. The International Federal of Library Associations and Institutions (IFLA) has expressed interest in indigenous librarianship. This includes programmes sponsored by two of its forty–five sections, Libraries Serving Disadvantaged Persons, and Library Services to Multicultural Populations.

In addition the IFLA Governing Board approved a resolution in 2002, now referred to as the IFLA Statement on Indigenous Traditional Knowledge. This is an acknowledgement of the value of tribal knowledge systems and the need to collect, document, preserve, and provide access to such knowledge. Note that applications of this statement must insure that indigenous peoples are involved directly in interpreting the guidelines.

The U.S. federal government provides some funding for tribal libraries through the Institute of Museum and Library Services (IMLS) and federal legislation in the form of the Library Services and Technology Act (LSTA). The IMLS Native American Library Grant programme provides two categories of grants. The two non–competitive grants are the Basic Grants, approximately $4, 000 per year for general operating expenditures, and Professional Assistance Grants, $2, 000 per year to support an honorarium and expenses of a consultant. Tribal libraries compete to receive the Enhancement grants of up to $150, 000 to expand services or work cooperatively with other libraries. In some cases the small IMLS Basic Grants are the only financial support that tribal community libraries receive.

IMLS also provides state library agencies with funding. In turn, the state libraries distribute the IMLS funding through various grants. For example, tribal libraries in Washington State have received subsidy grants to access databases. Public libraries in Arizona that partner with tribal libraries to extend services to underserved communities may receive funding through a competitive grant process.

The IMLS funded the Five State Project which provided financial support for the staff of tribal community libraries, archives, and museums to gather separately in Arizona, Colorado, Nevada, New Mexico, and Utah and together at one annual event. These regional meetings were expanded in 2002 with a national conference in Mesa, Arizona. Papers and workshops will be published in a monograph in 2004. The Five State Project was a rare example of a tribally centred continuing education opportunity.

In 1997, the Bill & Melinda Gates Foundation launched a U.S. Library Programme that has delivered 40, 000 computers at 10, 000 public library outlets serving low economic communities in the United States. In 2001 the Foundation unveiled its customized Native American Access to Technology Programme (NAATP) for the nineteen Pueblo, two Apache, and Navajo tribal communities in New Mexico, as well as tribes in Arizona, Colorado, and Utah. NAATP delivered computer equipment and software, some initial onsite training, and access to a technical assistance hotline for three years. By June 2003 the Foundation had provided nearly $7 million towards NAATP. The NAATP programme also included an Intern programme for students at tribal colleges and the University of Arizona's graduate School of Information Resources and Library Science (SIRLS).

The Arizona State Library, Archives and Public Records department provided additional funding in 2002/2003 to support staffing on–site technology interns at nine sites in Indian Country as a test to assess whether tribal communities would provide local support to continue the staff positions.

## AILA

The closest organization to a national tribal libraries organization is the American Indian Library Association (AILA). AILA, which has been in existence for nearly 25 years, represents tribal library interests to the American Library Association (ALA) and to the public at large. Because its mission is so broad, its impact on tribal library development is probably best felt through the efforts of individual AILA members who report on their work at membership meetings and in the American Indian Libraries Newsletter. AILA membership is consistently around 300, a number that includes institutional members that join to receive the print–only newsletter. Approximately 30 AILA members and interested observers attend bi–annual meetings held in conjunction with the ALA Midwinter Meetings and annual conferences. While AILA provides a contact point for some professional librarians interested in tribal libraries, few practicing tribal librarians are able to afford to costs associated with attending AILA business meetings.

AILA is officially affiliated with ALA. The ALA Office for Literacy and Outreach Services' Subcommittee on Library Services to American Indians is another venue for librarians to collaborate to develop conference programmes and otherwise increase the visibility of tribal library needs. Members of this committee have recently developed a webliography of resources on Native librarianship. Tribal community librarians who are unable to attend ALA conferences may attend state library conferences, such as the New Mexico Library Association and Arizona Library Association annual conferences, or regional meetings such as those planned by the Mountain Plains Library Association. Tribal school librarians may be involved in meetings of the National Indian Education Association (NIEA). Tribal college librarians may attend national general library conferences or the American Higher Education Consortium (AIHEC) annual conference for individuals involved in education at tribal college settings. California, Alaska, and New Mexico illustrate how states can work with tribal communities to advance library services.

Support and recognition of tribal libraries varies from state to state. California is the state with the greatest American Indian population—333, 000 people according to the 2000 U.S. census—and the largest number (150) of federally recognized tribal groups. In 2001/2002 the California State Library sponsored a "Tribal Library Census & Needs Assessment" of thirty–seven reservations in the southern region of the state. Results of this study found that just over half (53 percent) of the tribal communities had libraries and three–fourths (77 percent) of these libraries had open hours for the public. Only a third (38 percent) of the libraries had salaried personnel on site and none of these staff members had an entry–level professional degree or school media certification. Unfortunately, to those involved in tribal library development, these figures do not sound unusual. The Alaska State Library sponsored a workshop for Alaska Library Directors that resulted in a document referred to as the "Culturally Responsive Guidelines for Alaska Public Libraries." These guidelines cover the categories of the library environment, services and programmes, collections, and staff. Tribal libraries could also benefit from the creation or customizing of other planning documents, including output measures for tribal library settings and quantitative standards. Similarly, tribal librarians should work with community members to develop interpretations of reference and library instruction guidelines such as the Big6 for information literacy and the Reference and User Services Association's Guidelines for Behavioural Performance of Reference and Information Services Professionals.

The New Mexico Library Association is the only state library association with a membership unit devoted to Native librarianship, the Native American Libraries Special Interest Group (NALSIG). NALSIG established the New Mexico Friends of the Tribal Librarians, a non–profit organization that can lobby and fundraise to support tribal library efforts. The New Mexico tribal library community is also involved with promoting statewide library development efforts such as a recent referendum to increase general operating expenditures for community libraries through a General Obligation Bond.

In New Mexico the State Library also has special services for tribal libraries. Their Tribal Libraries Programme (TLP) receives $270, 000 per year from the New Mexico State budget to support tribal library services. TLP received additional support from the Bill & Melinda Gates Foundation to assist tribal library staff in converting their cataloging records to a common automation system. In addition, TLP provides small grants directly to tribal libraries and additional training.

## Tribal School Libraries

Approximately 50, 000 of the nearly 600, 000 Indian children in the United States attend the 185 schools managed by the federal Bureau of Indian Affairs (BIA). Children also attend public schools off reservation, private schools (including religious mission schools), or are homeschooled. Funding for tribal school construction typically excludes funding for school libraries. School library budgets are also usually low to nil, depending on the prerogative of the school principal.

Like other school media specialists, tribal school librarians are generally required to have teaching certification along with their library training. Since Native Americans have smaller numbers of secondary school and college or university graduates than people from other underrepresented groups, the pool of potential Native school librarians is initially small. The need for two degrees results in a double barrier for Native people to assume professional positions at tribal schools. As a result, Native school library staff tend to be in assistant or clerical positions. When local schools lack a clear understanding of the role and potential service of a school media specialist, the librarian or library assistant ends up serving multiple roles within the school setting. One library clerk at a tribal school in New Mexico served as the sole librarian, manager of a computer lab in a location apart from the library, lunch break playground monitor, school bus driver, and girls' basketball and track coach.

Tribal school librarians deserve a national consultant who can provide guidance on needs ranging from facilities planning to the development of culturally centred library instruction plans for Native children. Greater effort is needed to acculturate tribal school librarians into the profession of librarianship. Incentives should be provided locally for tribal school media centre staff to attend and participate in state and national library conferences and to take advantage of continuing education opportunities available to other information professionals.

### Tribal College Library Services

There are 33 tribal colleges within the United States. Since 1990, tribal college librarians gather annually at an institute organized by librarians at Montana State University—Bozeman. The Tribal College Librarians Professional Development Institute is a continuing education event with tours, presentations, and workshops.

Tribal colleges are ideal settings for promoting librarianship as a professional career. Yet, no tribal college offers an undergraduate major or minor in library studies. Few tribal colleges offer four–year degrees, so it is not surprising that no tribal college offers an American Library Association–accredited master's degree programme or school media centre certification. Students majoring in American Indian studies at one tribal college, Haskell Indian Nations University in Lawrence, Kansas, may enroll in one undergraduate class on tribal archives, but this educational opportunity is rare. Distance education programmes or substantial financial aid to attend in–residence programmes may be the answers to recruiting Native students to schools of library and information science.

There currently exist several grant or scholarship programmes to assist Native students to pursue graduate degrees in information studies or school media centres. These include the American Library Association's Spectrum Initiative Scholarships, and the Knowledge River Centre for the Study of Hispanic and American Indian Library and Information Issues at the University of Arizona. Over the five first years of the Spectrum Initiative, fewer than ten of the 277 initial scholarship recipients were Native students. Twelve, or half, of the first cohort of graduating Knowledge River students were Native. The American Indian Library Association has a new scholarship to assist a Native library school student.

Obviously, a variety of educational approaches are needed to increase the number of Native librarians in the workforce. These include degree–granting in–residence and distance delivery master's and bachelor's degrees as well as workshops and online courses that contribute to skills development without awarding an academic degree. The key is flexibility at all levels of programme development, from admissions and coursework to modes of delivery.

## Tribal Community Libraries

Public libraries on tribal homelands are referred to as tribal community libraries. Like other information settings, they have been greatly impacted by technology and especially by the arrival of public access computing. While they may receive one–time donations of equipment and software, they are often unable to afford upgrades. Staff at tribal community libraries also feel pressure to upgrade their skills, especially in areas related to technology troubleshooting.

Another pressure that tribal community libraries experience is the constant need to build community support. They need to develop a direct communication line to tribal governance so that their needs are known and so that they can tailor services that support tribal sovereignty initiatives. Some tribal community libraries are trying to initiative traditional programmes such as after school programmes for children and book clubs. Tribal libraries probably have yet to reach their potential as unique sites where community members can create content, preserve culture, and develop new skills.

## Recommendations for Funding and Training

As with American public libraries, tribal libraries must develop stable financial support at the local level. This involves tribal librarians engaging in well–developed and multi–faceted marketing efforts and developing coalitions with educational institutions and cultural heritage efforts. Tribal community libraries especially need to be "at the table" at tribal initiatives, especially those involved with literacy efforts and native language revitalization.

As colleges and universities are rediscovering community service and engaged citizenship, they are one category of potential fruitful collaborative partners for tribal libraries. The Universities of Michigan, Texas, and Washington provide three examples.

The School of Information at the University of Michigan secured funding from the Kellogg Foundation to provide technology training for tribal college librarians to develop websites for their libraries.

The School of Information also hosted a meeting on "Indigenous Digital Collectives," held in Hilo, Hawaii in 2001, providing an opportunity for indigenous librarians from around the world to meet with academics to initiate planning on collaborative efforts. This meeting resulted in the publication of a special issue of the online journal, *D–Lib Magazine*, in March 2002. The School also offers an annual Cultural Heritage Preservation Institute at Dine College in Tsaile, Arizona as a technology workshop for Navajo teachers and students.

The University of Washington's Student Access and Computing Group provided the Quileute Tribal School library with 20 computers they refurbished, along with technical support in the winter of 2002. A Native Professor and her students in the School of Information at the University of Texas at Austin developed "If I Can Read, I Can Do Anything" in the fall of 1998 for ALA President Sarah A.

Long. The programme has evolved from a pilot programme at one tribal school to a national reading club for Native children attending schools at or near reservations. By the summer of 2003, volunteers with "If I Can Read" had delivered over $100, 000 in new books to tribal school libraries, and helped organize a variety of activities promoting reading. These include a national art and writing contest, annual scary story online chats, donations of new dictionaries to children, and onsite cataloging.

Children at the 20 participating sites receive membership cards and reading incentives throughout the school year. "If I Can Read" staff includes a director with a half–time graduate research associate, a local team of graduate student volunteers, a national advisory board, and volunteers who serve as sponsors or liaisons to individual schools. Still, the largely volunteer–run project has focused more on collection development than on other needs of tribal school libraries, including continuing education and training and assistance in developing policy documents such as collection development policies.

At the beginning of the twenty–first century, the greatest accomplishments in tribal library development are reflected in regional efforts. Similarly, individuals involved with tribal communities are endeavoring to be included at large scale efforts to make sure that tribal library concerns are included in the development of new initiatives. It provides a virtual space for developing an online community plus content, such as sample policies and purchasing advice, for librarians providing public access computing. Online courses are available for those who desire to extend their skills in such areas as XML, HTML, and computer troubleshooting.

Tribal communities should seek partners in native language revitalization efforts. This includes collaborating with large–scale digitization efforts. One such effort is the International Children's Digital Library (ICDL). ICDL is a five–year research project managed by the University of Maryland and the Internet Archives. In addition to studying reading habits of children in five countries, the ICDL will digitize 10, 000 books for children. Books suitable for 3–13–year–olds will be selected and will be digitized in their entirety. This is an opportunity for tribal communities that have produced children's books with Native language text to have them professionally produced and made available to anyone who has access to the Internet.

This discussion has discussed several solutions to address the needs of tribal community libraries. Many of these involve targeting financial aid to improve facilities and support the infrastructure of personnel and technology. Although networks of Native information specialists and librarians exist, few individual librarians can afford to travel to conferences. The dearth of Native professional librarians must be addressed by marketing librarianship as a career in tribal communities and providing scholarships at all levels of higher education for Native students.

Partnerships among state libraries, library associations, universities, and tribal community library organizations have begun to form, but these relationships need to be nurtured and exploited. There is a vast body of knowledge among library and information science professionals and we must find the means to apply it to the needs of the tribal community. Guidelines describing collection development and the role of library personnel need to be tailored for Native libraries, so that they might be implemented even in tribal communities and schools without the funding for a professional librarian or certified media specialist. Library services in tribal communities are becoming more sophisticated but still lag in some aspects behind their peers in the library world at large. One reason for the disparity is the heterogeneous nature of their missions, governing bodies, and communities served. This diversity should also be celebrated and indulged. No two communities have the same resources, or needs.

## Creating a Library Plan for the Sami in Sweden

The work of researching and implementing a library plan for the Sami in Sweden is now complete. The whole process began as early as August 1994, when the Swedish Sami Parliament's Executive Council determined that the office of the Sami Library Consultant was to be moved from the Central Lending Library for Upper Norrland Province [*lan*] at the City Library of Umea to the Sami Parliament. Then, in February of 1995, a full plenary meeting of the Sami Parliament determined that the office of Sami Consultant was to be located in Jokkmokk, and that the Executive Council "should investigate the feasibility of establishing a Sami central library regarding financing, areas of responsibility, location, etc."

My position as Sami Library Consultant was inaugurated in March of 1996. At first, the main order of business was to get the programme going, as far as information services and project activity were concerned. The following year, it was decided to move the Sami depository library from Umea Jokkmokk as well, under the administration of the Library Consultant.

Then, in November 1998 the Sami Parliament's Executive Council resolved that the Library Consultant should work with the Sami Cultural Council to "investigate the feasibility of establishing a Sami central library regarding financing, areas of responsibility, location, etc."

The Sami Cultural Council on October 20th 1999 requested that the Library Consultant together with the department submit a memorandum concerning the investigation into a Sami Central Library and Library Plan for the Sami in Sweden. My office submitted the memorandum entitled "White Paper: A Sami Central Library/Library Plan for the Sami in Sweden" to the Cultural Council in March 2000, with a proposal for a commission, timeline, and budget for the investigation. The proposal was to complete the investigation in 12 months, to appoint a project director for the study, that the Library consultant was to be responsible for the study, that we engage an advisory group of 10 leaders of various relevant institutions, and that 540, 000 Swedish kronor be set aside for the study. The Sami Cultural Council accepted the White Paper on March 21st 2000. The Executive Council determined in June 2000 that Sami Parliamentarian Borje Allas would be appointed to lead the investigation into the question of a Sami Library Plan, with the Library Consultant as secretary of the study group. The Commission was required to submit its proposals within 12 months.

The year 2001 saw a new Sami Parliamentary election and a new Executive Council elected by the plenary meeting of the Parliament in December 2001. The new Executive Council resolved the following January that:

A mandate be made to the Sami Library Consultant to investigate the question of a Sami Library Plan for Sweden and that the study should:

- Investigate the need for a Sami Central Library and a general plan for Sami library development in Sweden
- Make an inventory of library resources related to the Sami that already exist in Sweden, the mandates of these institutions, and how a Sami library plan could function together with the existing library infrastructure in Sweden
- Make an inventory of the existing library plans and library resources within the Sami area outside of Sweden and propose possible forms of collaboration
- Investigate the best ways of reaching out to the Sami population with library services, as far as locations for libraries, bookmobiles and applications of new information technology are concerned
- To present a report with a proposal for a Library Plan and proposals for locations and funding

The commission is to be considered legally binding so long as funding can be arranged for the investigation.

The Library Consultant submitted an application for funding to the Swedish Cultural Council, and was awarded 200, 000 Swedish kronor. The Sami Cultural Council added 50, 000 Swedish kronor and the Sami Parliament's Executive Council set aside 50, 000 Swedish kronor from its budget.

In April 2001, the Library Consultant appointed an advisory group consisting of representatives from the Swedish Cultural Council, the Royal Library (the Swedish National Library), the university libraries of Lulea and Umea, the library of Mid–Sweden University College, as well as representatives from the 4 most northerly provincial libraries: Norrbotten, Vasterbotten, Jamtland and Vasternorrland.

The head librarian of the Norwegian Sami Parliament had a standing invitation to participate in the meetings of the advisory group. The first of these meetings were held in April 2001 in Umea to draw up the guidelines for the study. At the following meeting in Karasjok (Karasjoga) in Norway, it became clear that the Library Consultant could not work alone on this investigation, since it was difficult to combine it with the day–to–day work of his office. Based on a suggestion from the advisory group, it was decided to appoint Ann–Christine Haupt as project leader in a half–time position from October 2001 to May 2002.

The advisory group arranged a seminar in Pajala in Norrbotten in February 2003, in connection with the Sami Parliament's plenary meeting. The study itself was presented in complete form to the Sami Parliament's Executive Council at the beginning of March 2003, where the Council accepted the whole thing as presented, and finally sent it to the plenary meeting of the Sami Parliament at the beginning of June 2003, when the study was also accepted in full.

The Sami Parliament has this day, June 5th 2003, Resolution 28, resolved:

- That it shall accept the Library Plan for the Sami in Sweden in full as appended to this resolution,

- That the library services of the Sami Parliament be declared a regular undertaking of the Parliament and be included within its budget,
- That the Executive Council be required to work together with the Cultural Council to investigate the prerequisites and make a proposal for the establishment of a Library Executive Board or its equivalent.

In connection with this same plenary meeting, the Executive Council also enacted a number of other measures that were proposed by the Library Commission in the presentation of the study:

The Leader of the Commission and the advisory group propose that certain measures be enacted and completed already in 2003. These are:

1. The establishment of a Library Executive Board whose members are appointed by the Executive Council of the Sami Council. Under the leadership of the Library Board the following activities should be commenced in the course of 2003:
   a. To develop a plan of operations for 2004–2006, including a budget, building on the overall mission of the Sami Parliament and the Sami Library Plan.
   b. To initiate collaboration with the commissions that the Sami Parliament and the Swedish government have created regarding information strategies for the Sami and implement the Library Plan within these.
   c. To initiate a preliminary study of Sami publication activities in Sweden.
2. Collaboration with Ajtte [the main Sami cultural museum]:
   a. The Sami Library Consultant's office shall be moved to Ajtte by September 2003.
   b. The libraries of the Sami Parliament and ajtte shall develop a plan for coordination of their services.

The Library Plan affirms that the purpose of the plan is to:

> *Assure access by the Sami people to reading, information, education and recreation, as well as to reinforce the identity, language, culture, and research of the Sami people. The Library Plan shall also contribute to increasing an understanding of the Sami people and their culture from a Sami perspective.*

The Plan proposes to focus on three centres: Kiruna, Jokkmokk, and Ostersund, where the libraries also will be attached to specific Sami institutions. In Kiruna, the library will be attached to the Sami government offices and the future parliament building. In Jokkmokk, the library will be part of Ajtte, the Swedish mountain and Sami museum, while the third library will be associated with the South Sami cultural centre Gaaltje in Ostersund.

The plan is to have the system function as one library in a network, thus making use of the new information technology and the internet, as intended by the mandate to the commission. A parliamentary and government library will be developed in Kiruna where it will be possible to organize a virtual library with an extensive intranet for the personnel and elected members of the Sami parliament. Here it will also be possible to provide the politicians of the Sami parliament with an information service to support their parliamentary work. The existing collection at Ajtte will form the basis of the Jokkmokk library, as well as developing a service that will collaborate with research activities on the Sami and Sami affairs both in Sweden and abroad.

This is where the existing work with a Sami bibliography will be further developed, and in addition acquisitions and cataloging activities will be concentrated here. An open library and knowledge centre will be initiated from Jokkmokk. The first stage will involve the development of a centre for Sami culture at the newly constructed Aja house at Ajtte, where the overall responsibility for the Sami cultural buses and bookmobiles will also be located. A future goal will be to build up a library and knowledge centre for the South Sami culture to be attached to the South Sami Cultural Centre Gaaltje in Ostersund.

Bookmobile services will be administered in collaboration with the Sami parliament in Norway. Currently, there is a bookmobile cooperative operating in Vasterbotten in South Sami territory. Jokkmokk commune is in the midst of a Lule Sami bookmobile project in cooperation with Tysfjord commune in Norway.

The Library Plan also makes provision for library consultation as an important aspect of library activities, and it is therefore proposed to create a position as consultant for children's librarianship.

Regarding personnel resources, the commission has established that Sami library activities in Sweden include the following: one Sami library consultant, one bibliographer who has been employed at Ajtte for the past 1 ½ years for retrospective cataloging, and one research librarian salaried by Ajtte. For future development in Sami library services, the commission proposes two stages be prioritized. During the first stage, the following services and activities should be established:

- A Sami bibliographer/cataloguer
- A Sami parliamentary librarian
- A librarian for the development of the library and knowledge centre for North Sami culture
- A children's library consultant
- Measures for the promotion of literacy for various age groups
- Book publishing for children and young adults

The second and final stage would then add the following, according to the commission:

- A librarian for the development of the library and knowledge centre at Gaaltje for South Sami culture
- A literature consultant
- A research librarian
- An education consultant

The mandate stipulated that the commission should examine possible avenues for financing. Here, the advisory group was unanimous that the only means of funding could be through government appropriations. In its 2004–2006 budget application to the Swedish government under the rubric Sami Library Activities, the Sami parliament has requested 4.9 million Swedish kronor for new services. By 2010 it is estimated that the Sami Library will cost about 8 million Swedish kronor. The plan is for activities to be fully developed by 2015, at a cost of 21 million Swedish kronor.

The commission proposes that prime responsibility for Sami library and information services should be laid under the Sami parliament, and that the Sami Library would be responsible for the Sami parliament's information services in cooperation with the parliament. In addition, the Sami Library will function as parliamentary and government library for the administration and organization of the parliament's activities.

Finally, the commission proposes that the Sami Library be administered by an executive board appointed by the Sami parliament. Members of the executive board will be representatives of the libraries and politicians affected by these developments. The Sami Library will be located in Kiruna and Jokkmokk, and at a later date also in Ostersund, and will be led by one overall executive officer. According to the commission's mandate, the study was also to investigate the need for a central Sami library and a general library plan for the Sami in Sweden. The library consultant therefore developed two surveys in cooperation with the advisory group. One survey was directed to public libraries in the northernmost provinces and the other to 200 randomly selected members of the Sami voting register. The results of these surveys were published in appendices to the report of the commission.

The library survey showed us a picture of libraries that:

- Have acceptable knowledge about the Sami and Sami affairs
- Can provide their patrons with satisfactory information about the Sami

- Lack knowledge of the Sami languages
- Lack an overview of what has been published in the Sami languages or about the Sami people
- Lack well–developed routines for the acquisition of literature in the Sami languages
- Do not acquire the majority of literature published in the Sami languages
- Have developed their activities based on current actual demand for services, but
- Do have the willingness to educate their personnel and expand their activities

As far as the survey of the 200 randomly selected Sami voters is concerned, it is possible to draw the following conclusions:

The Sami voting register that was used to select the names included close to 7, 000 people, so that if all 200 had replied, it would only number about 3 percent of the total. As it turned out, 68 replied, which is equivalent to about 1 percent of all registered Sami voters. That obviously means that the basis is too low to be able to have any representative answers to the questions that were put.

However, we can understand that there nevertheless are some tendencies that come through. One result that can be deduced from the survey is that there are very many Sami who cannot read the Sami languages. 75 percent of the respondents must be said to be a very large number.

It is also clear that efforts really need to be initiated to preserve the Sami languages, and a part of these efforts must be endeavours to develop Sami literature. Furthermore, we clearly need extensive linguistic surveys to determine the extent of the Sami people's knowledge of the Sami languages. The statistics we have now are quite old and may also be inaccurate.

Sami people also do not have very many books in their homes, which could be explained by the fact that there are not so many books to go around, and certainly not that many in the linguistic group that one might belong to.

Going to the library to check out books is also not very prevalent. The comments say that people cannot read the Sami languages, after all, but also that they suspect that librarians are not competent to advise us, since they certainly cannot read Sami.

Some reported that they looked for Sami books in other places, such as the Sami League, or family or friends, bookstores, etc. There were not many who were interested in going to the Sami League's meeting places or Sami Centres to look for literature. On the other hand, those who were interested were that much more enthusiastic about it; the differences here are social: it was possible to meet other Sami there.

From the individual responses it is possible to deduce that the range of books that is available in the Sami languages is mediocre, and there is a need for a considerably broader choice. Then perhaps the languages have a chance to survive or candidly even to develop.

What will happen in the future with the library development plan? First of all, the measures for 2003 enacted by the Sami parliament in June are being put into place. The Library Consultant's office was relocated to Ajtte in August. The depository library's collection will be integrated with the Aja library, although the books will still be found in separate catalogs.

The Sami parliament books will be marked with the logo of the Sami parliament. A plan for the coordination of library activities of Ajtte and the Sami parliament is under development, along with a plan for the Sami parliament's library services to 2006.

The chair of the Sami cultural council has been in contact with me and encouraged me to write a memorandum to the Sami cultural council with a proposal for what the Library Board might look like as far as numbers and makeup are concerned. A proposal for the board's areas of responsibility is also expected to be included in this memorandum.

Collaboration with the commissions of inquiry ordered by the Swedish government and the Sami parliament regarding information priorities of concern to the Sami people is now being intensified, and attempts to get a preliminary study or a full inquiry into Sami publication activities in Sweden have been initiated.

As far as contacts with the central Swedish authorities are concerned, it is now up to the executive council of the Sami parliament to take the initiative. The Sami Library Consultant will naturally be prepared to actively provide any petitions that may be necessary to support their activities. Te Ara Tika: Maori and Libraries in New Zealand – Staying the Distance.

Ko te manu kai i te miro, nona te ngahere.

*Ko te manu kai i te matauranga, nona te ao.*

The bird that eats of the miro tree owns the forest.

The bird that feasts on knowledge owns the world.

The above *whakatauki* is a traditional Maori proverb, and was recently adopted by Te Rau Herenga o Aotearoa, the Library & Information Association of New Zealand Aotearoa [LIANZA]. Referring to the importance of knowledge as a tool for empowerment, the use of these words as a signature statement for the Association reflects something of the distance travelled by New Zealand libraries as they seek to meet the needs of Maori, the indigenous people of New Zealand Aotearoa.

This paper provides a broad overview of the journey taken by New Zealand libraries, in general terms, over the last 40 years relating to services to Maori. The journey has been an eventful one, guided by a changing environment and fuelled by urgent needs. Some of these events are described in this paper, together with a closer look at how one Library—Manukau Libraries—is seeking to respond to Maori information needs.

Since the early 1960s New Zealand librarians have expressed concern about the lack of engagement libraries have with Maori. In 1963 a report to the New Zealand Library Association noted that Maori were unaware of the range of library services available and consequently not using libraries in numbers comparable to the wider population. The report identified a need to improve services on several fronts and make greater efforts to recruit Maori into the library profession.

Thirty years later the Association initiated the *Te Ara Tika* project which sought to "promote the development of biculturalism in library services, and in the library and information profession."

In English, the term "te ara tika" translates into "the right path," the name specifically chosen to demonstrate the profession's commitment to following a path to a bicultural future.

The project consisted of two parts. Part one was an analysis conducted in 1993 of the activities, research and issues relating to biculturalism and services to Maori from the perspective of the library profession. Part two, completed in 1997, comprised of research directly into Maori opinion on libraries and Maori information needs. The *Te Ara Tika Guiding Voices* Report (1997) identified 6 main themes. The themes, ranked in order of prominence, were:

- Issues relating to Intellectual access and information literacy
- The need to focus on Maori youth, literacy and relationships between libraries and schools
- Issues relating to Maori staffing
- The need or desire to have Maori libraries
- The need to take libraries out to Maori communities and increase targeted promotion
- Issues relating to intellectual property.

The report concluded that the key issues were generally the same as those identified some 30 years prior. While acknowledging that many libraries were actively engaging with these issues, and implementing a variety of programmes and initiatives, what was lacking was the ability to measure the impact of these activities or chart progress.

While it is true that the key issues affecting Maori usage of libraries have remained largely unchanged to the present day, the last 40 years have certainly seen significant societal changes take place in New Zealand in social, cultural and political terms. This changing environment brought with it a more urgent impetus for libraries and Maori to engage with one another.

For example, prior to the 1960s, Maori society was still largely rural-based, with many Maori maintaining strong links to tribal heartlands, and a cultural confidence and fluency in the Maori language. It was therefore not surprising that Maori were not seen in great numbers as library users.

The 1950s and 60s however, heralded the beginning of a steady Maori migration to towns and cities, as rural living became difficult to sustain and employment opportunities more limited.

By the 1970s the Maori population had become predominantly urban-based, and, like many other colonised indigenous minorities throughout the world, were (and still are) experiencing chronic social problems. These include higher rates of unemployment, mortality and imprisonment, and lower rates of income, good health and educational achievement. These trends were not especially new, but given the new urban-based nature of Maoridom, the issues were more visible, and considered to be more acute.

As mentioned above, the comparatively poor social conditions of Maori are not unique to the New Zealand situation when considering the overall context of colonisation and experiences of indigenous minorities worldwide. However, there are some distinguishing factors which are relevant when considering the relationship with libraries.

The first of these relates to the way in which New Zealand was colonised in the early 19th century. Missionaries had established an early foothold in the country, and had developed an orthography for the Maori language. Thereafter, through missionary teachings, Maori rapidly became literate in their own language, generating a wealth of written material. Many of these writings are now held in research libraries throughout New Zealand.

By 1840 it was evident that New Zealand was becoming a significant destination for European settlement. Consequently, the British Crown entered into a Treaty with Maori, which established British rule over the country, while guaranteeing Maori ongoing ownership of their lands, fisheries and other possessions.

The Treaty of Waitangi is considered to be New Zealand's founding document of nationhood. By the late-19th century however, the intent of the Treaty had become largely disregarded due to the mounting pressures of European settlement. These pressures involved protracted warfare relating to land ownership, unfair government legislation, and a significant shift in demographics as the Maori population declined to become a minority. The template for ongoing Maori poverty was thus established.

Following the urbanisation of Maori, the significance of the Treaty of Waitangi re-emerged in the 1970s, along with a renaissance of Maori cultural pride and determination to address social problems. A Tribunal was established by the Government to hear claims under the Treaty of Waitangi.

An early claim upheld by the Waitangi Tribunal related to the Maori language. It was deemed that the actions of the Crown had seriously compromised the viability of the Maori language as a living language. Subsequently, in 1987, Maori was declared an official language of New Zealand. A Commission was established charged with the responsibility of fostering the language as a language of everyday use

By the late-1980s there were more than 500 claims lodged with the Waitangi Tribunal. In researching their claims, and tracing the processes by which land and other possessions were alienated, Maori were able to turn to the wealth of written material that had been produced by their ancestors in the late 19th century.

These writings were also a valuable resource for the resurgence of the Maori language. As much of this material was now held in the nation's research institutions, the need for libraries and Maori to engage with one another became inescapable.

Thus in 1992, in recognition of the need to better serve Maori, the Library Association of New Zealand Aotearoa, incorporated the Treaty of Waitangi into its mission statement and adopted a Maori name: Te Rau Herenga o Aotearoa ["the bound pages of New Zealand"]. The Te Ara Tika project was initiated, and a wave of activity swept through New Zealand libraries as various bicultural programmes, plans and strategies were implemented.

Of particular significance at this time, was the establishment of Te Ropu Whakahau, the Maori Library & Information Workers' Association. This group has worked closely alongside LIANZA over the last decade to ensure that the Treaty of Waitangi is promoted in library and information work. Approximately 200 Maori are thought to be working in libraries throughout New Zealand.

Earlier in this article, it was mentioned that many libraries throughout New Zealand have been actively implementing programmes and initiatives aimed at meeting the needs of Maori. One of the challenges however, has been the inability to measure the impact of these activities, or chart progress. In seeking to embark upon Te Ara Tika, a bicultural path to the future, how can libraries maintain the momentum and stay the distance without a road map?

The following is a brief account of one library's journey, and the development of a strategy, or map, to chart their progress with services to Maori.

Manukau City was established in 1965 and is located in the wider Auckland region in the northern part of New Zealand's North Island. The City is spread across an area of around 700 square kilometres—about the same size as Singapore—and is home to some 300, 000 people.

Covering both rural and urban zones, Manukau is one of New Zealand's largest and fastest-growing cities, with a culturally-diverse and young population. Roughly half of

Manukau City residents are of European descent, followed by Maori (16%), Pacific Islanders (27%) and Asians (15%). Thirty-five percent are under the age of twenty.

The City's diversity is reflected in its library service. In the New Zealand context, *Manukau Libraries* is one of the country's biggest public libraries. It is a dispersed system comprised of 12 community libraries, 5 volunteer rural libraries, a corporate library, a mobile book bus, and a research library. Over 220 staff are employed in 135 fulltime-equivalent positions.

In the 2002/2003 year more than 3 million items were issued from a total collection of just under 720, 000 items. Over 2.5 million visits were made to libraries across the city, with a further monthly average of 11, 000 visits to the Library's website. Usage of the Library's services continues to steadily grow every year, along with a programme of system expansion. Three more community libraries are scheduled to open over the next four years.

Manukau is home to the largest concentration of Maori population in New Zealand, with over 44, 000 residents claiming Maori ancestry. Accordingly, significant efforts have been made to develop services that are appropriate and relevant to the needs of Maori. In the late 1980's and early 1990's Manukau was among the first public libraries in New Zealand to establish Maori specialist staffing, implement signage in the Maori language, and introduce bicultural training programmes for staff.

For more than a decade there have been numerous initiatives, programmes and events aimed at increasing Maori usage of the Library. More recently there have been greater efforts made to track whether or not these activities are making a difference.

In 1996 the Library undertook its first extensive survey aimed at understanding the needs of Maori residents. A follow-up study was done in 2001 which gave the Library an opportunity to assess any movement of opinion or change in usage patterns over a five year period. The survey findings were generally encouraging. The 2001 study indicated that more Maori were using Manukau Libraries then before, as well as more regularly. Over half of the survey respondents had used the Library at least once during the preceding year, with the majority visiting fortnightly or monthly. This represented a 13% increase over the figures for 1996.

Maori Library users indicated a high level of satisfaction with the Library with around 80% rating the overall service as good or excellent. Opinions of the Library staff, their approachability and willingness to assist also rated positively. Against these positive results however, was a more worrying trend toward fewer Maori actually joining the Library, and a decrease in those who borrowed books to take home.

Both studies showed interesting differences between users and non-users of the Library. Library users were more likely to have an academic qualification, and be more actively involved in activities such as Maori language education and cultural performance groups.

Maori library users were also more likely to have some fluency in the Maori language than were non-users. Reasons cited by non-users for not using the Library included uncertainty over the use of technology, poor reading ability, and a disinclination to ask for assistance.

A new area of enquiry introduced in the 2001 survey was a section on Maori access to, and use of information technology. The study indicated that 44% of Maori households in the City owned a computer and printer, with ownership significantly higher amongst library users (54%) compared to non-users (34%). Approximately half of the survey respondents had access to the Internet, although a far lesser number considered themselves to be Internet literate.

In general terms, the study results were pleasing, indicating that Library services in Manukau are relevant and make a positive difference to the lives of Maori residents.

The studies are also useful tools for informing the ongoing development and planning of Maori services. In 2002 Manukau Libraries developed a Maori Service Strategy called *Te Ao*

*Marama*. The Strategy acknowledges the Treaty of Waitangi as the basis for developing organisational relationships with Maori in Manukau City. The expectation is that these relationships will be reflected in the way the Library is staffed and operated, in the development of collections and resources, and in the delivery of appropriate services.

The *Te Ao Marama* Strategy is structured on a framework based on internal and external processes. The internal processes relate to such things as recruitment, Maori staff support, staff training and collection development, while the external aspects include the delivery of targeted programmes and events, usage, promotion and presentation of Library collections and facilities, and ongoing liaison with Maori customers, residents and tribal groups.

*Te Ao Marama* also signalled the need for a Maori language strategy to implement a commitment to fostering the use and profile of the Maori language in the way the Library operates and in the delivery of services. A recent questionnaire indicated that staff are positive and willing to improve their Maori language abilities, ranging from mainly basic correct pronunciation through to full fluency. A training plan is currently being devised to support this.

Another recent and unique Maori service innovation relates to the Manukau Libraries website. Manukau Libraries is the only library in New Zealand to offer its website as a fully-bilingual service in English and Maori. The Maori language version of the site receives usage comparable to that of the Library's hardcopy Maori collection resources, with usage steadily increasing. A recent general customer survey indicated that there is greater awareness of the existence of the Library's web services among Maori residents, than the Manukau population generally.

This discussion has provided a general overview of some of the developments in New Zealand library services over the last several decades, as they relate to Maori services. New Zealand libraries have an important role to play in assisting Maori research efforts as they relate to Treaty claims, as well as supporting the resurgence of the Maori language. In responding to this role, many libraries throughout the 1980's and 1990's implemented a range of programmes and initiatives. However, it is difficult to ascertain the impact of these activities in terms of addressing key ongoing issues relating to access to library services, information literacy and Maori staffing.

Manukau Libraries is one example of a public library taking a proactive approach to serving a sizeable Maori population. The true challenge however, is to be active in a way that is meaningful, measurable and sustainable within a changing social environment, particularly as knowledge becomes an economic commodity in the Information Age. New Zealand libraries have made a strong start in establishing a pathway for the delivery of services to Maori. The challenge now, is to stay the distance.

# 6

# Libraries and the Information Movement

The purpose of this chapter is to review the developments, supportive research, and the major documents associated with the information literacy movement as it has developed since the late 1980s. An effort has been made to demonstrate that we as professionals are not alone in this interest but have colleagues with similar ideas across the field of education and from cognitive psychology. The review here should not be construed to mean that the authors support the notion that the constructivist approach is "the only way to teach or learn," since the reality of much educational practice points to a wide variety of successful teaching and learning styles.

This paper is divided into several sections. In the first, a variety of definitions of information literacy are given. This section is followed by a listing of the most prevalent information literacy models that are being used in the field. The assumption has been made that most readers will have ready access to those models and so they are not reproduced herc. The models in current use are derivations of important earlier work and so the authors have traced that development for the reader beginning with work done in Great Britain and its importation into the United States and into several other countries.

To show the relationship between what school library media specialists are proposing and other disciplines, related concepts and models have been included-some from persons who specialize in technology, others from cognitive psychologists.

Wherever possible, the authors have included the models found or at least abbreviations thereof. The last two sections of the paper focus on the research done in teaching information literacy as a process and then monitoring student behaviour during the research. These two areas have received the most attention in the past ten years.

At first, the authors were only going to summarize the papers from the Oregon and British Columbia Conferences, However, their interest and research led them much further. Searches of the authors' extensive libraries, plus back issues of *School Library Media Quarterly, Emergency Librarian* and *School Library Media Annual* were included. The authors plan a more comprehensive view in the near future.

## Historical Antecedents of Critical Thinking and the Field of School Libraries

Modern education borrowed rather than created the idea of critical thinking. Its roots are easily traced to the ideas of Plato and Aristotle and onward through Aquinas, Descartes, Bacon, Machiavelli, Hobbes, Locke, Newton, Boyle and many others. The scientific method, a system of knowing, has ruled much of the industrialized world in the 19th and 20th centuries and is considered a foundational element in the advance of society.

In education, the teacher as authority and the student as passive learner has held great weight in the classroom and was encouraged by the behaviourist work of B.F. Skinner. Many of the ideas of instructional development in the world of educational technology stemmed from the behaviourist viewpoint and led to notions that if instruction is carefully designed, anyone can master any concept of knowledge.

A second rival school of thought began with the work of John Dewey in the 1930s and Benjamin Bloom in 1956. Armed with developments in cognitive and brain research, educators created theories of inquiry or constructivism. This focus challenged teachers in restructured schools to leave their pulpits as sages on the stage to become guides on the side. Numerous reports and research studies have been released demonstrating that constructivist-based education is a major key to academic achievement. An example of such a report is a brief monograph by Newmann and Wehlage entitled: *Successful School Restructuring.*

In the field of school libraries, the same transformation has taken place. Early interest in the role of the library media specialist in instructional design, popularized first in Canada and then in the United States by Loertscher and Turner was known as 'resource-based teaching.'

That movement evolved into increased interest in information literacy (the library media version of constructivism and critical thinking).

The term 'resource-based learning' was popularized in the late 1980s signifying the adoption of information literacy principles in learning projects using a wide variety of information sources and technologies. Resource based learning is a school library term for inquiry-based learning or project-based learning, terms known more widely in the education field.

Meanwhile, library media specialists find themselves in a very interesting mix of philosophies and practices. Some teachers and full faculties have adopted a clear focus of either behaviourism or constructivism. Other schools allow a wide variety of teaching and learning styles to flourish in the same learning environment.

Thus, library media specialists must be able to operate comfortably in both camps as they try to bring the best materials and technology into the learning process.

## Definition

A variety of groups and persons defined information literacy in the last ten years. Most concentrate on a series of behaviours that a person possessing this quality might exhibit. In the 1989 American Library Association's statement, the following description is given:

To be information literate, a person must be able to recognize when information is needed and have the ability to locate, evaluate, and use effectively the information needed... Ultimately information literate people are those who have learned how to learn. They know how to learn because they know how information is organized, how to find information, and how to use information in such a way that others can learn from them.

In 1992, Doyle used the Delphi technique to gain consensus among scholars on the following definition:

Information literacy is the ability to access, evaluate and use information from a variety of sources.

By 1997, Holloway, Doyle and Lindsay added to the above definition by saying that "Information literacy is best thought of as a verb, a way of doing information." Then they translate this notion of a verb into the area of telecommunications:

Information literacy in telecommunications is achieved when learners know when to use online resources, how to access information competently, how to evaluate information for accuracy and significance, and how to use this information to communicate effectively. Learners who are able to do this have a life long skills to meet the challenges of the information age.

Woolls suggests that because information literacy is interwoven with critical thinking and information literacy requires the use of critical thinking skills, the role for the school library media specialist is much greater. She did a summary of various definitions of information literacy from a variety of current fields and found the following from the critical thinking literature:

> *Critical thinking is the intellectual disciplined process of actively and skillfully conceptualizing, applying, analyzing, synthesizing, and/or evaluating information gathered from, or generated by, observation, experience, reflection. reasoning, or communication, as a guide to belief and action.*

King, another critical thinking expert, says "The hallmark of a critical thinker is an inquiring mind." According to Moody, "There is a distinct difference, however between locating sources of information and locating and interpreting information within sources." She shares Beyer's list of major critical thinking skills:

*Distinguishing between verifiable facts and value claims.*

*Distinguishing relevant from irrelevant information, claims, or reasons.*

*Determining the factual accuracy of a statement.*

*Determining the credibility of a source.*

*Identifying ambiguous claims or arguments.*

*Identifying unstated assumptions.*

*Detecting bias.*

*Identifying logical fallacies.*

*Recognizing logical inconsistencies in a line of reasoning.*

*Determining the strength of an argument or claim.*

Quellmalz approached the subject from the related concept of higher-order thinking:

> *Students engage in purposeful, extended lines of thought during which they identify the task or problem type, define and clarify essential elements and terms, judge and connect relevant information, and evaluate the adequacy of information and procedures for drawing conclusions and of solving problems.*

After looking at all of the various definitions and perspectives, Woolls proposed that information literacy is a subset of the concept of critical thinking. She pictures the idea that information literacy is something that happens to a learner somewhere between *believing* and *doing*:

> *Eileen Daniel looked at the literatures both of the K-12 library arena and the academic library literature and found a striking overlap in the notions of information literacy skills, library and information handling skills, and computer skills. Academic librarians worry through their literature that students are ill-equipped to do simple things such as finding and using periodical articles, understanding the principles of computer searching, and how libraries are organized. They complain that students do not understand a process of investigation from formulating*

*a research question through the production of a product.*

Summing up all of the elements of the critical thinking literature, Callison and Tilley draw the following model illustrating the relationship between all the various definitions and perspectives:

## Current Models of Information Literacy in Popular Use (By Year of Introduction)

Of the many models that have appeared in the literature in the past 10 years, a few have gained substantial acceptance in the field. The following six models are presented in order of the year they were first published in the school library media literature.

### Stripling and Pitts Research Process Model, 1988

The Stripling/Pitts model gained wide acceptance upon publication. It guided students through each stage of creating a research paper, but at each stage, the student was asked to reflect upon what had just been done.

### The Kuhlthau Model of the Search Process, 1989

In 1989, Kuhlthau published her Search Process Model based upon a major research project done in high schools with students engaged in research. This model not only became popular with the library media profession but by 1997 was used in a number of library schools as a text showing how users face the research process not only as organized or disorganized investigators, but also their confidence level at various stages of their research.

### Eisenberg and Berkowitz The Big Six Skills, 1990

The Eisenberg/Berkowitz Big Skills model won instant attention because of its simplicity and ease of use by a wide cross section of the field. Since 1990, both creators of the model have done extensive speaking and travelling and have created The Big Six Listserv of persons in the field using the model. It is by far, the most well known model in the field and is being taught widely to students as a guide for their research.

### California School Library Association Information Literacy Model, 1994

The California model was published in a major guide which not only explained the model, but gave many clear suggestions how to incorporate it into a wide variety of instructional systems and content areas. It was published in a second edition in 1997 and incorporated major suggestions and guidance for teaching information literacy to English learners among others.

### Pappas and Tepe Pathways to Knowledge Information Skills Model, 1995

Teaming with the Follett Software Company, Pappas and Tepe created an elaborate double-page rendition of information literacy complete with recommended strategies, forms of expression, and methods of teaching and learning embedded in the model. The model was published in three sizable binders containing numerous full length units of instruction as demonstrations for how to apply the model.

### AASL and AECT Information Literacy Standards for Student Learning, 1996

As part of the effort to create new standards to replace Information Power, the Vision Committee of the Standards Project published a draft of their thinking to the profession for comment. A revised model in final form is due from the publisher some time in 1998.

## ANTECEDENTS OF CURRENT MODELS

To say that information literacy is new in the school library media field is not exactly true. Going back to the writing of Frances Henne in the 1960 *Standards for School Library Programmes*, she foresaw librarians integrating library skills instruction into classroom content and said the ultimate goal was the "synthesis of information, the extension of knowledge, the analysis and solution of problems, thinking, reflection, the satisfaction of curiosity, the development of trust, or the derivation of pleasure." The profession at large did not heed the forward-looking words of Henne. Instead, the predominant themes of library skills instruction from the 1960s to the 1990s concentrated on the finding and locating of information plus the orientation to the library as a place.

Three reviews of the history of the information literacy movement were found in the literature. Kuhlthau's was published first in 1987 followed by Doyle, in 1994 and most recently by Bruce in 1996.

The earliest use of the term "information literacy" is traced to a proposal written in 1974 by Paul Zurkowski for the National Commission on Libraries and Information Science. This report proposed the achievement of a universal information literacy goal by 1984.

Much excitement had arisen during the 1960s concerning the development of computer information systems and the exponential rise of an information-based society. By 1983, the *Nation at Risk* report was promoting the concept of a learning society.

Cooke traces the emergence of information literacy models for librarians to work done in Great Britain and published by Michael Marland in his 1981 book entitled *Information Skills in the Secondary Curriculum*. The nine steps to research formed the basis of much work done in that country and around the world:

1. WHAT DO I NEED TO DO?
   (formulated and analyze need)
2. WHERE COULD I GO?
   (identify and appraise likely sources)
3. HOW DO I GET TO THE INFORMATION?
   (trace and locate individual resources)
4. WHICH RESOURCES SHALL I USE?
   (examine, select and reject individual resources)
5. HOW SHALL I USE THE RESOURCES?
   (interrogate resources)
6. WHAT SHOULD I MAKE A RECORD OF?
   (recording and sorting information)

7. HAVE I GOT THE INFORMATION I NEED?

   (interpreting, analyzing, synthesizing, evaluating)

8. HOW SHOULD I PRESENT IT?

   (presenting, communicating)

9. WHAT HAVE I ACHIEVED?

   (evaluation)

This early work was part of a project initiated by the British Library Research and Development Department (28) and resulted in many important publications, particularly the work of Ann Irving (29) that reached the United States with her consultive work in the Treasure Mountain Research Retreat # 2.

Hughes and Rankin (30) had developed a model in 1986 in some work done with the Association for Supervision and Curriculum Development using the following seven steps:

*Plan;*

*Gather information;*

*Organize information;*

*Analyze information;*

*Extend and expand;*

*Synthesize and create;*

*Evaluate and apply.*

Using the work of Piage, Taba, and Ehrenberg, Huges also created a developmental structure of thinking skills and process model.

Also in 1986, Eleanor R. Kulleseid did a summary of research in reading and developmental Psychology with implication for practice. At that time, she was introducing the field to cognitive theories not well known in the library media world and which would become the basis of much of the work of information literacy as a process of inquiry learning. Mancall, Aaron, and Walker published a major article in 1986 entitled "Educating Students to Think: The Role of the School Library Media Programme." Their concept was of a programme that would help students develop thinking skills, pointed to research on how children and adolescents process information and ideas, and gave practical implications for developing information skills in various curricular areas.

Interest in information literacy was, by this time, gaining momentum around the world. This international interest was boosted by the publication of the United Nations' guidelines for the training of teachers in the integration of libraries and information skills into the curriculum by Hall. She recommended that all teachers be trained in information skills and that the school library concentrate on delivering these skills to students.

In 1987, Carol Kuhlthau published an extremely important document titled: *Information Skills for an Information Society: A review of Research* encouraging school library media specialists to carve out the emerging concept of information literacy as a foundational element of their programme. That same year, the Washington Library Media Association published one of the first state guides to information skills. They used a 12-step system to the research process and published a scope and sequence chart for K-12 education listing where each of the skills should be presented and finally mastered.

In 1988, the new national guidelines for school library media programmes, *Information Power,* declared that the mission of the school library media centre is "to ensure that students and staff are effective users of ideas and information," and called for the library media specialist to become a key participant in the learning process.

Kathleen Craver in the Fall of 1989 published a synthesis article summarizing research studies concerning critical thinking and their implication for library work. She urged the field to become interested in this area of research and to know how to improve the ability of students to find, to synthesize, and to apply information in everyday situations. In the same issue of *School Library Media Quarterly*, Carol Kuhlthau published her own summary of cognitive research and her information literacy model for the first time in the AASL literature. One of the most significant documents published in the entire library community was a statement on information literacy published by the American Library Association on January 10, 1989. Known simply as the *Final Report*, the document became the basis of much of the discussion about information literacy in both school and academic libraries around the world. After the emergence of this document, Patricia Breivik, the chair of the committee established the National Forum for Information Literacy whose purpose was to popularize the need for information literacy across many organizations and disciplines.

In September of 1989, the first Treasure Mountain Research Retreat was convened in Park City Utah. Since that time, five other such retreats have occurred. This gathering of school library media researchers and practitioners has provided a great boost to the intelligent discussion of research findings and looking toward the future of this profession. At the 1989 meeting, Kathleen Craver reviewed the research related to critical thinking.

Carol Kuhlthau also provided a look into her research on the information search process, Barbara Stein provided a glimpse into the world of cognitive learning styles, and Michael Eisenberg reviewed the research in the area of library and information skills.

In 1993, the Wisconsin Educational Media Association published a major document on information literacy that was adopted and published by AASL as a position paper. This paper outlined seven basic elements of the research process: defining the need for information; initiating the search strategy; locating the resources; accessing and comprehending the information; interpreting the information; communicating the information; and evaluating the product and process. The following year, the state of Colorado issued their *Model Information Literacy Guidelines* which gained national attention.

In 1994, a second major summary of the literature was published by Christina Doyle in her ERIC monograph, *Information Literacy in an Information Society: A Concept for the Information Age*. In this document, she reviewed the evolution of the concept of information literacy and demonstrated its relevance in national education goals and curricular concerns.

## Elaboration on Information Literacy Models

Kathy Brock published an elaboration on other models previously published models that combined a number of factors from mere instructing in the model, to coaching throughout the model, to facilitating a self-directed student.

O'Connell and Henri adapted earlier information literacy models from an Australian perspective by showing the core activities of the information process as central flanked by the stages of critical thinking and the basic elements of literacy. Their emphasis is to create a model that has meaning to teachers who are most closely linked to learners. Across the world, Wilson also worried that teachers should, but do not possess their own mental model of information literacy.

Loertscher redrew the popular models with the student at the centre, emphasizing that what was lacking in many of the models was the need for students to spend a great deal of time *consuming* the information they find by reading, viewing, and listening. Too many students do not feel they should spend time consuming; they jump over this step IMMDIATELY after information location as they rush toward product creation.

## Related Models and Applications

Numerous experts from related fields of cognitive psychology, education, and educational technology have been working on the constructivist ideas and putting forth their conceptions of how students can benefit from information literacy-related thinking. While the following models do not exhaust what is currently available in the literature, some major work has been pulled together.

## From Cognitive Psychology

In a study of cognition and complexity, Reeves proposed a model by which a student might plan to attack a subject about which the student knows very little. He advocates that teaching a student the model directly could help a student assess whether progress is being made from surface learning to deep learning. The model known as the Reeves Knowledge Management Tool consists of ten steps in three major levels:

**Foundations**

1. Build Background (key dates, events, people, places)
2. Know key words
3. Know key concepts/ideas

**Relationships**

4. Diagram parts of the topic (classes, categories, objects)
5. Diagram activities that take place in your topic (actions)
6. Diagram the environment of the topic (financial, political, technological, sociological, educational, economic, artistic religious, historical, location)

**Depth**

7. Draw analogies to something you already know (compare, contrast, describe)
8. Visualize (examine/create charts, tables, maps, diagrams)
9. Explain the topic to someone
10. Find themes, patterns, and trends

# 7

# Future of Library

Several authors are beginning to warn about major problems in accessing and using electronic information. Fitzgerald lists numerous problems affecting the quality of information gained from using the Internet. She then lists nine skills needed to effectively evaluate electronic information:

1. Adopt critical consciousness for all Internet interaction.
2. Establish prior knowledge through wide browsing, searching and reading.
3. Distinguish between fact and opinion.
4. Evaluate arguments.
5. Compare and contrast related pieces of information from different sites, sources and search engines.
6. Evaluate the reliability of online sources.
7. Identify and detect bias.
8. Learn to interpret the conventions of the Internet.
9. Examine assumptions.

## COMPUTER LITERACY AND INFORMATION LITERACY

Eisenberg and Johnson took the elements of the Big Six Model and created a checklist for the needed computer skills at each level of model. For example, for the task definition stage, learners should be able to use e-mail, desktop conferencing and idea generating software to help define an information problem. Their checklist covers a full spectrum of technical skills and any learner mastering the list would be considered a technology expert.

Penrod and Douglas define information technology literacy as the ability to:

- operate and communicate with technological devices;
- understand how subsystems fit together to form systems or networks;
- understand documentation and how to utilize applications software;
- understand the basic jargon or terminology of information technology;
- solve problems through the use of technology;
- identify and use alternate sources of information; discuss the history and future of information technology; and
- have some insight into the ethical and human impact issues of information technology.

## THE GLOBAL RESOURCES NETWORK

The Global Resources Network is a collaborative initiative of the major North American universities and research libraries to support international studies through the preservation and exchange of knowledge and source materials.

This article documents the history and development of the programme, and highlights three specific projects based at the Centre—Cooperative African Newspaper Project (AFRINUL); German–North American Resources Partnership (GNARP); Latin Americanist Research Resources Project (LARRP); and the Digital South Asia Library (DSAL). Taken as a whole, the Global Resources Network and its projects facilitate unprecedented access to new resources and provide a framework of collaboration that can be modeled for other collection programmes.

### Overview

Located at the Centre for Research Libraries (CRL) since January 2006, the Global Resources Network (GRN) is a collaborative initiative of the major North American universities and research libraries to support international studies through the preservation and exchange of knowledge and source materials. GRN was initially established by the Association of American Universities (AAU) and Association of Research Libraries (ARL) with support of the Andrew W. Mellon Foundation.

The GRN has two main goals:

- To expand the depth, quantity, and diversity of information resources from all world regions available to scholars and researchers.
- To achieve synergy among university and research library efforts to develop interrelated collections of international materials, through coordinated collecting and powerful systems for access, discovery, presentation, and delivery.

To achieve these goals, the GRN pursues several complementary activities. These include supporting activities that create widespread access to resources for international and area studies; preserving cultural, historical, and scientific information and evidence; and, building capabilities for informed stewardship of information resources.

The Global Resources Network (GRN) connects libraries in North America to institutions abroad through strong collaborative partnerships and sustainable programmes. Institutions interact with diverse partners and centres of excellence that share an interest in making their material available to researchers worldwide.

### History and Rationale

The Global Resources Network evolved through the recommendations and activities of a variety of collaborative efforts of the early 1990s, most notably the Association of Research Libraries' Foreign Acquisitions Project and the Association of American Universities' Research Libraries Project.

The ARL Foreign Acquisitions Project was charged with investigating the forces hindering the ability of North American research libraries to build and maintain international collections. Detailed studies confirmed that the collective ability of research institutions to keep pace with publishing from abroad was declining, and that many important works had not found their way into North American collections. Additionally, static or declining budgets compelled area studies librarians to focus acquisitions efforts increasingly on "core" materials, resulting in a greater duplication of collections among institutions and a corresponding decline in "non-core" or unique collections. The findings of the project were published in the significant report "Scholarship, Research Libraries, and Global Publishing."

The AAU Research Libraries Project began in 1992 in response to the Andrew W. Mellon Foundation's critical study on the state of research libraries in the United States, "University Libraries and Scholarly Communication." AAU established a series of task forces, one of which was the Task Force on Acquisition and Distribution of Foreign Language and Area Studies Materials.

In its final report issued in 1994, the task force drew upon the Mellon study and outlined the confluence of challenges to the acquisition of global materials: increasing budgetary constraints, the decline of purchasing power of the dollar in the global market, an increase in international publishing, and changes in research patterns that create new demands for foreign language materials. The Task Force concluded that the challenges could not adequately be addressed through intra-institutional solutions, and that the "the key to improving access to and delivery of international research resources is the creation of a network-based, distributed programme for coordinated development of foreign acquisitions for U.S. and Canadian research libraries."

Among the recommendations of the Task Force were:

- The major North American research universities and libraries should organize a distributed programme for access to foreign acquisitions. This programme should include the Library of Congress and foreign national and research libraries working together to organize a cooperative programme that shares the responsibility for acquiring, organizing, and facilitating access to foreign acquisitions.

- The major North American research universities and libraries should implement the programme through demonstration projects that aggressively test the barriers to distributed access and evaluate their impact on faculty.
- Universities should plan and fund the electronic infrastructure necessary to support the new avenues of access and delivery crucial to the success of a distributed North American collection.
- University leaders and their research librarians should articulate incentives to scholars and faculty for moving away from local and toward remote access, so that an individual institution's library may develop in-depth collections in a few selected areas, but provide remote access to many more in-depth collections.
- Planning and development of the distributed programme should focus special attention on meeting the needs of scholars and researchers and thereby build support among faculty.

The Task Force report included a proposal for three demonstration projects focusing on Germany, Japan, and Latin America, selected to test the viability of implementing a distributed, networked, coordinated collection management programme for foreign research materials. These were implemented by ARL in partnership with AAU, and a broader international programme was envisaged in ARL's "Strategic Plan for Improving Access to Global Information Resources in U.S. and Canadian Research Libraries."

**Expanding Access**

As envisioned by the AAU and ARL, the Global Resource Programme (GRP) was established to provide the organizational structure and catalyst for the development of several regional projects undertaken by subject to improve access to international research materials through cooperative structures, the use of new technologies, and information sharing. In December 1996, the Andrew W. Mellon Foundation awarded US$450, 000 to the newly created programme at ARL. The award enabled the project to expand the three initial projects and add three initiatives for South Asia, Southeast Asia, and Sub-Saharan Africa. The six pilot projects original created under the Global Resources Programme were:

- Cooperative African-Newspaper Project
- Digital South Asia Library
- German-North American Resources Partnership
- The Japan Project
- Latin Americanist Research Resources Project
- Southeast Asia Indexing Project

Originally intended to support three years of activity, the Mellon funding stimulated over five years of work focused on improving access to international research materials through cooperative structures and the use of new technologies. These projects, four of which are described in detail below, have excelled and continue to this date, with many obtaining additional funding and ongoing institutional support to expand their activities.

From 2003-2006, the Global Resources Programme entered a transitional phase in which number of important activities occurred. In 2003, the Global Resources Programme was reframed as the "Global Resources Network," with a new Advisory Committee and a new GRN Vision Statement. The new vision statement reinforced the overall goal of "ensuring seamless access to information resources from all parts of the world, through fluid and mutually beneficial exchanges that strengthen international education and scholarship." To achieve this, the GRN would pursue two complementary approaches in developing a new and more robust model for international information:

- A series of discrete projects would focus on significantly expanding the depth, breadth, quantity, range of formats, and variety of international information resources available to our students and scholars.

- A second, broad-based, long term and necessarily evolutionary programme would minimize unnecessary duplication among and across library collections.

### A Strategic Partnership

The relocation of GRN to CRL was a collaborative decision developed by the boards of both the Centre and ARL to bring the strongest resources to bear on the cooperative acquisition of critical international materials for students, faculty, and scholars at participating institutions. It was a natural fit, since the Centre had actively coordinated two of the six programmes — DSAL and AFRINUL — for several years, and had become the administrative home in 2004 to two other programmes — GNARP and LARRP. The objective was to capitalize on the Centre's solid track record for supporting and administering ongoing international projects such as the Area Studies Microform Projects the International Coalition on Newspapers Projects and the Foreign Newspaper Microfilm Project.

The decision to locate these institutions under one roof has proven beneficial to each project separately and as a group of associated initiatives. The Centre has begun to apply its expertise in project development and management to assist with fiscal administration, resources management, rights acquisition, licensing, and other project logistics. It will also seek opportunities to promote synergies, facilitate communications, and exploit efficiencies among and across all of the GRN projects as well as its own, related cooperative ventures.

Four GRN programmes based at the Centre — Cooperative African Newspaper Project (AFRINUL); German–North American Resources Partnership (GNARP); Latin Americanist Research Resources Project (LARRP); Digital South Asia Library (DSAL)— are profiled in the rest of this paper.

## COOPERATIVE AFRICAN NEWSPAPERS PROJECT

The inspiration for the Cooperative African Newspapers Project was born of discussions and strategic planning by members of the African Studies Association's Africana Librarians

Council (ALC). In 1994, the ALC prepared a "Report of the Africa Task Force... for the Association of Research Libraries Foreign Acquisitions Project," which recommended expanding cooperative efforts among African Studies libraries. The ALC, a long-standing committee focused on cooperative acquisition of materials published in or relating to Africa, sought a project that would benefit all libraries and researchers that used them.

The idea of focusing on newspaper acquisition, description, and preservation came early in brainstorming sessions. Newspapers published in Africa are consistently the only permanent, continuing publications that record political events in the countries of Africa. Articles, editorials, letters, announcements, cartoons, and advertising in newspapers provide a wealth of material for social, economic, and political research. These materials, which are notoriously difficult to collect, describe, and store, are vital to the historical record of Africa and an important component of all Africana collections in the U.S. Further impetus was given the project by ongoing ALC efforts to provide accurate and up-to-date information on newspapers collected in U.S. repositories. For many years, Northwestern University's Africana librarian, Mette Shayne, compiled an annual list of *African newspapers currently received by American libraries*. This resource greatly benefited scholars and librarians seeking contemporary sources for primary research.

The core of the Cooperative African Newspaper Project is an online database of holdings information for newspapers (all formats and all languages) published in sub-Saharan Africa. The African Newspaper Union List (AFRINUL) has been the primary deliverable of the project and one by which the ongoing effort is commonly referred. Located and administered by the Centre for Research Libraries, AFRINUL has been attracting growing interest from bibliographers, scholars, and instructors as a resource for African Studies students and faculty.

For some time, AFRINUL has included only Centre for Research Libraries' holdings and holdings reported in the most recent paper edition (1999) of *African Newspapers Currently Received*. Participants of the project have been gathering information on their own collections, but a low-barrier approach to entering information into the collaborative database was slow in developing. A major step forward occurred in the summer of 2004 when the AFRINUL administrative tool was tested with a limited number of titles from Northwestern University's extensive newspaper holdings of the Melville J. Herskovits Library of African Studies. Once the administrative testing was completed, member institutions were invited to submit their holdings.

The administrative tool allows authorized participants to add, edit, and remove bibliographic and holdings information relating to their local collections. Utilizing a simple, Web-based interface, users can input a conglomeration of information (standard bibliographic fields, contextual information, and combined holdings of print, microform, or electronic issues) into an aggregated record.

The information is immediately posted to the public search interface of AFRINUL, located at. From the beginning, AFRINUL has been based at the Centre for Research Libraries. Limited funding of the project at the outset required participants to rely on voluntary staff time to complete the project, a fact that has caused delay in its final implementation. However, the Title VI National Resource Centres for African Studies have since agreed to provide funding to cooperative projects such as AFRINUL.

Meanwhile, use of AFRINUL is growing and researchers are providing positive feedback on it. Researchers can access AFRINUL from both the CRL Web site at and from links on individual Web pages of a growing number of African studies libraries. AFRINUL participants have reported varying degrees of local publicity on institutional Web sites, in faculty and graduate student orientation programmes, in class and bibliographic instruction sessions, etc. AFRINUL continues to be an integral part of regular meetings of the Africana Librarians Council. The fall meetings of AFRINUL and ALC are held in conjunction with the annual meeting of the African Studies Association, and are publicized in the conference programme and open to all ASA members.

## The German–North American Resources Partnership

German is the native language of only three countries — Germany, Switzerland, and Austria — representing a small fraction of the world's population. However, the cultural, literary, industrial, and technical output of German-speaking communities makes it the third most important publishing power — after English and Chinese.

In the years since German reunification in 1990, German language publications and resources experienced robust growth in overall size, diversity, and other measures. In the first decade following reunification, a total of 82, 936 new titles were published in Germany, Switzerland, and Austria, an increase of 22 percent. A relatively high percentage of this production is valued for its scholarly content. The creation of Internet sources and resources is also booming in German-speaking countries, with new products and publicly supported sites becoming available almost daily. Many of these resources are of great interest to North American scholars.

## GNARP Origins

Recognizing this potential and the needs of German scholars on both sides of the Atlantic, the German-North American Resources Partnership (GNARP) was founded with a mission to improve transatlantic access to library and publishing resources— both physical and virtual.

GNARP's roots go back to the early 1990's AAU/ARL German Demonstration Project. A series of surveys undertaken by the Association of College and Research Libraries' (ACRL) Western European Studies Section (WESS) at the invitation of ARL indicated that a significant number of important research publications from Western Europe were not being acquired by any North American libraries. Subsequently an article was published documenting the results of one of these surveys. Since the German Demonstration Project was renamed the German Resources Project under the umbrella of the Global Resources Programme in the late 1990s (and subsequently "GNARP" in 2004), the project has made substantial progress in forging closer ties between North American and German libraries in the areas of bibliographic control, collection development, digitization initiatives, and document delivery.

The original purpose of GNARP was to serve as a vehicle for cooperative and collaborative collection development efforts within the United States and Canada, essentially to ensure that North American research libraries had comprehensive, minimally redundant collections of materials for the study of German society and culture available to their researchers and students — in effect trying to recreate the library of materials at the disposal of researchers in Germany. However, the vision has been expanded in recent years to encompass resources in all domains of scholarship, and to focus more on access and cooperation among North American and German libraries rather than outright acquisition. Comprised of more than 60 institutional members in the United States, Canada, and Germany, the partnership also performs a gateway function for German libraries seeking access to North American library resources. The recent transfer of operational responsibility to the Centre for Research Libraries in Chicago has enhanced GNARP's capacity to fulfil its goals and objectives.

## GNARP Projects and Initiatives

The following projects and initiatives exemplify how GNARP services and activities promote and fulfil the goals and objectives of the partnership.

## Contact Partnerships Project

GNARP fosters ongoing collaborative partnerships between German and North American institutions. Utilizing the framework of the *Deutsche Forschungsgemeinschaft* (DFG) Special Subject Collection Areas Plan, GNARP identified a number of subject areas, principally in the social sciences and humanities, for which to develop institutional partnerships.

By identifying the appropriate German institutions participating in the DFG National Research Collection System (*Sondersammelgebietssystemplan* — SSG) and pairing them with U.S. libraries with similar collection strengths, GNARP hopes to develop partnerships to expedite the location of information on collection strengths, facilitate the answering of in-depth reference questions among GNARP partners, and extend collaboration to other projects (*e.g.*, exchange of bibliographic and acquisition information, cooperative digitization efforts). The SSG partnerships was the subject of a symposium to be held October 5-7, 2006, in Frankfurt, Germany.

### Consortial Access to Electronic Resources

GNARP has successfully negotiated consortium rates for member access to important scholarly resources published in Germany or in the German language. The following recent examples illustrate the diverse nature of these collections.

***Xipolis***: A suite of online German-language reference sources, including the 24-volume *Brockhaus* encyclopedia, 10-volume *Duden* dictionary, and a number of specialist tools in disciplines such as literature, music, film, and economics.

***Digitale Bibliothek Deutscher Klassiker***: This resource brings together fully searchable digital editions of 133 titles in the *Bibliothek deutscher Klassiker* of the *Deutscher Klassiker Verlag* (DKV) series. The works include a broad array of materials ranging from the writings of medieval German mystic Meister Eckhart, to writings on war by Carl von Clausewitz and an online edition of the fairy tales of the Brothers Grimm.

***DigiZeitschriften***: Modeled after the JSTOR journal archive project, German academic libraries have launched an online archive of extended runs of German scholarly journals. An archive of over one million pages is planned for preservation, with more than 30 journals already available through the earliest issues.

***BDSL-Online***: The *Bibliographie der deutschen Sprach- und Literaturwissenschaft* (Bibliography of German Language and Literature Research) was started in 1957 by Hanns W. Eppelsheimer of the University of Frankfurt and continued by Clemens Kottelwesch. It is the largest and most authoritative index of published research on all areas of German philology.

### Services and Other Collaborations

***Catalogue Services:*** GNARP has converted from the RAK German cataloging standard to *AACR2* more than 15, 000

MARC records for the large microform set *Bibliothek der deutschen Literatur*. This collection contains microform reproductions of important German first editions, published by K.G. Saur, in the humanities and social sciences. The collection is held by approximately 35 U.S. and Canadian libraries.

GNARP also was instrumental in the cooperative translation of the *Anglo-American Cataloguing Rules* (*AACR2*) into German. The translation project was completed in 2002 and published by Saur Verlag.

***Cultural Expertise:*** The *Bildarchiv der Deutschen Kolonialgesellschaft* (Thesaurus of the Pictorial Archive of the German Colonial Society), hosted by the University of Frankfurt Library, is an online, fully searchable archive of 50, 000 nineteenth and early twentieth century photographs. In October 2003, GNARP received a request from colleagues in Frankfurt to help make the site searchable in English.

Helene Baumann of Duke University, the GNARP contact partner for African Studies, volunteered to lead the effort. With a Coutts Nijhoff grant from the Western European Studies Section (WESS) of ACRL, Baumann assisted in the translation and development of a searchable, online version of the Thesaurus. All of these projects mobilize the efforts of dozens of librarians at member institutions and CRL with the goal of expanding transatlantic access for the benefit of libraries and library users in both Europe and North America. GNARP strives to achieve reciprocity in relations between the German and North American research library communities, and seeks to involve more German colleagues in its management and leadership in order to better pave the way for meaningful partnerships.

## LATIN AMERICANIST RESEARCH RESOURCES PROJECT

The Latin Americanist Research Resources Project (LARRP) was launched in 1994 when a critical mass of 31 North American universities joined together to explore new ways of building Latin American Studies research collections. The alliance was forged by concern that the diversity of Latin American cultural and scholarly materials available to researchers was declining due to funding reductions and over-reliance on a handful of foreign book dealers. The collective response was to devise new approaches for acquiring Latin American materials and providing greater access to the materials held in U.S. repositories.

With support from the Association of American Universities (AAU) and the Association of Research Libraries (ARL), LARRP's concerns and planning were brought to the attention the larger arena of Latin American scholars, including the Latin American Network Information Centre (LANIC), the exemplary Latin American area studies programme at the University of Texas-Austin. An early LARRP decision to partner with LANIC resulted in collaboration on two important digital projects, summarized below.

### Latin American Periodicals Table of Contents (LAPTOC)

One of the primary LARRP objectives was to itemize the vast wealth of content locked up in library stacks. Participants found that the majority of Latin American journals were not indexed in the key scholarly periodical indexes. To address this issue, LARRP created a table of contents database in 1996 and required that all members contribute table of contents information from 11 journals not indexed elsewhere. Utilizing a remote Web-based administrative tool developed by LANIC, each member is able to input journal content information directly from their institution. Results have been impressive: after eight years, the LAPTOC database offers access to more than 230, 000 articles from more than 860 Latin American journals. The tables of content are freely available over the Web. Users from LARRP member institutions can request articles directly from their interlibrary loan departments through the database.

### Presidential Messages

The importance of official publications to scholars and the fact that they were not bound by copyright issues led the project to digitize Presidential Messages from Argentina (1810-1993) and Mexico (1821-1989). The LANIC provided Internet access to these indexed images through its Web site. The value of these messages among scholars is significant, as indicated by the 300, 000 hits the site received last year.

## Additional LARRP Projects

The initial LARRP projects were funded through the AAU and ARL by an Andrew W. Mellon Foundation grant. Follow-up funding through two Technological Innovation and Cooperation for Foreign Information Access (TICFIA) grants from the U.S. Department of Education enabled LARRP to redesign and upgrade the LAPTOC database to meet current database standards, including the following:

- A query module with robust searching capability
- Advanced searching features with e-mail export capacity
- Links to available full-text journal articles
- Enhanced bibliographic data on each journal
- A capacity for simultaneous updating of articles

The initial TICFIA grant (1999-2002), provided to LARRP through the University of Texas at Austin, also enabled LARRP to expand its membership into Latin America and to create an Internet portal for full-text resources. The membership expansion effort resulted in the addition of seven Latin American members and contributions to the LAPTOC database from more than 150 Latin American journals. The Internet portal led to the development of the open archives initiative described below.

## Distributed Resources

Following the initial digital projects, the participating institutions broadened their collecting activities to acquire secondary materials through the Distributed Resources project. To fund the effort, participating members were asked to voluntarily allocate seven percent of their annual Latin American Studies funds to acquire materials in a specific country or subject area. By the late 1990s, more than US$300, 000 a year was raised by 30 LARRP institutions for these materials. The project also energized bibliographers at participating institutions. CRL coordinates the dissemination of information about the project and its successes.

## Open Archives Initiative

Latin American specialists have long recognized that Latin American scholarly institutions produce important research that is seldom seen by interested scholars in other regions. The second TICFIA grant (2002-2005), funded this time through the University of California, Los Angeles, enabled LARRP partners to establish the Latin American Open Archives Project (LAOAP), which provides the scholarly community with access to a wide variety of Latin American reports, statistics, and surveys. The project utilizes the Open Archives Initiative Protocol for Metadata Harvesting — an emerging standard for providing access and enhance searching capabilities to digital resources — and enables desktop delivery worldwide of "grey literature" to social science scholars.

The LARRP efforts could not have been completed without the countless hours of labour contributed by scholars at member institutions. Further, the LARRP vision to improve access and acquisitions would not have happened without generous support from the AAU, ARL, Andrew W. Mellon Foundation, and the Department of Education. Taken together — the outside funding and the dedicated labour of so many — have moved Latin American Studies bibliography solidly into the digital realm and accorded the project legitimacy among libraries and scholars.

## Digital South Asia Library (by Gerald Hall)

Beginning in the early 1990s, American research libraries were confronted with a pressing problem. The decreasing value of the U.S. dollar and the increasing cost of all library acquisitions threatened the quantity and quality of acquisitions for area studies. As a result, a task force of the Association of American Universities Research Libraries Project proposed "the creation of a network-based, distributed programme for coordinated development of foreign acquisitions for U.S. and Canadian research libraries." The Digital South Asia Library (DSAL), became one of six programmes participating in the Global Resources Programme — originally developed by the Association of American Universities (AAU) together with the Association of Research Libraries (ARL) and initially supported by the Andrew W. Mellon Foundation — intended to address this problem. With subsequent funding from the U.S. Department of Education's Technological Innovation and Cooperation for Foreign Information Access (TICFIA) programme, DSAL has become widely recognized as an essential resource for the study of South Asia.

Since DSAL's launch as a two-year pilot project in 1997, collaboration has been an important hallmark of its success in improving access to significant research resources concerning South Asia for a broad audience encompassing scholars, policy makers, and the public at large. Led by the Centre for Research Libraries and the University of Chicago, DSAL maintains strong ties with institutions located in the U.S., South Asia, and Europe. Among DSAL's diverse partners are: the Library of Congress, the British Library, the Roja Muthiah Research Library in Chennai, Sundarayya Vignana Kendram in Hyderabad, Madan Puraskar Pustakalaya in Nepal, the University of Oxford, University of Cambridge, Columbia University, the South Asia Microform Project, the American Institute of Indian Studies, and the Committee on South Asian Libraries and Documentation. These institutions have contributed both resources and expertise to the construction of a significant digital library freely available to a broad audience via the Internet.

Arranged among eight broad categories, DSAL currently is the home of more than one hundred separate resources with more than a dozen other resources in various stages of development. A more detailed description of a few of these resources will illustrate the essential research tools being made available through DSAL. Among those tools is the *Imperial Gazetteer of India*, consisting of 26 volumes that comprise more than 25, 000 pages of text along with scores of detailed maps. Compiled during the course of six decades and published in several editions from 1881 until 1931, the *Gazetteer* is acknowledged as "one of the largest and most influential exercises in imperial information gathering undertaken in the nineteenth century." The *Gazetteer* provides critical descriptions of cultural, geographical and administrative districts of South

Asia under British rule. As with many of the resources on DSAL, there is an effort to provide users of the *Imperial Gazetteer* with formats that appear familiar but also allow for the increased functionality that a digital format permits. Users are presented with images of pages that look and function in a manner that resembles the original volumes but at the same time can undertake full-text searches. In other resources, full-text searching is accompanied by the possibility of complex proximity searching. Furthermore, in the production of digital resources, DSAL has attempted to plan for the future and the implementation of new capacities. Provisions have been made for the integration of geographical information systems to better link the historical and statistical data contained there with cartographic representations of the subcontinent such as those found in *A Historical Atlas of South Asia*, edited by Joseph E. Schwartzberg, currently in the latter stages of development for DSAL.

Another important DSAL resource that exemplifies the benefits of close collaboration is the digital version of the *National Bibliography of Indian Literature* (NBIL). The NBIL is a select bibliography of literary texts in 22 languages compiled by a group of distinguished language specialists under the direction of B.S. Kesavan, a former director of the National Library of India. The NBIL implementation of DSAL provides not only the bibliographic details for more than 55, 000 titles included in the original print edition but also additional information on those titles that were included in the Microfilming of Indian Publications Projects (MIPP) undertaken by the Library of Congress with the National Library of India that have been acquired by the South Asian Microform Project (SAMP) and housed at CRL.

The linking of bibliographic information with holdings information is an essential tool for scholars, and DSAL — with support from the Ford Foundation, the U.S. Department of Education, and the National Endowment for the Humanities — is expanding this concept beyond the select corpus represented by the NBIL in order to develop a South Asian Union Catalogue (SAUC). The SAUC intends to gather existing bibliographic records from partners such as the Library of Congress and the British Library and combine them with new cataloging to create an historical bibliography of books and periodicals published in South Asia since 1556. The SAUC will also be a union catalogue in which libraries from around the world will be able to register their holdings and fill an important *lacuna* for research on South Asia.

These essential resources for the study of South Asian literature in numerous languages are augmented by the Digital Dictionaries of South Asia (DDSA) hosted by DSAL. A project of the South Asia Language and Area Centre of the University of Chicago, Columbia University, and the Triangle South Asia Consortium in North Carolina, DDSA currently provides 27 digital dictionaries for the study of South Asian languages. In addition to textual entries, these dictionaries include sound files with pronunciations by native speakers. The ongoing development of linguistic materials continues with funding to the CRL from the U.S. Department of Education for the digital conversion and delivery of audio recordings from the Linguistic Survey of India. Compiled by Sir George Abraham Grierson during three decades from 1898 until 1928, the survey comprised 19 folio volumes amounting to almost 8, 000 pages and described 179 languages and 544 dialects spoken in the subcontinent. The entry for each language and dialect included a version of the parable of the prodigal son, an oral narrative or statement, and an established vocabulary of words and phrases. These entries were then set within their social, historical, and scholarly contexts. The audio recordings that accompanied the survey are a rare and fragile treasure that DSAL and its collaborators will help to preserve and make available to a wider audience.

Another of the lesser known jewels for the study of South Asia already available at DSAL is the American Institute of Indian Studies Centre for Art and Archaeology Photo Archive. Founded in 1961, the American Institute of Indian Studies (AIIS) is a consortium of U.S. universities and colleges engaged in research in South Asia. Among its numerous activities in support of scholarship, the AIIS maintains research centres and facilities in South Asia and is a member of the Council of

American Overseas Research Centres (CAORC). At the Centre for Art and Archaeology in Gurgaon, India the AIIS houses an archive of more than 120, 000 photographs and colour slides documenting South Asian art and archaeology. The renowned collection forms the basis of the monumental multivolume *Encyclopaedia of Indian Temple Architecture.*

The collection of a large database of art from Indian monuments will, it is hoped, not only inform existing scholarship but also foster new approaches to understanding art and architecture. By presenting scholars with a large corpus to consider and compare, it is hoped that the wider contexts of production and meaning will be analyzed and explained. Among the more fascinating recent uses of the AIIS photo archive is a project, spearhead by a team of scientists at the *Eidgenossische Technische Hochschule Zürich* (ETH Zurich) to restore a pair of the colossal fifth century Buddha statues in Afghanistan that were destroyed by the Taliban in 2001. The ETH Zurich team used photographs from the AIIS Centre for Art and Archaeology Photo Archive to help create a computer reconstruction of the Great Buddha that can serve as an exact model for the eventual restoration of the monument. In this way, the AIIS collection on DSAL has contributed to the stewardship of the cultural heritage of South Asia.

In the spring of 2005, CRL was awarded a grant from the U.S. Department of Education through the Technological Innovation and Cooperation for Foreign Information Access (TICFIA) programme to continue the work of DSAL in improving access to vital resources on South Asia. This project, funded at US$788, 000 for the four years of its duration, builds upon the foundation and experience of DSAL through its three previous grant phases. In addition to efforts such as the South Asia Union Catalogue and the Linguistic Survey mentioned above, the grant project will pursue preservation and indexing of highly select periodicals published in South Asia, and will begin to construct a framework to support international electronic article delivery on demand from the South Asian subcontinent to readers in the U.S. Through these activities, DSAL will continue to foster and coordinate the collaboration of a variety of partners in order to provide new and innovative resources for scholarship.

## Conclusion

GRN fosters, supports, and coordinates discrete projects among North American and overseas participants to build cooperative collections and access mechanisms. The GRN also provides a framework for leadership and strategies to maximize the diversity of acquired resources and support enhanced access to existing collections. The projects described above are examples of partnerships that can serve as models for activity in other subjects, regions, or languages. The "Network" aspect of the GRN means that the projects are committed to working together to share expertise, technology, and best practices. Within the GRN projects, several types of common activities exist where sharing of expertise and resources might yield savings and other benefits. Those common activities include (but are not limited to):

## IDENTIFICATION/DISCOVERY OF RESOURCES

- Projects engaging in the construction and delivery of union lists. These include AFRINUL, DSAL, the SEA Indexing Project, and the Japan Project's Union List of Japanese Serials and Newspapers. Related non-GRN projects that feature this activity include the International Coalition on Newspapers (ICON), the South Asia Union Catalogue initiative (funded by the Ford Foundation, National Endowment for the Humanities, and Department of Education), and Middle East Research Journals (MERJ) project of the Digital Library for International Research (DLIR).
- Projects enhancing access through the creation of electronic indexes and tables of contents, such as LARRP, DSAL, and the SEA Indexing Project. MERJ also aims to deliver such content.
- Projects exposing and aggregating research resources via technologies such as the Open Archives Initiative. This activity is included in current grant-funded phases of DSAL, the SEA Indexing Project, and LARRP.

- Projects improving access to and interoperability of discovery tools through instructional techniques, professional training, or assistance with bibliographic control. This includes GNARP's translation of *AACR2* rules and subsequent training. Related projects include the North American Coordinating Council (NCC) on Japanese Library Resource's training initiatives and the South Asia Union Catalogue training conferences in India.

## Interlibrary Loan/Document Delivery

- Projects facilitating arrangements among participating libraries for the delivery of returnable and non-returnable items. These include the Japan Project, GNARP, and LARRP. Conceivably, AFRINUL and the SEA Indexing Project could extend into this activity.

## Cooperative Collection Development and Distribution

- Projects engaging in coordinated, purposeful direction of collecting responsibilities among partners. Such examples include the distributed collection component of LARRP, the partnership agreements of GNARP, and the related NCC Multi–Volume Sets project. The CRL–administered Area Studies Microform Projects are another form of cooperative collection and access to be considered as models of activity.

## Development of Digital Collections and Electronic Resources

- Projects actively engaging in digitization of resources for display or delivery over the Web. These include DSAL and LARRP. Related projects include CRL's Brazilian Government Document Digitization Project, DLIR, and increasing activity by the AMPs.
- Projects acquiring or licensing digital content for participants' use. These include GNARP, current efforts being explored by LARRP, and efforts by and the related NCC Digital Resources Committee.

Sharing of expertise and resources among such projects would do much to extend the scope and scale of GRN activities. Already, a few of the projects are moving beyond area-specific projects to become more interconnected programmes sharing diverse resources. GNARP extends far beyond access to "German studies" resources, focusing broadly on bi-national cooperation among German and North American libraries to share materials across multiple subject areas.

Similarly, the Japan Project's Global ILL Framework seeks to expand its audience to include other institutions and individuals beyond those seeking Japanese resources. DSAL, GNARP, and LARRP are focusing on extending the number of participants in the projects both from North America and from the regions of interest. Participation may conceivably extend into other world regions as well, as in the case of the British Library and University of Sydney with DSAL.

The Centre for Research Libraries is committed to fostering the cross-regional applicability of activities and models.

Because an increasing amount of advanced research spans multiple regions, CRL will favour activities that can be applied to preserving materials from multiple regions and that support interdisciplinary and cross-cultural research. CRL's role is to facilitate sharing of expertise, equipment, technologies, and other resources for the preservation of critical source materials among region-based and discipline-based projects.

8

# Organising the Library

Libraries personnel at all levels of the organization are responsible for developing and maintaining a culture supportive of and committed to diversity. However, in order to expedite implementation of the plan and provide support and guidance, the Diversity Task Force recommends that the establishment of a Diversity Officer position and a standing Diversity Committee be the first actions taken. The Diversity Officer and Committee should begin action on the "within 6 months" items immediately as they are of the highest priority. The remaining action items where implementation is recommended within twelve months should be prioritized by the Committee. Where funds and workload implications of others are incurred in the execution of the Plan, the responsible party(ies) will develop a plan.

## RECRUITMENT OF STAFF FROM DIVERSE BACKGROUNDS

***Goal:*** To increase the diversity of the Libraries' workforce at all levels of the organization.

### Action Items

***Implementation:*** Diversity Officer; Diversity Committee; Administrative Officer Responsible for Personnel (AORP); Staff Development

### Within 6 Months

o Review our recruitment policies and procedures so that they support the UW Libraries commitment to diversity

- o Initiate a conversation between the iSchool Diversity Committee and the Libraries Diversity Committee to explore collaboration
- o Investigate the costs and effectiveness of residency programmes for minority librarians and develop a proposal if appropriate (2005-2006)

**Within 12 Months**

- o Establish monitoring programme for staff who may want to pursue a library degree, collaborating with the i-School
- o Work with the University to take advantage of hiring opportunities that promote a diverse Libraries staff
- o Proactively promote UW Libraries as a place in which to work
- o Establish opportunities for students interested in working in libraries as a career to participate in mentored work programmes

## RETENTION OF STAFF FROM DIVERSE BACKGROUNDS

***Goal:*** Promote an inclusive and supportive workplace culture as an important element in retaining a diverse staff

***Action Items:*** Within 12 Months

- o Support opportunities for professional development and/ or growth, and monitoring/networking for all staff

***Implementation:*** Diversity Officer; Diversity Committee; Libraries Council; Staff Development; Librarian Advisory Programme (LAP)

- o Facilitate connections between new hires and groups/ resources at the university and in the community

***Implementation:*** Diversity Committee; Diversity Officer; Staff Development Officer, UL Staff

- o Work with the University to enhance salary and compensation flexibility to retain a diverse library staff

***Implementation:*** Dean of the Libraries; AORP

## ORGANIZATIONAL CULTURE

***Goal:*** To incorporate awareness of the value and importance of diversity at all levels of the Libraries so that staff recognize their responsibility in maintaining a culture supportive of and committed to diversity; provide a supportive and safe working and learning environment

### Action Items

***Implementation:*** Diversity Officer; Diversity Committee; Staff Development

### Within 6 Months

- o Provide ongoing staff training to foster individual responsibility for maintenance of a supportive and safe working and learning environment, with particular attention to the role of supervisors and managers to eliminate or remedy inequities when they are identified
- o Highlight and promote the diversity of the libraries staff through programmes and publications throughout the organization, *i.e.* Inforum, Library Directions, and LSA
- o Enhance the Staff Development collection with diversity related materials including academic librarianship, higher education and organizational development

## SERVICES TO CONSTITUENTS

***Goal:*** To enrich the quality of life and advance intellectual discovery by connecting people of diverse backgrounds and ethnicities with knowledge

***Action Items:*** Within 6 Months

- o Develop and implement ongoing staff training in order to improve staff members' abilities to provide excellent service to all our diverse users, especially with regards to primary language barriers and physical/mental disabilities.

***Implementation:*** Staff Development Officer; Diversity Committee; RISG and other public service groups

- o To ensure compliance with Section 508 of the Americans with Disabilities Act, attempt to procure accessible information technology products and electronic resources. If an accessible product cannot be found, ask vendors about their plans for making future versions of their products accessible and let them know that accessibility is a consideration for purchase.

***Implementation:*** CMS; Diversity Officer

- o Review University of Washington Libraries' publications, website, and service policies for their accessibility to disabled users.

***Implementation:*** WSC; RISG, Publications Committee

**Within 12 Months**

- o Develop and maintain collections to support diversity in the current and changing UW curriculum

***Implementation:*** IRC; Liaisons; Cataloging Policy Committee; Metadata Implementation Group

- o Increase outreach to UW and external communities through library resources, services, collections, web resources and exhibits related to diversity; including the use of multilingual web pages and other publications as appropriate.

***Implementation:*** WSC; Liaisons; IRC

- o Provide services and spaces that nurture and support academic success for our diverse student community

5. Organizational Structure of Diversity in the Libraries

***Goal:*** To create a standing Diversity Committee, reporting directly to the Dean of University Libraries

***Membership:***

- o Half of the committee membership should come from the Task Force to ensure continuity
- o The Staff Development Officer and the Assessment Officer will serve as ex officio members of the Committee to aid in communication, implementation, and benchmarking.

- o Consider the inclusion of 1 member from outside the Libraries

Elements to consider for inclusion in the charge to the Diversity Committee:

- o Coordinate implementation of the diversity plan
- o Promote the inclusion of diversity into our culture/ organizational values
- o Review and assess the diversity plan and staff/ community needs annually, including the establishment of appropriate benchmarks to measure and ensure progress in achieving the goals and action items
- o Work with other library individuals and groups to identify and take advantage of opportunities related to diversity
- o Provide a "diversity toolkit" for Libraries staff to use in outreach
- o Establish and maintain a website and use other appropriate methods of communicating with staff and community about diversity

***Goal:*** To establish the position of the Diversity Officer

Responsibilities of the Diversity Officer, based on an initial 2 year half-time appointment include:

- o Chair the Diversity Committee
- o Provide oversight for the Libraries' diversity efforts
- o Serve as official liaison to UW offices and departments, *i.e.* Office of Minority Affairs on behalf of the UW Libraries and the Diversity Committee
- o Work with the Diversity Committee and others in identifying areas of needed support within the Libraries, *i.e.* training
- o Assist in identifying opportunities for libraries staff involvement in diversity activities on campus and outreach to the community

- o Be involved in professional association diversity programmes/committees
- o Assist individuals, management and library units in achieving goals of the diversity plan and other diversity initiatives
- o Serve ex-officio on Libraries Council

It is the recommendation of the Task Force that a review of the Diversity Officer be conducted after 2 years. This review, involving Libraries Cabinet and the Diversity Committee, should include consideration of the placement of the position in the organization as well as the time commitment of the position.

## A STRATEGIC PLAN FOR THE UNIVERSITY OF IOWA

### Institutional Strategies

This chapter contains a short list of institutional-level strategies, ones for which primary responsibility for implementation lies with the central administration. These strategies are designed to shape selected features of the University's environment and have broad positive effects that cut across most of the seven University goals. Each strategy is a response to particularly important opportunities or challenges posed by the environment of the University. In some cases, these institutional-level strategies are the source of resources for the goal-specific strategies of the book. This list of major institutional strategies takes into account both the University's environment and long-term aspirations and goals during the next five years.

Develop an enrolment management system to meet quality and diversity objectives while maintaining access for all qualified Iowa students. Continue efforts to create a more diverse, high quality, national and international student body by vigorous and broader recruitment of students to achieve these aims: (a) enroll more Iowa students who are in the top 10 percent of their graduating class, (b) maintain the proportion of out-of-state students at approximately 40 percent with broad geographic and ethnic representation including more undergraduate international students, and (c) increase the proportion of U. S. ethnic minorities to at least 10 percent. Strengthen the capacity of academic and nonacademic units (*e.g.*, student services) to serve the needs of a more diverse student body. Identify and control the factors that influence students' decisions to enroll in and to complete degree programmes in a timely manner through improved financial aid, student services, and academic advising.

The University of Iowa has made strong gains in the diversity and quality of its student body but must continue this effort as a central priority over the next five years. This strategy will raise the quality of education for all students and enhance the national and international stature of the institution. A more diverse University community will expose students to the heterogeneity of viewpoint and background important for living in the modern world. Given the small minority population of Iowa and the accelerating growth of the minority population of the nation, a diverse student body is of special importance to the quality of the undergraduate educational experience at the University. As a long-term goal, the University seeks proportional minority enrolments that fall about midway between minority representation in Iowa and national populations.

Implementing this strategy will require continued student recruitment efforts both within and outside the state and the support of external constituencies for an appropriately broad representation of out-of-state students, including international students. Under the current demographic circumstances, as long as the needs of Iowa students are met, the University should maintain the current mix of in-state and out-of-state students. Increasing the proportion of undergraduate students from other countries will enhance awareness of global perspectives and complement other efforts to increase cultural diversity. Issues and resources related to enrolling more international undergraduate students are considered by the Committee on International Programmes' strategic plan.

Student financial aid, a complex and changing issue, is a vital component of enrolment management and must be integrated with efforts to attract a diverse, high quality student body. Institutional sources are an increasing component of financial aid while federal sources are decreasing and families are committing a larger proportion of their incomes to financing higher education. The major goal in allocating financial aid funds has been and should continue to be insuring access to the University for as many qualified students as possible. In order to promote quality and diversity, more scholarships based solely on merit, or a combination of need and merit, should be considered. In addition, greater investment in the Honours Programme, the Undergraduate Scholar Assistant (USA) Programme, and the Presidential Scholars Programme is recommended along with reinstatement of the Deans Scholar Programme.

The Strategic Planning Committee recommends that the University pursue a more active enrolment management policy. Closer coordination and cooperation among the existing University offices that deal with admissions and student services, under the direction of the Office of the Provost, will improve the effectiveness of enrolment management. Individual colleges should specify optimum programme size and enrolment goals consistent with the resources available to maintain quality.

Maintain the current student and staffing levels and the present size of the physical plant, but closely examine the distribution of resources across colleges and programmes to improve the match between student demands and instructional resources. Use institutional resources to recruit the highest quality new faculty and staff and to retain the most productive members of the current faculty and staff.

Experience over the past two decades strongly suggests that the present enrolment of 27, 000 is about the limit for maintaining quality education within the context of the University's current human and physical resources. Growth of a few hundred students, evenly distributed over University programmes, would probably not seriously impair quality, but it is clear that an increase of a thousand students or more (as demonstrated during the late 1980's) strains physical resources, limits access to classes, and delays graduation. If large enrolment increases were to occur, they would have to be matched with increases in classroom and residence space, teaching faculty, and student-service staff to maintain access and quality in instructional programmes. The University has made significant gains in improving student-faculty ratios over the past five years, through growth in faculty numbers, decreases in enrolments, and greater commitment of faculty effort to undergraduate instruction.

Further improvements require more faculty and/or redistribution of faculty to areas of highest student demand. It is clear that the most serious difficulties in meeting student needs in terms of class availability, class sizes, and faculty supervision occur as a result of shifts in relative popularity of particular majors or disciplines. Although the University has some mechanisms for adjusting to changing demands, they are often slow and depend on the pace of retirements and resignations. The University should improve means of making rapid adjustments, both within and across colleges, such as appropriate use of flexible assignments, cross-listing of courses, joint appointments, and temporary appointments.

If the University is to be successful in its "Top Ten" aspiration, it must hire and retain the best faculty. Hiring distinguished faculty at the senior level is expensive, but it must be done in critical situations in order to maintain quality in distinguished programmes or to provide key leadership to push emerging programmes to a higher level of achievement.

Even more critical is the need to identify and retain the very best faculty at Iowa. University resources should be allocated in carefully selected instances to retain the most distinguished and productive faculty members-a policy that is often more economical than losing top faculty and hiring replacements. Increasing the number of named chairs and professorships is one way to recognize and support outstanding faculty.

Develop a high performance, unified, University-wide electronic communications infrastructure. As rapidly as possible, the University should complete the fibre-optic "backbone" network, establish technical standards for services, coordinate management of all electronic communication systems, and provide access to the University community with appropriate instructional support.

The immediate availability of state-of-the-art, integrated electronic communications will have a great impact on all the missions of the University. Instruction, research, service to the state, internal business operations, cost savings, and efficiency can all be improved by a uniform base of coordinated communication services. These include voice, video, data, and telemetry services with full interconnectivity throughout the UI campus and linkage to the Iowa Communications Network and worldwide networks.

The first step-completion of the "backbone" fibre-optic network connecting primary locations-is now underway, but much more needs to be done. Many buildings require rewiring. Terminals and computers must be updated or added and classroom facilities modernized. An institution-wide information architecture must be developed and implemented, and management of the vast array of services, technical standards, and financial support must be updated. In particular, support for training faculty, staff, and students in new skills will be essential to the successful implementation of a comprehensive communications system. It is vital that the University obtain continued state support for rapid implementation of a modern communications infrastructure.

The establishment of a high performance information network will lead to other communications improvements by facilitating information gathering, exchange of ideas, and coordination of services and planning. Use of electronic bulletin boards, e-mail, file transfer, data banks, and other features of modern computer-based communication systems aids students, scholars, and staff in their daily activities. Only if the University is fully connected electronically will its resources be available to the citizens of the state for education and services. As members of the University community develop the necessary new technological skills, they will gain access to new tools for their work and learning.

Improve support for the professional development of faculty and staff by (a) strengthening the capacity of departments and programmes to support teaching, research, and service activities of faculty and staff; (b) maintaining a strong and vital Developmental Assignment programme; and (c) improving recognition of the contributions of faculty and staff.

In the highly competitive era of the 1990s, there is a need not only to recruit outstanding faculty and staff but also to develop active measures to retain them. In order to improve retention, raise morale, reduce recruitment costs, and increase performance, the University must develop sufficient resources to enable all its faculty and staff to develop their potential to the fullest. Some of the measures may be symbolic (*e.g.*, recognizing the accomplishments of more persons by expanding award programmes); some would involve greater support for improved working conditions and professional activities (*e.g.*, the infrastructure of departments); others would require the targeting of funds for specific professional-development activities (*e.g.*, travel to professional meetings and tuition assistance for staff members). This strategy responds, in part, to the erosion of certain forms of support over the last 15 years due to repeated budgetary reversions from which the University still has not recovered. It calls for a balance between hiring distinguished persons from elsewhere and assisting current faculty and staff in their efforts to reach their potential.

This 1989 strategy is repeated here, with little change, because it is the one which appears to have been the least fully implemented over the past five years, even though the need for more support for professional development has grown and become even more obvious. Indeed, with noteworthy exceptions, recognition of staff and faculty accomplishments has become pro forma and the Developmental Assignment programme has supported fewer faculty projects in recent years. Even while faculty members have committed more of their efforts to instruction, support for teaching in the form of general expense budgets, library materials, teaching and laboratory assistants, and classroom facilities has stagnated. The lack of professional travel funds has raised obstacles to academic advancement; increases are necessary if the University is to achieve its "Top Ten" aspiration. Travel funds support continuing professional education, recruitment of future faculty members and students, visibility and recognition of Iowa scholars, and the impact of Iowa views on national and international issues and policies. The University needs a coordinated programme of professional development that would include acquisition of contemporary computer and management skills, the upgrading of disciplinary knowledge, and continued improvement of effective teaching skills. The proposed Centre for Teaching offers a potential contribution to developing and enhancing professional skills; it should be implemented as soon as possible and monitored for effectiveness. Another programme that should be expanded is the awarding of Instructional Computing Funds to support development of computer materials for classroom use.

Use the "Criteria for Institutional Enhancements and Reductions" to reallocate resources and create funds for responding to innovative proposals, raising quality, and generating flexible resources.

In today's competitive climate, strategy of focus in academic programmes is essential, even for the largest universities. As an institution smaller than most of its peers, The University of Iowa must decide which programmes and subprogrammes it can support at a high level of quality and which programmes it must leave for other institutions. In a process of continuous programme review, now in place throughout the University, hard decisions must be made about the allocation of resources. The absence of flexible monies in the colleges and in the central administration seriously hampers the ability of the institution to respond to special opportunities and innovative proposals. This strategy is designed to encourage faculty, staff, and students with ideas and proposals to put them forward for consideration and also ensure that they come to the attention of both collegiate and central administrators.

The Strategic Planning Steering Committee has developed "Criteria for Institutional Enhancements and Reductions" the present Strategic Planning Committee recommends vigorous application of the Criteria. The intent of the Criteria is to focus the limited resources of the University and to raise the quality of its programmes through a process of review and revision.

Overall, this strategy takes account of the fact that a significant amount of the money to implement plans at the University and collegiate levels will have to come from internal sources. With the application of this strategy, two purposes will be served: (a) the highest quality programmes can be maintained and emerging programmes can receive resources that will enhance their quality and move them into the top ranks, and (b) lagging programmes can be eliminated, consolidated, or downsized to free resources for stronger programmes and new initiatives. One recent example of the application of this strategy is the initiation of the Central Investment Fund for Research Enhancement (CIFRE) system in the Office of the Vice President for Research, permitting flexible awards to the most outstanding proposals.

To rebuild and improve core resources and the infrastructure over the next five years, give priority among state funding requests to University libraries, information technology, equipment for teaching and research, and the physical infrastructure.

The financial needs of the University Libraries continue to be a paramount concern among all members of the University community, impacting both instruction and scholarship. Library resources and staffing are an important indicator of institutional ranking; the 20-year decline in Association of Research Libraries rankings must be reversed if the University of Iowa is to make progress toward its "Top Ten" aspiration. Consequently, a significant increase in the base budget of the University Libraries remains a priority. Support for information technology, detailed in Strategy III, complements Library support as well as facilitating many other aspects of the University.

Because the pace of capital additions to the University is slower now than during the past two decades, it is timely to use capital funds to eliminate the backlog of deferred maintenance and to improve the quality of classroom facilities throughout the campus. (The opening of the Pappajohn Business Administration Building has served to highlight the need to upgrade existing classrooms.) Upgrading existing facilities also provides an opportunity to serve several other goals such as improving access for persons with disabilities, increasing safety, and conserving energy. The University has made onsiderable progress in these areas over the past five years, but it must continue to emphasize this strategy to avoid loss of momentum.

Strive to develop a climate of process review and continuous improvement in the quality and efficiency of University services, both academic and non-academic, by establishing methods of gathering information, reviewing costs, receiving suggestions, and recommending changes within each first-level planning unit.

Over time, any large organization accumulates inefficiencies and unnecessary requirements that require periodic examination and challenge. Students, staff, and faculty often raise questions about the continued need for certain pieces of paperwork or for programme requirements; they sometimes have suggestions for cost savings. As we move to greater use of electronic communication and data bases, are there changes in our record-keeping or management practices that we should implement? Should some functions be decentralized or, alternatively, can scattered services be collected in a single office with cost savings or improvement in quality? As we examine academic programmes for quality and focus, we should also examine our management and service offices for improvements. The challenge is how to implement a process of examination and evaluation, using knowledge and suggestions from all members of the University community to enhance the quality and efficiency of the services we provide to each other. The best method of proceeding is likely to vary from one unit to another, but we call on each division of the University to develop a process of quality and cost review. While recognizing that most University units are understaffed, we believe it is possible to use the experience and creativity of faculty, staff, and students to improve the functioning of all offices. We recommend that each first-level planning unit report on quality improvements and cost savings as part of its annual strategic planning progress reports.

Examine the academic and administrative structure of colleges, including the positioning of departments within colleges, for improved efficiency, communication among academic units, and responsiveness to educational needs. Colleges, departments, and nondepart-mentalized programmes, units, and services are reviewed on a regular basis throughout the University.

Self-studies and reviews of individual units may raise questions about reorganization, but it is difficult to act on such suggestions because other departments or units that may be affected by reorganization are not reviewed simultaneously. At present, the University has no process in place for reviewing the overall structure of its academic programmes at the same time. Examining the total set of academic units and programmes can revitalize needed collaborations and prune nonfunctional relationships maintained only for historical reasons.

A systematic review of the overall academic structure of the University should be undertaken periodically. During the past five years, the central administration of the University has been reorganized; in the current planning cycle, an examination of collegiate and departmental structures appears timely. Questions to be examined should include the placement of programmes in appropriate colleges, the need to phase out some programmes or initiate new ones, consolidation of small units or division of large ones, and the relationships between colleges and departments that support shared or joint programmes. Is the present location of departments and programmes within colleges optimal? Should one or more colleges be restructured? Are the connections among colleges functioning optimally? Do present departmental structures appropriately represent scholarly disciplines and use resources effectively to educate students at all levels? Are the present structures the best ones to support faculty research and scholarship?

Enhance the University's external relationships and visibility with its various constituencies.

Universities are becoming increasingly accountable to their external constituencies which range from alumni to governmental agencies. As private funding, through both individual donations and corporate research support, has become a larger proportion of The University of Iowa's resources, so too have the demands for responsiveness escalated. The University must continue to explore innovative ways of building and strengthening ties to its many constituencies if we are to respond to the needs of our external audiences and increase opportunities for financial support and cooperation with the private sector. As part of that effort, the University should increase its emphasis on alumni relations and UI Foundation fund-raising activities, while encouraging expanded student and faculty contacts with the business community for the furtherance of employment and research opportunities.

The University, through all members of the UI community, must listen to and speak to many publics. It is clear that the University enjoys wide-spread public support and admiration throughout the state and the region, but many members of the diverse constituencies that we serve either do not understand all of our many missions, or disagree with the priorities that we set. Therefore, it is our continuing responsibility to provide more information, to show how our efforts serve all citizens, and to cooperate with other educational and service organizations in the state. We must increase the effectiveness of our outreach and communications efforts at all levels of the University, by making even more coordinated use of departmental and collegiate newsletters and such institutional channels as the Office of State Relations, the University radio stations, and the facilities of University Relations and The University of Iowa Hospitals and Clinics' office of public affairs. We must listen carefully to the concerns of all Iowans, acknowledging their investment in the advancement of The University of Iowa.

Examine the consequences of health care reform for the University with particular attention to the health science colleges and The University of Iowa Hospitals and Clinics. Encourage additional cooperative agreements to insure adequate patient referral and actions to coordinate educational programmes across the health colleges.

While the direct impact of changes in the health care system falls primarily on the UI health colleges and The University of Iowa Hospitals and Clinics, the entire University will be affected by modifications in funding, service delivery, and patient referral. All members of the community must become better informed about reform proposals and recognize the consequences for local institutions and units. There are uncertainties about how educational programmes in the health science colleges will be funded, how an adequate patient flow will be maintained, and how the administration and provision of health care will be structured in the future.

A major change in administrative structure, grouping the health science colleges and the health care units under a Vice President for Health Sciences, has enhanced the University's ability to cope with health care reform. We endorse the new arrangement and urge the entire University community to become knowledgeable about the health care reform movement. Administrative officials must continue their efforts to position the UI to the best advantage in a rapidly changing environment and to explore new health care options for the University community.

Develop proposals for more extensive use of the Oakdale Research Campus.

The use of the Oakdale Campus, as a site for programmes supporting technology transfer and as a home for selected academic research and service units, has grown over the past two decades, but there exists the potential for even greater use of this land asset. At a time when there is not much unused land on the main campus, room for future development is available at Oakdale. A master plan for the physical development of land and infrastructure on the Oakdale Campus has been prepared and approved. In consultation with pro-spective users and community groups, relevant administrators should prepare a programmatic vision for Oakdale analyzing the advantages and disadvantages of an Oakdale location and identifying University programmes that might flourish there.

**Summary**

Eleven institutional strategies are recommended for implementation over the next five years. In some cases, these strategies continue efforts started five years ago; others represent new initiatives. A few require allocation of additional financial resources; others require only the will to carry out the proposed recommendations. Many of the strategies complement or support recommendations from first-level planning units; others represent challenges to the first-level units to coordinate their efforts with University-wide strategies. All will require support and leadership from the central administration. All, we believe, will significantly benefit the University.

## THE HARVARD SELF-ENRICHING LIBRARY FACILITIES (SELF) PROJECT

We have developed a research agenda based on the design and implementation of a "Self-Enriching Library Facilities" (SELF) technology. By developing and exploiting the online, interactive features of a digital library, SELF systems allow users to contribute to the archive, adding useful, organized information as a natural part of the work they already do. In particular, users will easily be able to enter evaluative comments, add links between related works, and contribute their own data, manipulations, analytical results, and software to the library.

Because the system will capture and incorporate users' knowledge and tools, the quality of the library will be continually enriched and its capabilities will be progressively enhanced. Instead of serving as passive repositories, the SELF technology will convert libraries into information sources that grow as users employ them. Self-enrichment, the capacity to incorporate users' contributions, distinguishes the SELF approach from many other digital library designs. Instead of devoting resources to expensive one-time digitization of printed materials, the SELF project will invest primarily in tools to capture the extensive knowledge, analyses, and information routinely created by users. Tools will be provided to allow users to contribute easily. In addition to improving digital libraries automatically, SELF tools will improve the practice and quality of scientific research: they will enhance tracking of research by an individual researcher (playing a role similar to that of a natural scientist's laboratory notebook) and make it possible to replicate the research of others.

The proposed research project will develop facilities that subject the fundamental features of this self-enriching library vision to intensive empirical evaluation. These features include:

1. A work environment that facilitates users' contributions to the database
2. A user interface that supports contribution submission by users
3. A client/server architecture that is extensible to new hardware platforms and to new types of data, including users' contributions
4. Mechanisms for certifying information and protecting users' intellectual property by authenticating users' identities and limiting access rights

The primary users of the testbed will be social scientists, using data archives from the Inter-university Consortium for Political and Social Research (ICPSR, the largest collection of social science data in the world), and the Harvard On-Line Library Catalogue, HOLLIS, of Harvard University (the largest university library in the world). Social scientists from all over the country are expected to participate in the design and evaluation of the tools and systems to be developed.

An important goal of the project is to create tools and procedures and to gain an understanding of user behaviour that extends to all types of digital library use, not only to research by scholars in the social sciences. The system will be extensible to multiple network configurations including the Internet and cable TV, to other data archives including image and video servers, and to other types of users including grade-school pupils and casual browsers.

## Project Rationale

The profound change in media that the transition from paper to digital libraries represent will undoubtedly be accompanied by equally profound changes in the intellectual organization and day to day use of our libraries. During discussions of possible pilot digital library applications at Harvard we decided to focus on one important aspect of this change. Using traditional libraries is a one-way process whereby users retrieve materials from the library. Indeed, usage actually degrades (through normal wear-and-tear) rather than enhances paper-based collections. Through SELF technology, digital libraries offer the possibility of blurring the distinction between users and librarians since both will be able to contribute to the collection. The collection which we propose using in our initial digital library implementation is the datasets distributed by ICPSR (the Inter-university Consortium for Political and Social Research), a membership collaborative which collects and distributes social science data of numerous types. Harvard makes very heavy use of ICPSR data, with researchers spread across many schools and academic departments. Several aspects of the present use of ICPSR datasets which make the SELF model attractive include:

- Significant effort is frequently required to make use of these datasets, effort in part duplicated by each subsequent user;
- Researchers frequently spend considerable effort creating derivative datasets, new derived variables, etc., while using the datasets, efforts again frequently duplicated by other users; and
- It has been shown that it is frequently difficult to replicate research results reported in the literature, in part because the complex manipulations used to derive results are hard to document and recreate.

Discussions with empirical data researchers revealed a great willingness to make available through automated contribution to the digital library various products of their research, especially if some of the burdens of making this information available were resolved by the SELF project. Specifically, the SELF library model will enable researchers to make at least three types of contributions:

- *Derivative Datasets and Software*: This addresses the issues of duplicate effort, and provides ways to document the research process which yielded a given research result.

- Evaluative commentary, providing commentary by experts about given objects in the digital library (such as cells, variables, observations, datasets, or software).
- Linkages between objects in the digital library, allowing "webs" or networks of links between various objects in a collection.

The latter two types of contribution are applicable to library materials beyond datasets, and address two shortcomings of traditional library catalogs:

- Current library catalogs provide users with little information to help them decide which of the items in a collection retrieved in a search is most likely to be of use. This seeming neutrality of catalogs, where each holding is implicitly attributed equal importance or potential usefulness, has many justifications but is beginning to be questioned in the library field. After all, we have no reason but tradition to prefer this equal weighting scheme to the infinite variety of other possibilities. For example, some institutions are experimenting with including book reviews in their catalogs. Weighting schemes may be particularly important for very large libraries, such as Harvard, where the probability of any volume being used may be exceedingly low (about half of all books in the largest Harvard library have never been checked out).
- Budgets constrain how much effort libraries can invest to enhance the retrievability of catalogue data. Permitting users to build "links" between related materials in a catalogue allows the use of popular "hyperlinking" techniques in catalogs without requiring additional library resources to add such data during the cataloging process. By "deputizing" users as expert librarians, we can significantly increase the level of effort invested in catalogue building and enhancement without corresponding increases in library staff and budget.

### Architectural Overview of the Proposed SELF Library

The SELF library is based on the client/server system architecture, and has four basic components: the user client software, a metadata or catalogue server, a data store server, and a contribution acceptance server. Figure outlines the architecture.

The most difficult and sophisticated component is the client. Client functions include:

- Support for traditional word and phrase catalogue searching, as implemented in the Z39.50 information retrieval protocol. In the SELF model collection use begins with a catalogue search.
- Support for following hypertext links between data records in the metadata store, as implemented today in such systems as the WorldWideWeb. Links are used in the SELF system after a relevant catalogue record is found for retrieving evaluative commentary about an object, metadata or catalogue data about other related objects in the collection (including contributed derivative datasets and software), and extended information about datasets (description of a survey, data element lists, etc.).
- Facilities which make it easy during the research process for users to accumulate information about related items in the collection and evaluations of objects in the collection, and to contribute this information to the SELF library at an appropriate time.
- Facilities for retrieving digital objects from the collection.

We believe that the user interface is one of the most critical elements in the design of the digital library, and research into the effective design of the client software is a major element in the SELF project.

The metadata server contains traditional library catalogue data for objects in digital library, enhanced with commentary, links to related data and publications, extended information about datasets including such things as data element list, etc.

The server will support two retrieval protocols: Z39.50 search/retrieval, and HTTP for following links from the catalogue records to other relevant data.

The data store servers will be tailored to the nature of the digital objects they contain. Different access protocols, different retrieval functions, different security/billing facilities will be needed depending on the materials stored. While the SELF project will initially provide only statistical research datasets, the architecture allows for a variety of data store servers, and we assume that during the project other types of digital materials relevant to users of the SELF library (such as electronic text, video, audio, etc.) will become available and will be incorporated into the system.

The contribution acceptance server will automate the process of incorporating user contributions into the SELF library. Contributions will include additions to existing catalogue records, links between catalogue records, and new materials for the data store along with appropriate metadata. One of the major issues to be resolved about the contribution process is the degree to which validation of contribution can be automated, and the degree to which a manual "editorial" process is needed.

## Major Research Issues to be Addressed

The proposed research project will subject the fundamental features of this self-enriching library vision to intensive testing. These features include:

- *Interactive User Interface:* Two complementary forms of information-finding tools will be integrated into a single coherent interface. Users will be able to use the precision of traditional keyword and phrase searching, and after locating one relevant item in the catalogue pursue related materials through hypertext linking. Hypertext techniques will also be used to provide access to enriched catalogue data, such as evaluative commentary and descriptions of data set formatting and content. In addition, the same interface will provide facilities for the user to accumulate information throughout the research process. This information can be easily contributed subsequently, enriching both the catalogue and the collection. Finally, the interface will support communication in limited sublanguages such as TV remote-control protocol for cable.

- *The "bibliography" of Datasets*: Libraries have largely standardized on an international basis the rules and data formats for describing printed materials. Similar consensus does not yet exist for describing datasets, and different conventions are growing up in different communities. One aspect of the SELF project is to analyze these various conventions for use in digital library systems.
- *Context-rich Work Environment:* Context-tracking software will be used to support and encourage users to make contributions to the database. Authentication, security, and access-control mechanisms that understand context will be devised.
- *Security/authentication:* The use of the ICPSR data, combined with the desire to make the SELF library accessible to users beyond Harvard, raises interesting security issues. ICPSR data is freely available to researchers in any ICPSR member institution. Providing access to non-Harvard users therefore requires a system to validate institutional affiliations over the network. Our project incorporates research into the construction of an inter-institutional authentication system.
- *Scalable Client/server Architecture:* The architecture will be extensible in the future to servers that incorporate various kinds of users' contributions and to new types of published data, and it will leverage existing searching capabilities. The additions may be in various data types, including text, numeric tables, graphics, and video.
- *Information Certification:* Users' contributions can be properly evaluated, filtered, classified, or edited to enhance their value to other users.
- *Intellectual-property Management:* While the ICPSR provides one model for ownership/access for digital

materials, any robust digital library system must be able to encompass materials under a range of different intellectual property-rights protocols. The present lack of guidance in intellectual property management has held back the ICPSR (and many other archives) in pursuing advanced services based on digital library concepts. We will work with ICPSR to solve these problems in their case, while attempting to provide more generally applicable solutions. In particular, the new legal challenge of incorporating users' contributions in a digital library will be studied. The proposed research is expected to result in frameworks for handling financing and intellectual-property management issues.

**The Testbed and its Three-Layer Model**

The proposed SELF project will develop a testbed to support the research work. Figure depicts a three-layer model of the testbed:

- *Usage Layer:* A set of applications for the testbed. Each application is associated with a specific set of users and tools that the testbed will support.
- *Data Layer:* A collection of datasets that the testbed possesses.
- *Infrastructure Layer:* Includes all the hardware and software facilities that are applicable to a large number of data stores and applications. These facilities include networking configurations, clients, servers, user interface, work environments, as well as mechanisms for assuring security, authentication and information certification, the protection of intellectual property rights, etc.

The primary users of the testbed under this proposal will be social scientists, using the ICPSR data archives, the Harvard University library catalogue.

Social scientists include political scientists, economists, anthropologists, sociologists, geographers, and scholars from many other areas using data from the ICPSR. The SELF library catalogue will draw materials from many sources at Harvard (materials relevant to social science research in all formats, not just datasets, will be included in the catalogue), and, given the depth of Harvard's collections, will be a significant resource for social scientists well beyond Harvard.

Because the catalogue will be accessible over the Internet, our beta test users will come from all over the U.S. These social scientists will participate in and evaluate, in depth, the tools and systems to be researched and developed under this project. The shaded boxes in the figure indicate these core activities of the project.

Results of the proposed research under this project will be most useful if they are applicable to other fields and different types of users.

We shall insure that the system is extensible at each of the three layers. At the infrastructure layer, we will allow (in addition to the Internet) cable networks, based on the Ethernet and TCP/IP protocols, to provide access to households and business offices at speeds ranging from 0.5 to 10 Megabits/sec. At the data layer, we will ensure that the SELF system can incorporate other datasets beyond ICPSR and the Harvard library catalogue. We also hope to provide facilities for including datasets based on audio as well as static and full motion video. At the usage layer, via cable access, we will experiment with introducing the SELF system to people outside of the research community. These users will most likely be consumers rather than producers of contributions submitted to the data archive, and will in general use communication-limited sublanguages such as remote TV control protocols. The unshaded boxes in Figure indicate all these extended activities to ensure the testbed's architectural generality.

**Testbed Development Plan**

The testbed will be developed according to the following schedule:

- Year 1: (1) Metadata server with URL (Uniform Resource Locators) linkage capability, (2) ICPSR data server, and

(3) Microsoft Windows-based clients using both MOSAIC and Notes.

- Year 2: (1) Opening of the testbed to selected researchers around the world via the Internet, and high-speed access (*i.e.*, Ethernet speed) to local users in the Greater Boston area through cable services, and (2) implementation of users' contributions.
- Year 3: (1) Integration of the client with advanced work environment and user interface facilities to facilitate users' contributions, (2) second-generation servers (*e.g.*, servers documents like magazine articles, video, and copyrighted materials) and (3) servers implementing results of research on security and intellectual property.
- Year 4: Evaluation of system and user experience to identify effectiveness, limitations, areas for improvement, and possible extensions for the SELF technology.

**Concluding Remarks**

The SELF project is a cooperative effort involving Harvard researchers with a number of institutions having complementary expertise in areas relevant to digital libraries, including user interface design (Lotus Notes, NCSA), metadata and data servers (OCLC, CIESIN), digital information collections (CIESIN, ICPSR), and networking infrastructure (Continental Cablevision).

The project proposes the development of a library system with an in depth catalogue of social science materials linked to a digital collection initially composed of social science datasets from the ICPSR. This library would be of relevance to a wide range of researchers at Harvard and elsewhere, and could expect to receive a significant level of use from students and scholars in many disciplines.

The project is based on the proposition that, unlike traditional libraries, digital libraries can accept information from, as well as dispense information to, users, and that such libraries can be improved and enriched through use. In particular, as applied to social science datasets, such a library can reduce effort for users by capturing the results of earlier work, can help address the difficulties of research replicability, and can provide enhanced catalogue services through expert user input.

The enhanced catalogue features would be applicable to libraries of any sort. Technically, the project proposes an architecture that is extensible to digital collections of any sort, and in fact one project participant (CIESIN) will apply the same architecture to a collection of significantly different materials, ensuring that our developments will be generalizable.

The design combines two modes of information retrieval for catalogue or metadata: word or phrase searching, and hypertext linkage. Primary emphasis is placed on the design of a user's working environment that both simplifies system use and provides for the facile capture of research by-products which can be subsequently shared with other users. Lastly, the project intends to address the problems of security and intellectual property rights control in a multi-institutional environment.

In summary, we have designed the SELF project to be immediately useful to the vast numbers of social and political researchers in these numerous related academic fields. Our testbed will therefore be a real-world application that will help real-world users.

If our application is successful, SELF technology will also fundamentally restructure the practice and improve the quality of scientific research throughout the social sciences and other areas that rely on secondary data analyses. The proposed SELF technology is generic in the sense that it can benefit a variety of mainstream digital library technologies of the future beyond this single application.

## LIBRARY FACILITIES FOR THE MENTALLY CHALLENGED

Under the guidance of Federal legislation, Dr. Robert Lowe, Director of the North Jersey Developmental Centre (NJDC), applied for and received a $10, 000 grant to establish a library and resource centre for his facility that serves just under 500 mentally challenged adults.

Our company had experienced marked success in the development of a special library for institutionalized adults afflicted with problems attendant to old age, and we were selected to develop Dr. Lowe's facility because of our past accomplishments.

The unique opportunity to start a library for the developmentally disabled presented one of the major challenges that was ever faced by our twelve year old corporation. Research in collection development took us through many areas of the country and varied functional settings.

Suitable and adaptable furniture, furnishings, and interior designs were chosen from many sources. Throughout the first six months of learning and implementation we were inspired by the awareness that mental health can lead to the mastery of ordinary tasks and that needs and interests are the same regardless of developmental levels.

## Methodology

Our first action was to tour the NJDC facility, both the area selected for the library as well as the living, working, and school quarters. We then obtained a profile of the population from the school principal: degree of retardation, age range, sex, cultural background, and ambulatory level.

This helped us evaluate the facility and determine what material in the existing collection to weed, what furniture and shelving would be needed, and what special equipment such as computers would be advisable.

When we first saw the 30 foot by 40 foot classroom (9.1 meters x 12.1 meters) that was designated for the library setting it was shabby, dirty and covered with the dust of disuse. Old equipment, outdated and inappropriate material, sagging shelves, overgrown plants, broken blinds, and dilapidated furnishings filled the space with depressing neglect. The room had been closed for library use for more than two years and the programmes that once existed were now abandoned. To begin our rehabilitation we appraised the area for size and location and we found that the space would adequately serve the needs of the school. We then weeded almost all of the books, all of the magazines, all of the cassettes, and threw away the faded decorations. What remained were two shelving ranges, one bulletin board and one librarian's desk.

The floor area was opened up and rearranged with wall stacks, a supply closet and magazine racks. Tables and chairs in white with primary colour accents enlivened the atmosphere. New and colour coordinated blinds, display areas, and a professional corner for the librarian were included in the interior design.

Maximum floor space was allowed for wheelchairs and other mobility aids. American Libraries Association posters and flags blanketed the exposed walls. The walls were painted, the floors were polished, the lighting was enhanced. The new look was fresh and appealing and bid a warm welcome to the residents.

**Collection Development**

Our first problem was one of money. Out of the $10, 000 total grant funds, only $2, 000 was earmarked for the collection and $8, 000 for our services. Although the allocation for professional consulting was completely unrealistic, we were excited by the prospect of this assignment and agreed to abrogate our standard fee and accept the contract proscribed by the grant.

Another requirement of the grant was that all of the residents had to be served regardless of the degree of their retardation. Most material in current use for the retarded population fell into two subject categories: a) instructional manuals for caregivers and parents, and b) children's books. For obvious reasons neither suited the needs of the targeted adult population in our project.

We believed that interest and emphasis should be in multi media format, particularly since some clients had multiple disabilities and communication would be more successful through the use of two or more senses. The difficulty lay not only in trying to find suitable material, but in trying to spend $2, 000 in collection development that could easily absorb $20, 000.

The preparation of the opening day collection demanded a great deal of time. Our initial task was to search for a similar facility to be used as a model. We felt that if we found an established site that already had a library we would have a base on which to build.

The immediate tri state area (New Jersey, New York, Pennsylvania) was thought to be geographically broad enough to find at least one special library serving a handicapped population and a field trip to the site would be convenient for travel.

We found no library in any of the facilities in our general geographical area and we expanded our search nationally. We contacted adult literacy groups, publishers, state and federal governments, organizations for the disabled, English as a second language (ESL) groups, Association of Retarded Citizens, school and public libraries, academic libraries and university research departments.

We estimate that more than 200 telephone calls were made over a period of a month. One of the best sources of information came from individuals who were related directly or indirectly to a mentally challenged person. They informed us of materials that were suitable, adaptable, and stimulating to the handicapped adult. They shared their experiences, reinforcing our research that children's subjects were inappropriate for our audience and that adult themes could be understood and enjoyed if presented to the reader using a simple vocabulary and many illustrations.

After exhausting every lead made available to us, we finally realized that our contract was indeed for a pilot project. This meant that we had no proven source of information on which to draw and that our work would be an original effort. We then visited facilities within the state that catered to mentally challenged adults and interviewed directors and supervisors of education. Although none of the facilities had a library or resource centre, the directors were expansive regarding what they would like to see in a library if they had one of their own. They were extremely interested in the outcome of our project with the hope of replicating some of our ideas should funding become available for their own resources.

One of the most successful field trips was to Montgomery County in the State of Maryland. Montgomery County has an advanced and highly successful English as a Second Language (ESL) programme and we believed that much of their material might be suitable for our needs.

One of the pleasant surprises encountered at our meeting was that we learned that some of the hand bound books in their collection had been written by the ESL students themselves. The subjects included sewing, nature, life skills, simple biography and were catalogued according to difficulty with different coloured spine labels. We adopted and maintained this method of classification.

Many publishers were called first the major names such as Random House, Scribners, Houghton Mifflin, Viking Penguin. When we narrowed the search down to small specialty houses such as New Readers Press we finally achieved some results. Our inquiry was focused on two questions only, "Do you publish material with high interest and low reading ability?" and "Is it illustrated?" We requested catalogs and also looked for selection and reviews in Library Journal, Choice, Wilson Library Bulletin Booklist and various publications from international book distributors. Finally a bibliography was developed that was representative of the interests of our target population.

**The New Library**

1. Besides being aesthetically attractive, the new library now has regularly scheduled classes.
2. The caregivers are being trained to assist in helping with material selection.
3. We have been told that the residents look forward to their visits.

4. The setting is the centre for other types of activities, *i.e.*, a new programme of physical awareness has been instituted.
5. The material is helping to broaden the interest of the clients.
6. A new grant for an additional $10, 000 has been received to expand the collection.
7. Recommendations for a permanent part time librarian have been made.
8. The facility will soon be opened to a non residential special needs school in the area that has no library on its site. We were especially pleased that our facility was recognized by another state service.
9. There is now a computer for library use. With the many Windows applications and touch screen programmes available, it is expected that the next major advancement will be in teaching fundamentals of simple automation to as many residents as possible.
10. We are hoping that the special education teachers and therapists will now become involved with programmes in the library setting.

**Conclusion**

A brief outline of our findings follows:

1. Little or no money is budgeted for media centres in either private or public institutions that cater to the mentally handicapped.
2. Grant money comes from the public sector. We found no private grants dedicated to this purpose.
3. While the most specialized material adaptable to developmentally disabled adults is high interest/low ability, it may not always be appropriate. Selectivity is essential to appropriate library development.
4. Very few publishers print material that covers subject matter of interest to retarded adults.

5. Training in the distribution and selection of material should have the benefit of a professional librarian's knowledge and experience.
6. Media centres for the handicapped should be model community environments, enhancing and expanding life skills which habilitate the clients. A crucial aspect is to normalize, humanize, and de institutionalize.
7. Technological advancements have increased the availability of information to the handicapped. Assistive devices are in a dynamic state of redevelopment. Page turners, mechanized wheel chairs, magnifiers, and innumerable other aids are changing the lives of the handicapped. The technology of microcomputers, exemplified by touch screens and voice activation, allow for a wealth of physical and intellectual experiences heretofore unavailable.
8. Anyone currently entering the field of special library development focusing on adults with disabilities is a pioneer.

# 9

# The New Law of Libraries

The Library which is to be spoken of in these pages, is all unlike the halls which a Spencer or a Huth fills with treasure beyond price. The age of great libraries has gone by, and where a collector of the old school survives, he is usually a man of enormous wealth, who might, if he pleased, be distinguished in parliament, in society, on the turf itself, or in any of the pursuits where unlimited supplies of money are strictly necessary. The old amateurs, whom La Bruyere was wont to sneer at, were not satisfied unless they possessed many thousands of books. For a collector like Cardinal Mazarin, Naude bought up the whole stock of many a bookseller, and left great towns as bare of printed paper as if a tornado had passed, and blown the leaves away. In our modern times, as the industrious Bibliophile Jacob, says, the fashion of book-collecting has changed; "from the vast hall that it was, the library of the amateur has shrunk to a closet, to a mere book-case. Nothing but a neat article of furniture is needed now, where a great gallery or a long suite of rooms was once required.

The book has become, as it were, a jewel, and is kept in a kind of jewel-case." It is not quantity of pages, nor lofty piles of ordinary binding, nor theological folios and classic quartos, that the modern amateur desires. He is content with but a few books of distinction and elegance, masterpieces of printing and binding, or relics of famous old collectors, of statesmen, philosophers, beautiful dead ladies; or, again, he buys illustrated books, or first editions of the modern classics. No one, not the Duc d'Aumale, or M. James Rothschild himself, with his 100 books worth 40,000 pounds, can possess very many copies of books which are inevitably rare.

Thus the adviser who would offer suggestions to the amateur, need scarcely write, like Naude and the old authorities, about the size and due position of the library. He need hardly warn the builder to make the salle face the east, "because the eastern winds, being warm and dry of their nature, greatly temper the air, fortify the senses, make subtle the humours, purify the spirits, preserve a healthy disposition of the whole body, and, to say all in one word, are most wholesome and salubrious." The east wind, like the fashion of book- collecting, has altered in character a good deal since the days when Naude was librarian to Cardinal Mazarin. One might as well repeat the learned Isidorus his counsels about the panels of green marble (that refreshes the eye), and Boethius his censures on library walls of ivory and glass, as fall back on the ancient ideas of librarians dead and gone.

The amateur, then, is the person we have in our eye, and especially the bibliophile who has but lately been bitten with this pleasant mania of collecting. We would teach him how to arrange and keep his books orderly and in good case, and would tell him what to buy and what to avoid. By the LIBRARY we do not understand a study where no one goes, and where the master of the house keeps his boots, an assortment of walking-sticks, the "Waverley Novels," "Pearson on the Creed," "Hume's Essays," and a collection of sermons. In, alas! too many English homes, the Library is no more than this, and each generation passes without adding a book, except now and then a Bradshaw or a railway novel, to the collection on the shelves.

The success, perhaps, of circulating libraries, or, it may be, the Aryan tendencies of our race, "which does not read, and lives in the open air," have made books the rarest of possessions in many houses. There are relics of the age before circulating libraries, there are fragments of the lettered store of some scholarly great-grandfather, and these, with a few odd numbers of magazines, a few primers and manuals, some sermons and novels, make up the ordinary library of an English household. But the amateur, whom we have in our thoughts, can never be satisfied with these commonplace supplies. He has a taste for books more or less rare, and for books neatly bound; in short, for books, in the fabrication of which ART has not been absent. He loves to have his study, like Montaigne's, remote from the interruption of servants, wife, and children; a kind of shrine, where he may be at home with himself, with the illustrious dead, and with the genius of literature.

The room may look east, west, or south, provided that it be dry, warm, light, and airy. Among the many enemies of books the first great foe is DAMP, and we must describe the necessary precautions to be taken against this peril. We will suppose that the amateur keeps his ordinary working books, modern tomes, and all that serve him as literary tools, on open shelves. These may reach the roof, if he has books to fill them, and it is only necessary to see that the back of the bookcases are slightly removed from contact with the walls.

The more precious and beautifully bound treasures will naturally be stored in a case with closely-fitting glass-doors. The shelves should be lined with velvet or chamois leather, that the delicate edges of the books may not suffer from contact with the wood. A leather lining, fitted to the back of the case, will also help to keep out humidity. Most writers recommend that the bookcases should be made of wood close in the grain, such as well-seasoned oak; or, for smaller tabernacles of literature, of mahogany, satin-wood lined with cedar, ebony, and so forth. These close-grained woods are less easily penetrated by insects, and it is fancied that bookworms dislike the aromatic scents of cedar, sandal wood, and Russia leather.

There was once a bibliophile who said that a man could only love one book at a time, and the darling of the moment he used to carry about in a charming leather case. Others, men of few books, preserve them in long boxes with glass fronts, which may be removed from place to place as readily as the household gods of Laban. But the amateur who not only worships but reads books, needs larger receptacles; and in the open oak cases for modern authors, and for books with common modern papers and bindings, in the closed armoire for books of rarity and price, he will find, we think, the most useful mode of arranging his treasures. His shelves will decline in height from the lowest, where huge folios stand at case, to the top ranges, while Elzevirs repose on a level with the eye. It is well that each upper shelf should have a leather fringe to keep the dust away.

As to the shape of the bookcases, and the furniture, and ornaments of the library, every amateur will please himself. Perhaps the satin-wood or mahogany tabernacles of rare books are best made after the model of what furniture-dealers indifferently call the "Queen Anne" or the "Chippendale" style. There is a pleasant quaintness in the carved architectural ornaments of the top, and the inlaid flowers of marquetry go well with the pretty florid editions of the last century, the books that were illustrated by Stothard and Gravelot.

Ebony suits theological tomes very well, especially when they are bound in white vellum. As to furniture, people who can afford it will imitate the arrangements of Lucullus, in Mr. Hill Burton's charming volume "The Book-hunter" (Blackwood, Edinburgh, 1862).—"Everything is of perfect finish,—the mahogany-railed gallery, the tiny ladders, the broad winged lecterns, with leathern cushions on the edges to keep the wood from grazing the rich bindings, the books themselves, each shelf uniform with its facings, or rather backings, like well-dressed lines at a review."

The late Sir William Stirling-Maxwell, a famous bibliophile, invented a very nice library chair. It is most comfortable to sit on; and, as the top of the back is broad and flat, it can be used as a ladder of two high steps, when one wants to reach a book on a lofty shelf.

A kind of square revolving bookcase, an American invention, manufactured by Messrs. Trubner, is useful to the working man of letters. Made in oak, stained green, it is not unsightly. As to ornaments, every man to his taste. You may have a "pallid bust of Pallas" above your classical collection, or fill the niches in a shrine of old French light literature, pastoral and comedy, with delicate shepherdesses in Chelsea china. On such matters a modest writer, like Mr. Jingle when Mr. Pickwick ordered dinner, "will not presume to dictate."

Next to damp, dust and dirt are the chief enemies of books. At short intervals, books and shelves ought to be dusted by the amateur himself. Even Dr. Johnson, who was careless of his person, and of volumes lent to him, was careful about the cleanliness of his own books. Boswell found him one day with big gloves on his hands beating the dust out of his library, as was his custom. There is nothing so hideous as a dirty thumb-mark on a white page. These marks are commonly made, not because the reader has unwashed hands, but because the dust which settles on the top edge of books falls in, and is smudged when they are opened. Gilt-top edges should be smoothed with a handkerchief, and a small brush should be kept for brushing the tops of books with rough edges, before they are opened.

But it were well that all books had the top edge gilt. There is no better preservative against dust. Dust not only dirties books, it seems to supply what Mr. Spencer would call a fitting environment for bookworms. The works of bookworms speak for themselves, and are manifest to all. How many a rare and valuable volume is spoiled by neat round holes drilled through cover and leaves! But as to the nature of your worm, authorities differ greatly. The ancients knew this plague, of which Lucian speaks. Mr. Blades mentions a white bookworm, slain by the librarian of the Bodleian. In Byzantium the black sort prevailed. Evenus, the grammarian, wrote an epigram against the black bookworm ("Anthol. Pal.," ix. 251):

Pest of the Muses, devourer of pages, in crannies that lurkest, Fruits of the Muses to taint, labour of learning to spoil; Wherefore, oh black-fleshed worm! wert thou born for the evil thou workest? Wherefore thine own foul form shap'st thou with envious toil?

The learned Mentzelius says he hath heard the bookworm crow like a cock unto his mate, and "I knew not," says he, "whether some local fowl was clamouring or whether there was but a beating in mine ears. Even at that moment, all uncertain as I was, I perceived, in the paper whereon I was writing, a little insect that ceased not to carol like very chanticleer, until, taking a magnifying glass, I assiduously observed him. He is about the bigness of a mite, and carries a grey crest, and the head low, bowed over the bosom; as to his crowing noise, it comes of his clashing his wings against each other with an incessant din." Thus far Mentzelius, and more to the same purpose, as may be read in the "Memoirs of famous Foreign Academies" (Dijon, 1755-59, 13 vol. in quarto).

But, in our times, the learned Mr. Blades having a desire to exhibit bookworms in the body to the Caxtonians at the Caxton celebration, could find few men that had so much as seen a bookworm, much less heard him utter his native wood-notes wild. Yet, in his "Enemies of Books," he describes some rare encounters with the worm. Dirty books, damp books, dusty books, and books that the owner never opens, are most exposed to the enemy; and "the worm, the proud worm, is the conqueror still," as a didactic poet sings, in an ode on man's mortality. As we have quoted Mentzelius, it may not be amiss to give D'Alembert's theory of bookworms: "I believe," he says, "that a little beetle lays her eggs in books in August, thence is hatched a mite, like the cheese-mite, which devours books merely because it is compelled to gnaw its way out into the air." Bookworms like the paste which binders employ, but D'Alembert adds that they cannot endure absinthe. Mr. Blades finds too that they disdain to devour our adulterate modern paper.

"Say, shall I sing of rats," asked Grainger, when reading to Johnson his epic, the "Sugar-cane." "No," said the Doctor; and though rats are the foe of the bibliophile, at least as much as of the sugar- planter, we do not propose to sing of them. M. Fertiault has done so already in "Les Sonnets d'un Bibliophile," where the reader must be pleased with the beautiful etchings of rats devouring an illuminated MS., and battening on morocco bindings stamped with the bees of De Thou. It is unnecessary and it would be undignified, to give hints on rat-catching, but the amateur must not forget that these animals have a passion for bindings.

The book-collector must avoid gas, which deposits a filthy coat of oil that catches dust. Mr. Blades found that three jets of gas in a small room soon reduced the leather on his book-shelves to a powder of the consistency of snuff, and made the backs of books come away in his hand. Shaded lamps give the best and most suitable light for the library. As to the risks which books run at the hands of the owner himself, we surely need not repeat the advice of Richard de Bury. Living in an age when tubs (if not unknown as M. Michelet declares) were far from being common, the old collector inveighed against the dirty hands of readers, and against their habit of marking their place in a book with filthy straws, or setting down a beer pot in the middle of the volume to keep the pages open.

But the amateur, however refined himself, must beware of men who love not fly leaves neither regard margins, but write notes over the latter, and light their pipes with the former. After seeing the wreck of a book which these persons have been busy with, one appreciates the fine Greek hyperbole. The Greeks did not speak of "thumbing" but of "walking up and down" on a volume.

To such fellows it matters not that they make a book dirty and greasy, cutting the pages with their fingers, and holding the boards over the fire till they crack. All these slatternly practices, though they destroy a book as surely as the flames of Caesar's soldiers at Alexandria, seem fine manly acts to the grobians who use them. What says Jules Janin, who has written "Contre l'indifference des Philistins," "il faut a l'homme sage et studieux un tome honourable et digne de sa louange."

The amateur, and all decent men, will beware of lending books to such rude workers; and this consideration brings us to these great foes of books, the borrowers and robbers. The lending of books, and of other property, has been defended by some great authorities; thus Panurge himself says, "it would prove much more easy in nature to have fish entertained in the air, and bullocks fed in the bottom of the ocean, than to support or tolerate a rascally rabble of people that will not lend." Pirckheimer, too, for whom Albert Durer designed a bookplate, was a lender, and took for his device Sibi et Amicis; and Jo. Grolierii et amicorum, was the motto of the renowned Grolier, whom mistaken writers vainly but frequently report to have been a bookbinder. But as Mr. Leicester Warren says, in his "Study of Book-plates" (Pearson, 1880), "Christian Charles de Savigny leaves all the rest behind, exclaiming non mihi sed aliis." But the majority of amateurs have chosen wiser, though more churlish devices, as "the ungodly borroweth and payeth not again," or "go to them that sell, and buy for yourselves." David Garrick engraved on his bookplate, beside a bust of Shakspeare, these words of Menage, "La premiere chose qu'on doit faire, quand on a emprunte' un livre, c'est de le lire, afin de pouvoir le rendre plutot." But the borrower is so minded that the last thing he thinks of is to read a borrowed book, and the penultimate subject of his reflections is its restoration. Menage (Menagiana, Paris, 1729, vol. i. p. 265), mentions, as if it were a notable misdeed, this of Angelo Politian's, "he borrowed a 'Lucretius' from Pomponius Laetus, and kept it for four years." Four years! in the sight of the borrower it is but a moment. Menage reports that a friend kept his "Pausanias" for three years, whereas four months was long enough.

"At quarto saltem mense redire decet."

There is no satisfaction in lending a book; for it is rarely that borrowers, while they deface your volumes, gather honey for new stores, as De Quincey did, and Coleridge, and even Dr. Johnson, who "greased and dogs-eared such volumes as were confided to his tender mercies, with the same indifference wherewith he singed his own wigs." But there is a race of mortals more annoying to a conscientious man than borrowers. These are the spontaneous lenders, who insist that you shall borrow their tomes. For my own part, when I am oppressed with the charity of such, I lock their books up in a drawer, and behold them not again till the day of their return. There is no security against borrowers, unless a man like Guibert de Pixerecourt steadfastly refuses to lend. The device of Pixerecourt was un livre est un ami qui ne change jamais. But he knew that our books change when they have been borrowed, like our friends when they have been married; when "a lady borrows them," as the fairy queen says in the ballad of "Tamlane."

"But had I kenn'd, Tamlane," she says, "A lady wad borrowed thee, I wad ta'en out thy twa gray een, Put in twa een o' tree!

"Had I but kenn'd, Tamlane," she says, "Before ye came frae hame, I wad ta'en out your heart o' flesh, Put in a heart o' stane!"

Above the lintel of his library door, Pixerecourt had this couplet carved -

"Tel est le triste sort de tout livre prete, Souvent il est perdu, toujours il est gate."

M. Paul Lacroix says he would not have lent a book to his own daughter. Once Lacroix asked for the loan of a work of little value. Pixerecourt frowned, and led his friend beneath the doorway, pointing to the motto. "Yes," said M. Lacroix, "but I thought that verse applied to every one but me." So Pixerecourt made him a present of the volume.

We cannot all imitate this "immense" but unamiable amateur. Therefore, bibliophiles have consoled themselves with the inventions of book-plates, quaint representations, perhaps heraldic, perhaps fanciful, of their claims to the possession of their own dear volumes. Mr. Leicester Warren and M. Poulet Malassis have written the history of these slender works of art, and each bibliophile may have his own engraved, and may formulate his own anathemas on people who borrow and restore not again. The process is futile, but may comfort the heart, like the curses against thieves which the Greeks were wont to scratch on leaden tablets, and deposit in the temple of Demeter. Each amateur can exercise his own taste in the design of a bookplate; and for such as love and collect rare editions of "Homer," I venture to suggest this motto, which may move the heart of the borrower to send back an Aldine copy of the epic-

Mr. William Blades, in his pleasant volume, "The Enemies of Books" (Trubner), makes no account of the book-thief or biblioklept. "If they injure the owners," says Mr. Blades, with real tolerance, "they do no harm to the books themselves, by merely transferring them from one set of book-shelves to another." This sentence has naturally caused us to reflect on the ethical character of the biblioklept. He is not always a bad man. In old times, when language had its delicacies, and moralists were not devoid of sensibility, the French did not say "un voleur de livres," but "un chipeur de livres;" as the papers call lady shoplifters "kleptomaniacs." There are distinctions. M. Jules Janin mentions a great Parisian bookseller who had an amiable weakness. He was a bibliokleptomaniac. His first motion when he saw a book within reach was to put it in his pocket. Every one knew his habit, and when a volume was lost at a sale the auctioneer duly announced it, and knocked it down to the enthusiast, who regularly paid the price. When he went to a private view of books about to be sold, the officials at the door would ask him, as he was going out, if he did not happen to have an Elzevir Horace or an Aldine Ovid in his pocket. Then he would search those receptacles and exclaim, "Yes, yes, here it is; so much obliged to you; I am so absent." M. Janin mentions an English noble, a "Sir Fitzgerald," who had the same tastes, but who unluckily fell into the hands of the police. Yet M. Janin has a tenderness for the book-stealer, who, after all, is a lover of books. The moral position of the malefactor is so delicate and difficult that we shall attempt to treat of it in the severe, though rococo, manner of Aristotle's "Ethics." Here follows an extract from the lost Aristotelian treatise "Concerning Books":-

"Among the contemplative virtues we reckon the love of books. Now this virtue, like courage or liberality, has its mean, its excess, and its defect. The defect is indifference, and the man who is defective as to the love of books has no name in common parlance. Therefore, we may call him the Robustious Philistine. This man will cut the leaves of his own or his friend's volumes with the butter- knife at breakfast. Also he is just the person wilfully to mistake the double sense of the term 'fly-leaves,' and to stick the 'fly- leaves' of his volumes full of fly-hooks. He also loves dogs'-ears, and marks his place with his pipe when he shuts a book in a hurry; or he will set the leg of his chair on a page to keep it open.

He praises those who tear off margins for pipe-lights, and he makes cigarettes with the tissue-paper that covers engravings. When his books are bound, he sees that the margin is cut to the quick. He tells you too, that 'HE buys books to read them.' But he does not say why he thinks it needful to spoil them. Also he will drag off bindings—or should we perhaps call this crime, or brutality, rather than mere vice? for vice is essentially human, but to tear off bindings is bestial. Thus they still speak of a certain monster who lived during the French Revolution, and who, having purchased volumes attired in morocco, and stamped with the devices of the oligarchs, would rip off the leather or vellum, and throw them into the fire or out of the window, saying that 'now he could read with unwashed hands at his ease.' Such a person, then, is the man indifferent to books, and he sins by way of defect, being deficient in the contemplative virtue of book-loving.

As to the man who is exactly in the right mean, we call him the book-lover. His happiness consists not in reading, which is an active virtue, but in the contemplation of bindings, and illustrations, and title-pages. Thus his felicity partakes of the nature of the bliss we attribute to the gods, for that also is contemplative, and we call the book- lover 'happy,' and even 'blessed,' but within the limits of mortal happiness. But, just as in the matter of absence of fear there is a mean which we call courage, and a defect which we call cowardice, and an excess which is known as foolhardiness; so it is in the case of the love of books.

As to the mean, we have seen that it is the virtue of the true book-lover, while the defect constitutes the sin of the Robustious Philistine. But the extreme is found in covetousness, and the covetous man who is in the extreme state of book-loving, is the biblioklept, or book-stealer. Now his vice shows itself, not in contemplation (for of contemplation there can be no excess), but in action. For books are procured, as we say, by purchase, or by barter, and these are voluntary exchanges, both the seller and the buyer being willing to deal. But books are, again, procured in another way, by involuntary contract—that is, when the owner of the book is unwilling to part with it, but he whose own the book is not is determined to take it.

The book-stealer is such a man as this, and he possesses himself of books with which the owner does not intend to part, by virtue of a series of involuntary contracts. Again, the question may be raised, whether is the Robustious Philistine who despises books, or the biblioklept who adores them out of measure and excessively, the worse citizen? Now, if we are to look to the consequences of actions only (as the followers of Bentham advise), clearly the Robustious Philistine is the worse citizen, for he mangles, and dirties, and destroys books which it is the interest of the State to preserve. But the biblioklept treasures and adorns the books he has acquired; and when he dies, or goes to prison, the State receives the benefit at his sale. Thus Libri, who was the greatest of biblioklepts, rescued many of the books he stole from dirt and misuse, and had them bound royally in purple and gold. Also, it may be argued that books naturally belong to him who can appreciate them; and if good books are in a dull or indifferent man's keeping, this is the sort of slavery which we call "unnatural" in our POLITICS, and which is not to be endured. Shall we say, then, that the Robustious Philistine is the worse citizen, while the Biblioklept is the worse man? But this is perhaps matter for a separate disquisition."

This fragment of the lost Aristotelian treatise "Concerning Books," shows what a difficulty the Stagirite had in determining the precise nature of the moral offence of the biblioklept. Indeed, both as a collector and as an intuitive moralist, Aristotle must have found it rather difficult to condemn the book-thief. He, doubtless, went on to draw distinctions between the man who steals books to sell them again for mere pecuniary profit (which he would call "chrematistic," or "unnatural," book-stealing), and the man who steals them because he feels that he is their proper and natural possessor. The same distinction is taken by Jules Janin, who was a more constant student of Horace than of Aristotle. In his imaginary dialogue of bibliophiles, Janin introduces a character who announces the death of M. Libri.

The tolerant person who brings the sad news proposes "to cast a few flowers on the melancholy tomb. He was a bibliophile, after all. What do you say to it? Many a good fellow has stolen books, and died in grace at the last." "Yes," replies the president of the club, "but the good fellows did not sell the books they stole. .. Cest une grande honte, une grande misere." This Libri was an Inspector-General of French Libraries under Louis Philippe. When he was tried, in 1848, it was calculated that the sum of his known thefts amounted to 20,000 pounds. Many of his robberies escaped notice at the time. It is not long since Lord Ashburnham, according to a French journal, "Le Livre," found in his collection some fragments of a Pentateuch. These relics had been in the possession of the Lyons Library, whence Libri stole them in 1847. The late Lord Ashburnham bought them, without the faintest idea of Libri's dishonesty; and when, after eleven years, the present peer discovered the proper owners of his treasure, he immediately restored the Pentateuch to the Lyons Library.

Many eminent characters have been biblioklepts. When Innocent X. was still Monsignor Pamphilio, he stole a book—so says Tallemant des Reaux—from Du Monstier, the painter. The amusing thing is that Du Monstier himself was a book-thief. He used to tell how he had lifted a book, of which he had long been in search, from a stall on the Pont-Neuf; "but," says Tallemant (whom Janin does not seem to have consulted), "there are many people who don't think it thieving to steal a book unless you sell it afterwards." But Du Monstier took a less liberal view where his own books were concerned. The Cardinal Barberini came to Paris as legate, and brought in his suite Monsignor Pamphilio, who afterwards became Innocent X. The Cardinal paid a visit to Du Monstier in his studio, where Monsignor Pamphilio spied, on a table, "L'Histoire du Concile de Trent"—the good edition, the London one. "What a pity," thought the young ecclesiastic, "that such a man should be, by some accident, the possessor of so valuable a book." With these sentiments Monsignor Pamphilio slipped the work under his soutane. But little Du Monstier observed him, and said furiously to the Cardinal, that a holy man should not bring thieves and robbers in his company. With these words, and with others of a violent and libellous character, he recovered the "History of the Council of Trent," and kicked out the future Pope. Amelot de la Houssaie traces to this incident the hatred borne by Innocent X. to the Crown and the people of France. Another Pope, while only a cardinal, stole a book from Menage—so M. Janin reports—but we have not been able to discover Menage's own account of the larceny.

The anecdotist is not so truthful that cardinals need flush a deeper scarlet, like the roses in Bion's "Lament for Adonis," on account of a scandal resting on the authority of Menage. Among Royal persons, Catherine de Medici, according to

Brantome, was a biblioklept. "The Marshal Strozzi had a very fine library, and after his death the Queen-Mother seized it, promising some day to pay the value to his son, who never got a farthing of the money." The Ptolemies, too, were thieves on a large scale. A department of the Alexandrian Library was called "The Books from the Ships," and was filled with rare volumes stolen from passengers in vessels that touched at the port. True, the owners were given copies of their ancient MSS., but the exchange, as Aristotle says, was an "involuntary" one, and not distinct from robbery.

The great pattern of biblioklepts, a man who carried his passion to the most regrettable excesses, was a Spanish priest, Don Vincente, of the convent of Pobla, in Aragon. When the Spanish revolution despoiled the convent libraries, Don Vincente established himself at Barcelona, under the pillars of Los Encantes, where are the stalls of the merchants of bric-a-brac and the seats of them that sell books. In a gloomy den the Don stored up treasures which he hated to sell. Once he was present at an auction where he was out-bid in the competition for a rare, perhaps a unique, volume. Three nights after that, the people of Barcelona were awakened by cries of "Fire!" The house and shop of the man who had bought "Ordinacions per los gloriosos reys de Arago" were blazing. When the fire was extinguished, the body of the owner of the house was found, with a pipe in his blackened hand, and some money beside him.

Every one said, "He must have set the house on fire with a spark from his pipe." Time went on, and week by week the police found the bodies of slain men, now in the street, now in a ditch, now in the river. There were young men and old, all had been harmless and inoffensive in their lives, and—all had been bibliophiles. A dagger in an invisible hand had reached their hearts but the assassin had spared their purses, money, and rings. An organised search was made in the city, and the shop of Don Vincente was examined. There, in a hidden recess, the police discovered the copy of "Ordinacions per los gloriosis reys de Arago," which ought by rights to have been burned with the house of its purchaser. Don Vincente was asked how he got the book. He replied in a quiet voice, demanded that his collection should be made over to the Barcelona Library, and then confessed a long array of crimes. He had strangled his rival, stolen the "Ordinacions," and burned the house. The slain men were people who had bought from him books which he really could not bear to part with. At his trial his counsel tried to prove that his confession was false, and that he might have got his books by honest means.

It was objected that there was in the world only one book printed by Lambert Palmart in 1482, and that the prisoner must have stolen this, the only copy, from the library where it was treasured. The defendant's counsel proved that there was another copy in the Louvre; that, therefore, there might be more, and that the defendant's might have been honestly procured. Here Don Vincente, previously callous, uttered an hysterical cry. Said the Alcalde:- "At last, Vincente, you begin to understand the enormity of your offence?" "Ah, Senor Alcalde, my error was clumsy indeed. If you only knew how miserable I am!" "If human justice prove inflexible, there is another justice whose pity is inexhaustible. Repentance is never too late." "Ah, Senor Alcalde, but my copy was not unique!" With the story of this impenitent thief we may close the roll of biblioklepts, though Dibdin pretends that Garrick was of the company, and stole Alleyne's books at Dulwich.

There is a thievish nature more hateful than even the biblioklept. The Book-Ghoul is he who combines the larceny of the biblioklept with the abominable wickedness of breaking up and mutilating the volumes from which he steals. He is a collector of title-pages, frontispieces, illustrations, and book-plates. He prowls furtively among public and private libraries, inserting wetted threads, which slowly eat away the illustrations he covets; and he broods, like the obscene demon of Arabian superstitions, over the fragments of the mighty dead. His disgusting tastes vary. He prepares books for the American market. Christmas books are sold in the States stuffed with pictures cut out of honest volumes. Here is a quotation from an American paper:-

"Another style of Christmas book which deserves to be mentioned, though it is out of the reach of any but the very rich, is the historical or literary work enriched with inserted plates. There has never, to our knowledge, been anything offered in America so supremely excellent as the $5000 book on Washington, we think— exhibited by Boston last year, but not a few fine specimens of books of this class are at present offered to purchasers. Scribner has a beautiful copy of Forster's 'Life of Dickens,' enlarged from three volumes octavo to nine volumes quarto, by taking to pieces, remounting, and inlaying. It contains some eight hundred engravings, portraits, views, playbills, title-pages, catalogues, proof illustrations from Dickens's works, a set of the Onwhyn plates, rare engravings by Cruikshank and 'Phiz,' and autograph letters. Though this volume does not compare with Harvey's Dickens, offered for $1750 two years ago, it is an excellent specimen of books of this sort, and the veriest tyro in bibliographical affairs knows how scarce are becoming the early editions of Dickens's works and the plates illustrating them. Anything about Dickens in the beginning of his career is a sound investment from a business point of view.

Another work of the same sort, valued at $240, is Lady Trevelyan's edition of Macaulay, illustrated with portraits, many of them very rare. Even cheaper, all things considered, is an extra- illustrated copy of the 'Histoire de la Gravure,' which, besides its seventy-three reproductions of old engravings, is enriched with two hundred fine specimens of the early engravers, many of the impressions being in first and second states. At $155 such a book is really a bargain, especially for any one who is forming a collection of engravings. Another delightful work is the library edition of Bray's 'Evelyn,' illustrated with some two hundred and fifty portraits and views, and valued at $175; and still another is Boydell's 'Milton,' with plates after Westall, and further illustrations in the shape of twenty-eight portraits of the painter and one hundred and eighty-one plates, and many of them before letter. The price of this book is $325."

But few book-ghouls are worse than the moral ghoul. He defaces, with a pen, the passages, in some precious volume, which do not meet his idea of moral propriety. I have a Pine's "Horace," with the engravings from gems, which has fallen into the hands of a moral ghoul. Not only has he obliterated the verses which hurt his delicate sense, but he has actually scraped away portions of the classical figures, and "the breasts of the nymphs in the brake." The soul of Tartuffe had entered into the body of a sinner of the last century. The antiquarian ghoul steals title-pages and colophons. The aesthetic ghoul cuts illuminated initials out of manuscripts. The petty, trivial, and almost idiotic ghoul of our own days, sponges the fly-leaves and boards of books for the purpose of cribbing the book-plates. An old "Complaint of a Bookplate," in dread of the wet sponge of the enemy, has been discovered by Mr. Austin Dobson:-

The Book-plate's Petition. By a Gentleman of the Temple.

While cynic CHARLES still trimm'd the vane 'Twixt Querouaille and Castlemaine, In days that shocked JOHN EVELYN, My First Possessor fix'd me in. In days of Dutchmen and of frost, The narrow sea with JAMES I cross'd, Returning when once more began The Age of Saturn and of ANNE. I am a part of all the past; I knew the GEORGES, first and last; I have been oft where else was none Save the great wig of ADDISON; And seen on shelves beneath me grope The little eager form of POPE. I lost the Third that own'd me when French NOAILLES fled at Dettingen; The year JAMES WOLFE surpris'd Quebec, The Fourth in hunting broke his neck; The day that WILLIAM HOGARTH dy'd, The Fifth one found me in Cheapside.

This was a Scholar, one of those Whose Greek is sounder than their hose; He lov'd old Books and nappy ale, So liv'd at Streatham, next to THRALE. 'Twas there this stain of grease I boast Was made by Dr. JOHNSON'S toast. (He did it, as I think, for Spite; My Master call'd him Jacobite!) And now that I so long today Have rested post discrimina, Safe in the brass-wir'd book-case where I watch'd the Vicar's whit'ning hair, Must I these travell'd bones inter In some Collector's sepulchre! Must I be torn from hence and thrown With frontispiece and colophon! With vagrant E's, and I's, and O's, The spoil of plunder'd Folios! With scraps and snippets that to ME Are naught but kitchen company! Nay, rather, FRIEND, this favour grant me: Tear me at once; but don't transplant me.

CHELTENHAM, Sept. 31, 1792.

The conceited ghoul writes his notes across our fair white margins, in pencil, or in more baneful ink. Or he spills his ink bottle at large over the pages, as Andre Chenier's friend served his copy of Malherbe. It is scarcely necessary to warn the amateur against the society of book-ghouls, who are generally snuffy and foul in appearance, and by no means so insinuating as that fair lady-ghoul, Amina, of the Arabian Nights.

Another enemy of books must be mentioned with the delicacy that befits the topic. Almost all women are the inveterate foes, not of novels, of course, nor peerages and popular volumes of history, but of books worthy of the name. It is true that Isabelle d'Este, and Madame de Pompadour, and Madame de Maintenon, were collectors; and, doubtless, there are other brilliant exceptions to a general rule. But, broadly speaking, women detest the books which the collector desires and admires. First, they don't understand them; second, they are jealous of their mysterious charms; third, books cost money; and it really is a hard thing for a lady to see money expended on what seems a dingy old binding, or yellow paper scored with crabbed characters.

Thus ladies wage a skirmishing war against booksellers' catalogues, and history speaks of husbands who have had to practise the guile of smugglers when they conveyed a new purchase across their own frontier. Thus many married men are reduced to collecting Elzevirs, which go readily into the pocket, for you cannot smuggle a folio volume easily. This inveterate dislike of books often produces a very deplorable result when an old collector dies.

His "womankind," as the Antiquary called them, sell all his treasures for the price of waste-paper, to the nearest country bookseller. It is a melancholy duty which forces one to introduce such topics into a volume on "Art at Home." But this little work will not have been written in vain if it persuades ladies who inherit books not to sell them hastily, without taking good and disinterested opinion as to their value. They often dispose of treasures worth thousands, for a ten pound note, and take pride in the bargain. Here, let history mention with due honour the paragon of her sex and the pattern to all wives of book-collecting men— Madame Fertiault. It is thus that she addresses her lord in a charming triolet ("Les Amoureux du Livre," p. xxxv):-

"Le livre a ton esprit. .. tant mieux! Moi, j'ai ton coeur, et sans partage. Puis-je desirer davantage? Le livre a ton esprit. .. tant mieux! Heureuse de te voir joyeux, Je t'en voudrais. .. tout un etage. Le livre a ton esprit. .. tant mieux! Moi, j'ai ton coeur, et sans partage."

Books rule thy mind, so let it be! Thy heart is mine, and mine alone. What more can I require of thee? Books rule thy mind, so let it be! Contented when thy bliss I see, I wish a world of books thine own. Books rule thy mind, so let it be! Thy heart is mine, and mine alone.

There is one method of preserving books, which, alas, only tempts the borrower, the stealer, the rat, and the bookworm; but which is absolutely necessary as a defence against dust and neglect. This is binding. The bookbinder's art too often destroys books when the artist is careless, but it is the only mode of preventing our volumes from falling to pieces, and from being some day disregarded as waste-paper. A well-bound book, especially a book from a famous collection, has its price, even if its literary contents be of trifling value. A leather coat fashioned by Derome, or Le Gascon, or Duseuil, will win respect and careful handling for one specimen of an edition whereof all the others have perished. Nothing is so slatternly as the aspect of a book merely stitched, in the French fashion, when the threads begin to stretch, and the paper covers to curl and be torn.

Worse consequences follow, whole sheets are lost, the volume becomes worthless, and the owner must often be at the expense of purchasing another copy, if he can, for the edition may now be out of print. Thus binding of some sort not only adds a grace to the library, presenting to the eye the cheerful gilded rows of our volumes, but is a positive economy. In the case of our cloth-covered English works, the need of binding is not so immediately obvious. But our publishers have a taste for clothing their editions in tender tones of colour, stamped, often, with landscapes printed in gold, in white, or what not. Covers like this, may or may not please the eye while they are new and clean, but they soon become dirty and hideous. When a book is covered in cloth of a good dark tint it may be allowed to remain unbound, but the primrose and lilac hues soon call out for the aid of the binder.

Much has been written of late about book-binding. In a later part of this manual we shall have something to say about historical examples of the art, and the performances of the great masters. At present one must begin by giving the practical rule, that a book should be bound in harmony with its character and its value. The bibliophile, if he could give the rein to his passions, would bind every book he cares to possess in a full coat of morocco, or (if it did not age so fast) of Russia leather. But to do this is beyond the power of most of us. Only works of great rarity or value should be full bound in morocco. If we have the luck to light on a Shakespeare quarto, on some masterpiece of Aldus Manutius, by all means let us entrust it to the most competent binder, and instruct him to do justice to the volume. Let old English books, as More's "Utopia," have a cover of stamped and blazoned calf.

Let the binder clothe an early Rabelais or Marot in the style favoured by Grolier, in leather tooled with geometrical patterns. Let a Moliere or Corneille be bound in the graceful contemporary style of Le Gascon, where the lace-like pattern of the gilding resembles the Venetian point-lace, for which La Fontaine liked to ruin himself. Let a binding, a la fanfare, in the style of Thouvenin, denote a novelist of the last century, let panelled Russia leather array a folio of Shakespeare, and let English works of a hundred years ago be clothed in the sturdy fashion of Roger Payne. Again, the bibliophile may prefer to have the leather stamped with his arms and crest, like de Thou, Henri III., D'Hoym, Madame du Barry, and most of the collectors of the seventeenth and eighteenth centuries.

Yet there are books of great price which one would hesitate to bind in new covers. An Aldine or an Elzevir, in its old vellum or paper wrapper, with uncut leaves, should be left just as it came from the presses of the great printers. In this condition it is a far more interesting relic. But a morocco case may be made for the book, and lettered properly on the back, so that the volume, though really unbound, may take its place with the bound books on the shelves. A copy of any of Shelley's poems, in the original wrappers, should I venture to think be treated thus, and so should the original editions of Keats's and of Mr. Tennyson's works. A collector, who is also an author, will perhaps like to have copies of his own works in morocco, for their coats will give them a chance of surviving the storms of time.

But most other books, not of the highest rarity and interest, will be sufficiently clothed in half-bindings, that is, with leather backs and corners, while the rest of the cover is of cloth or paper, or whatever other substance seems most appropriate. An Oxford tutor used to give half-binding as an example of what Aristotle calls, or "shabbiness," and when we recommend such coverings for books it is as a counsel of expediency, not of perfection. But we cannot all be millionaires; and, let it be remembered, the really wise amateur will never be extravagant, nor let his taste lead him into "the ignoble melancholy of pecuniary embarrassment." Let the example of Charles Nodier be our warning; nay, let us remember that while Nodier could get out of debt by selling his collection, OURS will probably not fetch anything like what we gave for it.

In half-bindings there is a good deal of room for the exercise of the collector's taste. M. Octave Uzanne, in a tract called "Les Caprices d'un Bibliophile," gives some hints on this topic, which may be taken or let alone. M. Uzanne has noticed the monotony, and the want of meaning and suggestion in ordinary half-bindings. The paper or cloth which covers the greater part of the surface of half-bound books is usually inartistic and even ugly. He proposes to use old scraps of brocade, embroidery, Venice velvet, or what not; and doubtless a covering made of some dead fair lady's train goes well with a romance by Crebillon, and engravings by Marillier. "Voici un cartonnage Pompadour de notre invention," says M. Uzanne, with pride; but he observes that it needs a strong will to make a bookbinder execute such orders.

For another class of books, which our honest English shelves reject with disgust, M. Uzanne proposes a binding of the skin of the boa constrictor; undoubtedly appropriate and "admonishing." The leathers of China and Japan, with their strange tints and gilded devices may be used for books of fantasy, like "Gaspard de la Nuit," or the "Opium Eater," or Poe's poems, or the verses of Gerard de Nerval. Here, in short, is an almost unexplored field for the taste of the bibliophile, who, with some expenditure of time, and not much of money, may make half-binding an art, and give modern books a peculiar and appropriate raiment.

M. Ambrose Firmin Didot has left some notes on a more serious topic,—the colours to be chosen when books are full-bound in morocco. Thus he would have the "Iliad" clothed in red, the "Odyssey" in blue, because the old Greek rhapsodists wore a scarlet cloak when they recited the Wrath of Achilles, a blue one when they chanted of the Return of Odysseus. The writings of the great dignitaries of the Church, M. Didot would array in violet; scarlet goes well with the productions of cardinals; philosophers have their sober suit of black morocco, poets like Panard may be dressed in rose colour. A collector of this sort would like, were it possible, to attire Goldsmith's poems in a "coat of Tyrian bloom, satin grain." As an antithesis to these extravagant fancies, we may add that for ordinary books no binding is cheaper, neater, and more durable, than a coat of buckram.

The conditions of a well bound book may be tersely enumerated. The binding should unite solidity and elegance. The book should open easily, and remain open at any page you please. It should never be necessary, in reading, to squeeze back the covers; and no book, however expensively bound, has been properly treated, if it does not open with ease. It is a mistake to send recently printed books to the binder, especially books which contain engravings. The printing ink dries slowly, and, in the process called "beating," the text is often transferred to the opposite page. M. Rouveyre recommends that one or two years should pass before the binding of a newly printed book. The owner will, of course, implore the binder to, spare the margins; and, almost equally of course, the binder, durus arator, will cut them down with his abominable plough. One is almost tempted to say that margins should always be left untouched, for if once the binder begins to clip he is unable to resist the seductive joy, and cuts the paper to the quick, even into the printed matter.

Mr. Blades tells a very sad story of a nobleman who handed over some Caxtons to a provincial binder, and received them back MINUS 500 pounds worth of margin. Margins make a book worth perhaps 400 pounds, while their absence reduces the same volume to the box marked "all these at fourpence." Intonsis capillis, with locks unshorn, as Motteley the old dealer used to say, an Elzevir in its paper wrapper may be worth more than the same tome in morocco, stamped with Longepierre's fleece of gold. But these things are indifferent to bookbinders, new and old. There lies on the table, as I write, "Les Provinciales, ou Les Lettres Ecrites par Louis de Montalte a un Provincial de ses amis, & aux R.R. P.P. Jesuites. A Cologne, Ches PIERRE de la VALLEE, M.DC.LVIII."

It is the Elzevir edition, or what passes for such; but the binder has cut down the margin so that the words "Les Provinciales" almost touch the top of the page. Often the wretch—he lived, judging by his style, in Derome's time, before the Revolution—has sliced into the head- titles of the pages. Thus the book, with its old red morocco cover and gilded flowers on the back, is no proper companion for "Les Pensees de M. PASCAL (Wolfganck, 1672)," which some sober Dutchman has left with a fair allowance of margin, an inch "taller" in its vellum coat than its neighbour in morocco. Here once more, is "LES FASCHEUX, Comedie de I. B. P. MOLIERE, Representee sur Le Theatre du Palais Royal. A Paris, Chez GABRIEL QUINET, au Palais, dans la Galerie des Prisonniers, a l'Ange Gabriel, M.DCLXIII. Avec privilege du Roy." What a crowd of pleasant memories the bibliophile, and he only, finds in these dry words of the title. Quinet, the bookseller, lived "au Palais," in that pretty old arcade where Corneille cast the scene of his comedy, "La Galerie du Palais."

In the Geneva edition of Corneille, 1774, you can see Gravelot's engraving of the place; it is a print full of exquisite charm (engraved by Le Mure in 1762). Here is the long arcade, in shape exactly like the galleries of the Bodleian Library at Oxford. The bookseller's booth is arched over, and is open at front and side. Dorimant and Cleante are looking out; one leans on the books on the window-sill, the other lounges at the door, and they watch the pretty Hippolyte who is chaffering with the lace-seller at the opposite shop. "Ce visage vaut mieux que toutes vos chansons," says Dorimant to the bookseller. So they loitered, and bought books, and flirted in their lace ruffles, and ribbons, and flowing locks, and wide canons, when Moliere was young, and when this little old book was new, and lying on the shelves of honest Quinet in the Palace Gallery. The very title-page, and pagination, not of this second edition, but of the first of "Les Fascheux," had their own fortunes, for the dedication to Fouquet was perforce withdrawn. That favourite entertained La Valliere and the King with the comedy at his house of Vaux, and then instantly fell from power and favour, and, losing his place and his freedom, naturally lost the flattery of a dedication. But retombons a nos coches, as Montaigne says.

This pleasant little copy of the play, which is a kind of relic of Moliere and his old world, has been ruthlessly bound up with a treatise, "Des Pierres Precieuses," published by Didot in 1776. Now the play is naturally a larger book than the treatise on precious stones, so the binder has cut down the margins to the size of those of the work on amethysts and rubies. As the Italian tyrant chained the dead and the living together, as Procrustes maimed his victims on his cruel bed, so a hard-hearted French binder has tied up, and mutilated, and spoiled the old play, which otherwise would have had considerable value as well as interest.

We have tried to teach the beginner how to keep his books neat and clean; what men and monsters he should avoid; how he should guard himself against borrowers, bookworms, damp, and dirt. But we are sometimes compelled to buy books already dirty and dingy, foxed, or spotted with red, worn by greasy hands, stained with ink spots, or covered with MS. notes. The art of man has found a remedy for these defects. I have never myself tried to wash a book, and this care is best left to professional hands. But the French and English writers give various recipes for cleaning old books, which the amateur may try on any old rubbish out of the fourpenny box of a bookstall, till he finds that he can trust his own manipulations.

There are "fat stains" on books, as thumb marks, traces of oil (the midnight oil), flakes of old pasty crust left in old Shakespeares, and candle drippings. There are "thin stains," as of mud, scaling-wax, ink, dust, and damp. To clean a book you first carefully unbind it, take off the old covers, cut the old stitching, and separate sheet from sheet. Then take a page with "fat stains" of any kind of grease (except finger-marks), pass a hot flat iron over it, and press on it a clean piece of blotting paper till the paper sucks up the grease. Then charge a camel-hair brush with heated turpentine, and pass it over the places that were stained.

If the paper loses its colour press softly over it a delicate handkerchief, soaked in heated spirits of wine. Finger-marks you will cover with clean soap, leave this on for some hours, and then rub with a sponge filled with hot water. Afterwards dip in weak acid and water, and then soak the page in a bath of clean water. Ink-stained pages you will first dip in a strong solution of oxalic acid and then in hydrochloric acid mixed in six times its quantity of water. Then bathe in clean water and allow to dry slowly.

Some English recipes may also be given. "Grease or wax spots," says Hannett, in "Bibliopegia," "may be removed by washing the part with ether, chloroform, or benzine, and placing it between pieces of white blotting paper, then pass a hot iron over it." "Chlorine water," says the same writer, removes ink stains, and bleaches the paper at the same time. Of chloride of lime, "a piece the size of a nut" (a cocoa nut or a hazel nut?) in a pint of water, may be applied with a camel's hair pencil, and plenty of patience. To polish old bindings, "take the yolk of an egg, beat it up with a fork, apply it with a sponge, having first cleaned the leather with a dry flannel." The following, says a writer in "Notes and Queries," with perfect truth, is "an easier if not a better method; purchase some bookbinder's varnish," and use it as you did the rudimentary omelette of the former recipe. Vellum covers may be cleaned with soap and water, or in bad cases by a weak solution of salts of lemon. Lastly, the collector should acquire such books as Lowndes's "Bibliography," Brunet's "Manuel," and as many priced catalogues as he can secure. The catalogues of Mr. Quaritch, Mr. Bohn, M. Fontaine, M.M. Morgand et Fatout, are excellent guides to a knowledge of the market value of books. Other special works, as Renouard's for Aldines, Willems's for Elzevirs, and Cohen's for French engravings, will be mentioned in their proper place. Dibdin's books are inaccurate and long-winded, but may occasionally be dipped into with pleasure.

### The Books of The Collector

The easiest way to bring order into the chaos of desirable books, is, doubtless, to begin historically with manuscripts. Almost every age that has left any literary remains, has bequeathed to us relics which are cherished by collectors. We may leave the clay books of the Chaldeans out of the account. These tomes resemble nothing so much as sticks of chocolate, and, however useful they may be to the student, the clay MSS. of Assurbanipal are not coveted by the collector. He finds his earliest objects of desire in illuminated manuscripts.

The art of decorating manuscripts is as old as Egypt; but we need not linger over the beautiful papyri, which are silent books to all but a few Egyptologists. Greece, out of all her tomes, has left us but a few ill-written papyri. Roman and early Byzantine art are represented by a "Virgil," and fragments of an "Iliad"; the drawings in the latter have been reproduced in a splendid volume (Milan 1819), and shew Greek art passing into barbarism. The illumination of MSS. was a favourite art in the later empire, and is said to have been practised by Boethius. The iconoclasts of the Eastern empire destroyed the books which contained representations of saints and of the persons of the Trinity, and the monk Lazarus, a famous artist, was cruelly tortured for his skill in illuminating sacred works. The art was decaying in Western Europe when Charlemagne sought for painters of MSS. in England and Ireland, where the monks, in their monasteries, had developed a style with original qualities. The library of Corpus Christi at Cambridge, contains some of the earliest and most beautiful of extant English MSS.

These parchments, stained purple or violet, and inscribed with characters of gold; are too often beyond the reach of the amateur for whom we write. The MSS. which he can hope to acquire are neither very early nor very sumptuous, and, as a rule, MSS. of secular books are apt to be out of his reach.

Yet a collection of MSS. has this great advantage over a collection of printed books, that every item in it is absolutely unique, no two MSS. being ever really the same. This circumstance alone would entitle a good collection of MSS. to very high consideration on the part of book-collectors. But, in addition to the great expense of such a collection, there is another and even more serious drawback. It is sometimes impossible, and is often extremely difficult, to tell whether a MS. is perfect or not. This difficulty can only be got over by an amount of learning on the part of the collector to which, unfortunately, he is too often a stranger. On the other hand, the advantages of collecting MSS. are sometimes very great.

In addition to the pleasure—a pleasure at once literary and artistic—which the study of illuminated MSS. affords, there is the certainty that, as years go on, the value of such a collection increases in a proportion altogether marvellous.

I will take two examples to prove this point. Some years ago an eminent collector gave the price of 30 pounds for a small French book of Hours, painted in grisaille. It was in a country town that he met with this treasure, for a treasure he considered the book, in spite of its being of the very latest school of illumination. When his collection was dispersed a few years ago this one book fetched 260 pounds.

In the celebrated Perkins sale, in 1873, a magnificent early MS., part of which was written in gold on a purple ground, and which was dated in the catalogue "ninth or tenth century," but was in reality of the end of the tenth or beginning of the eleventh, was sold for 565 pounds to a dealer. It found its way into Mr. Bragge's collection, at what price I do not know, and was resold, three years later, for 780 pounds.

Any person desirous of making a collection of illuminated MSS., should study seriously for some time at the British Museum, or some such place, until he is thoroughly acquainted

(1) with the styles of writing in use in the Middle Ages, so that he can at a glance make a fairly accurate estimate of the age of the book submitted to him; and (2) with the proper means of collating the several kinds of service-books, which, in nine cases out of ten, were those chosen for illumination. A knowledge of the styles of writing can be acquired at second hand in a book lately published by Mr. Charles Trice Martin, F.S.A., being a new edition of "Astle's Progress of Writing." Still better, of course, is the actual inspection and comparison of books to which a date can be with some degree of certainty assigned.

It is very common for the age of a book to be misstated in the catalogues of sales, for the simple reason that the older the writing, the plainer, in all probability, it is. Let the student compare writing of the twelfth century with that of the sixteenth, and he will be able to judge at once of the truth of this assertion. I had once the good fortune to "pick up" a small Testament of the early part of the twelfth century, if not older, which was catalogued as belonging to the fifteenth, a date which would have made it of very moderate value.

With regard to the second point, the collation of MSS., I fear there is no royal road to knowing whether a book is perfect or imperfect. In some cases the catchwords remain at the foot of the pages. It is then of course easy to see if a page is lost, but where no such clue is given the student's only chance is to be fully acquainted with what a book OUGHT to contain. He can only do this when he has a knowledge of the different kinds of service-books which were in use, and of their most usual contents.

I am indebted to a paper, read by the late Sir William Tite at a meeting of the Society of Antiquaries, for the collation of "Books of Hours," but there are many kinds of MSS. besides these, and it is well to know something of them. The Horae, or Books of Hours, were the latest development of the service-books used at an earlier period. They cannot, in fact, be strictly called service-books, being intended only for private devotion.

But in the thirteenth century and before it, Psalters were in use for this purpose, and the collation of a Psalter is in truth more important than that of a Book of Hours. It will be well for a student, therefore, to begin with Psalters, as he can then get up the Hours in their elementary form. I subjoin a bibliographical account of both kinds of MSS. In the famous Exhibition at the Burlington Club in 1874, a number of volumes was arranged to show how persistent one type of the age could be. The form of the decorations, and the arrangement of the figures in borders, once invented, was fixed for generations.

In a Psalter of the thirteenth century there was, under the month of January in the calendar, a picture of a grotesque little figure warming himself at a stove. The hearth below, the chimney-pot above, on which a stork was feeding her brood, with the intermediate chimney shaft used as a border, looked like a scientific preparation from the interior anatomy of a house of the period. In one of the latest of the MSS. exhibited on that occasion was the self-same design again. The little man was no longer a grotesque, and the picture had all the high finish and completeness in drawing that we might expect in the workmanship of a contemporary of Van Eyck. There was a full series of intermediate books, showing the gradual growth of the picture.

With regard to chronology, it may be roughly asserted that the earliest books which occur are Psalters of the thirteenth century. Next to them come Bibles, of which an enormous issue took place before the middle of the fourteenth century. These are followed by an endless series of books of Hours, which, as the sixteenth century is reached, appear in several vernacular languages. Those in English, being both very rare and of great importance in liturgical history, are of a value altogether out of proportion to the beauty of their illuminations. Side by side with this succession are the Evangelistina, which, like the example mentioned above, are of the highest merit, beauty, and value; followed by sermons and homilies, and the Breviary, which itself shows signs of growth as the years go on.

The real Missal, with which all illuminated books used to be confounded, is of rare occurrence, but I have given a collation of it also. Besides these devotional or religious books, I must mention chronicles and romances, and the semi-religious and moral allegories, such as the "Pelerinage de l'Ame," which is said to have given Bunyan the machinery of the "Pilgrim's Progress." Chaucer's and Gower's poetry exists in many MSS., as does the "Polychronicon" of Higden; but, as a rule, the mediaeval chronicles are of single origin, and were not copied. To collate MSS. of these kinds is quite impossible, unless by carefully reading them, and seeing that the pages run on without break.

I should advise the young collector who wishes to make sure of success not to be too catholic in his tastes at first, but to confine his attention to a single period and a single school. I should also advise him to make from time to time a careful catalogue of what he buys, and to preserve it even after he has weeded out certain items. He will then be able to make a clear comparative estimate of the importance and value of his collection, and by studying one species at a time, to become thoroughly conversant with what it can teach him. When he has, so to speak, burnt his fingers once or twice, he will find himself able to distinguish at sight what no amount of teaching by word of mouth or by writing could ever possibly impart to any advantage.

One thing I should like if possible to impress very strongly upon the reader. That is the fact that a MS. which is not absolutely perfect, if it is in a genuine state, is of much more value than one which has been made perfect by the skill of a modern restorer. The more skilful he is, that is to say the better he can forge the style of the original, the more worthless he renders the volume.

Printing seems to have superseded the art of the illuminator more promptly and completely in England than on the Continent. The dames galantes of Brantome's memoirs took pleasure in illuminated Books of Hours, suited to the nature of their devotions. As late as the time of Louis XIV., Bussy Rabutin had a volume of the same kind, illuminated with portraits of "saints," of his own canonisation. The most famous of these modern examples of costly MSS. was "La Guirlande de Julie," a collection of madrigals by various courtly hands, presented to the illustrious Julie, daughter of the Marquise de Rambouillet, most distinguished of the Precieuses, and wife of the Duc de Montausier, the supposed original of Moliere's Alceste.

The MS. was copied on vellum by Nicholas Jarry, the great calligraph of his time. The flowers on the margin were painted by Robert. Not long ago a French amateur was so lucky as to discover the MS. book of prayers of Julie's noble mother, the Marquise de Rambouillet. The Marquise wrote these prayers for her own devotions, and Jarry, the illuminator, declared that he found them most edifying, and delightful to study. The manuscript is written on vellum by the famous Jarry, contains a portrait of the fair Julie herself, and is bound in morocco by Le Gascon. The happy collector who possesses the volume now, heard vaguely that a manuscript of some interest was being exposed for sale at a trifling price in the shop of a country bookseller. The description of the book, casual as it was, made mention of the monogram on the cover. This was enough for the amateur. He rushed to a railway station, travelled some three hundred miles, reached the country town, hastened to the bookseller's shop, and found that the book had been withdrawn by its owner. Happily the possessor, unconscious of his bliss, was at home. The amateur sought him out, paid the small sum demanded, and returned to Paris in triumph. Thus, even in the region of manuscript-collecting, there are extraordinary prizes for the intelligent collector.

## To Know if a Manuscript is Perfect

If the manuscript is of English or French writing of the twelfth, thirteenth, fourteenth, or fifteenth centuries, it is probably either—(1) a Bible, (2) a Psalter, (3) a book of Hours, or (4), but rarely, a Missal. It is not worth while to give the collation of a gradual, or a hymnal, or a processional, or a breviary, or any of the fifty different kinds of service-books which are occasionally met with, but which are never twice the same.

To collate one of them, the reader must go carefully through the book, seeing that the catch-words, if there are any, answer to the head lines; and if there are "signatures," that is, if the foot of the leaves of a sheet of parchment has any mark for enabling the binder to "gather" them correctly, going through them, and seeing that each signed leaf has its corresponding "blank."

1. To collate a Bible, it will be necessary first to go through the catch-words, if any, and signatures, as above; then to notice the contents. The first page should contain the Epistle of St. Jerome to the reader. It will be observed that there is nothing of the nature of a title-page, but I have often seen title-pages supplied by some ignorant imitator in the last century, with the idea that the book was imperfect without one. The books of the Bible follow in order—but the order not only differs from ours, but differs in different copies.

The Apocryphal books are always included. The New Testament usually follows on the Old without any break; and the book concludes with an index of the Hebrew names and their signification in Latin, intended to help preachers to the figurative meaning of the biblical types and parables. The last line of the Bible itself usually contains a colophon, in which sometimes the name of the writer is given, sometimes the length of time it has taken him to write, and sometimes merely the "Explicit. Laus Deo," which has found its way into many modern books. This colophon, which comes as a rule immediately before the index, often contains curious notes, hexameters giving the names of all the books, biographical or local memoranda, and should always be looked for by the collector. One such line occurs to me. It is in a Bible written in Italy in the thirteenth century -

"Qui scripsit scribat. Vergilius spe domini vivat."

Vergilius was, no doubt, in this case the scribe. The Latin and the writing are often equally crabbed. In the Bodleian there is a Bible with this colophon -

"Finito libro referemus gratias Christo m.cc.lxv. indict. viij. Ego Lafracus de Pacis de Cmoa scriptor scripsi."

This was also written in Italy. English colophons are often very quaint—"Qui scripsit hunc librum fiat collocatus in Paradisum," is an example. The following gives us the name of one Master Gerard, who, in the fourteenth century, thus poetically described his ownership:- "Si Ge ponatur—et rar simul associatur - Et dus reddatur—cui pertinet ita vocatur."

In a Bible written in England, in the British Museum, there is a long colophon, in which, after the name of the writer—"hunc librum scripsit Wills de Hales,"—there is a prayer for Ralph of Nebham, who had called Hales to the writing of the book, followed by a date- -"Fes. fuit liber anno M.cc.i. quarto ab incarnatione domini."

In this Bible the books of the New Testament were in the following order:- the Evangelists, the Acts, the Epistles of S. Peter, S. James, and S. John, the Epistles of S. Paul, and the Apocalypse. In a Bible at Brussels I found the colophon after the index:- "Hic expliciunt interpretationes Hebrayorum nominum Do gris qui potens est p. sup. omia." Some of these Bibles are of marvellously small dimensions. The smallest I ever saw was at Ghent, but it was very imperfect. I have one in which there are thirteen lines of writing in an inch of the column. The order of the books of the New Testament in Bibles of the thirteenth century is usually according to one or other of the three following arrangements:-

(1) The Evangelists, Romans to Hebrews, Acts, Epistles of S. Peter, S. James, and S. John, Apocalypse.

(2) The Evangelists, Acts, Epistles of S. Peter, S. James, and S. John, Epistles of S. Paul, Apocalypse. This is the most common.

(3) The Evangelists, Acts, Epistles of S. Peter, S. James, and S. John, Apocalypse, and Epistles of S. Paul.

On the fly leaves of these old Bibles there are often very curious inscriptions. In one I have this:- "Haec biblia emi Haquinas prior monasterii Hatharbiensis de dono domini regis Norwegie." Who was this King of Norway who, in 1310, gave the Prior of Hatherby money to buy a Bible, which was probably written at Canterbury? And who was Haquinas? His name has a Norwegian sound, and reminds us of St. Thomas of that surname. In another manuscript I have seen

"Articula Fidei:- Nascitur, abluitur, patitur, descendit at ima Surgit et ascendit, veniens discernere cuncta."

In another this:-

"Sacramenta ecclesiae:- Abluo, fumo, cibo, piget, ordinat, uxor et ungit."

I will conclude these notes on MS. Bibles with the following colophon from a copy written in Italy in the fifteenth century:-

"Finito libro vivamus semper in Christo - Si semper in Christo carebimus ultimo leto. Explicit Deo gratias; Amen. Stephanus de Tantaldis scripsit in pergamo."

The "Psalter" of the thirteenth century is usually to be considered a forerunner of the "Book of Hours." It always contains, and usually commences with, a Calendar, in which are written against certain days the "obits" of benefactors and others, so that a well- filled Psalter often becomes a historical document of high value and importance. The first page of the psalms is ornamented with a huge B, which often fills the whole page, and contains a representation of David and Goliath ingeniously fitted to the shape of the letter. At the end are usually to be found the hymns of the Three Children, and others from the Bible together with the Te Deum; and sometimes, in late examples, a litany. In some psalters the calendar is at the end. These Psalters, and the Bibles described above, are very frequently of English work; more frequently, that is, than the books of Hours and Missals. The study of the Scriptures was evidently more popular in England than in the other countries of Europe during the Middle Ages; and the early success of the Reformers here, must in part, no doubt, be attributed to the wide circulation of the Bible even before it had been translated from the Latin. I need hardly, perhaps, observe that even fragments of a Psalter, a Testament, or a Bible in English, are so precious as to be practically invaluable.

We are indebted to Sir W. Tite for the following collation of a Flemish "Book of Hours":-

1. The Calendar.
2. Gospels of the Nativity and the Resurrection.
3. Preliminary Prayers (inserted occasionally).
4. Horae—(Nocturns and Matins).

5. (Lauds).
6. (Prime).
7. (Tierce).
8. (Sexte).
9. (None).
10. (Vespers).
11. (Compline).
12. The seven penitential Psalms
13. The Litany.
14. Hours of the Cross.
15. Hours of the Holy Spirit.
16. Office of the Dead.
17. The Fifteen Joys of B. V. M.
18. The seven requests to our Lord.
19. Prayers and Suffrages to various Saints.
20. Several prayers, petitions, and devotions.

This is an unusually full example, but the calendar, the hours, the seven psalms, and the litany, are in almost all the MSS. The buyer must look carefully to see that no miniatures have been cut out; but it is only by counting the leaves in their gatherings that he can make sure. This is often impossible without breaking the binding.

The most valuable "Horae" are those written in England. Some are of the English use (Sarum or York, or whatever it may happen to be), but were written abroad, especially in Normandy, for the English market. These are also valuable, even when imperfect. Look for the page before the commencement of the Hours (No. 4 in the list above), and at the end will be found a line in red,—"Incipit Horae secundum usum Sarum," or otherwise, as the case may be.

. Missals do not often occur, and are not only very valuable but very difficult to collate, unless furnished with catch-words or signatures. But no Missal is complete without the Canon of the Mass, usually in the middle of the book, and if there are any illuminations throughout the volume, there will be a full page Crucifixion, facing the Canon. Missals of large size and completeness contain—(1) a Calendar; (2) "the proper of the Season;" (3) the ordinary and Canon of the Mass; (4) the Communal of Saints; (5) the proper of Saints and special occasions; (6) the lessons, epistles, and gospels; with (7) some hymns, "proses," and canticles. This is Sir W. Tite's list; but, as he remarks, MS. Missals seldom contain so much. The collector will look for the Canon, which is invariable.

Breviaries run to an immense length, and are seldom illuminated. It would be impossible to give them any kind of collation, and the same may be said of many other kinds of old service-books, and of the chronicles, poems, romances, and herbals, in which mediaeval literature abounded, and which the collector must judge as best he can.

The name of "missal" is commonly and falsely given to all old service-books by the booksellers, but the collector will easily distinguish one when he sees it, from the notes I have given. In a Sarum Missal, at Alnwick, there is a colophon quoted by my lamented friend Dr. Rock in his "Textile Fabrics." It is appropriate both to the labours of the old scribes and also to those of their modern readers:-

"Librum Scribendo—Jon Whas Monachus laborabat - Et mane Surgendo—multum corpus macerabat."

It is one of the charms of manuscripts that they illustrate, in their minute way, all the art, and even the social condition, of the period in which they were produced. Apostles, saints, and prophets wear the contemporary costume, and Jonah, when thrown to the hungry whale, wears doublet and trunk hose. The ornaments illustrate the architectural taste of the day. The backgrounds change from diapered patterns to landscapes, as the modern way of looking at nature penetrates the monasteries and reaches the scriptorium where the illuminator sits and refreshes his eyes with the sight of the slender trees and blue distant hills. Printed books have not such resources.

They can only show varieties of type, quaint frontispieces, printers' devices, and fleurons at the heads of chapters. These attractions, and even the engravings of a later day, seem meagre enough compared with the allurements of manuscripts. Yet printed books must almost always make the greater part of a collection, and it may be well to give some rules as to the features that distinguish the productions of the early press. But no amount of "rules" is worth six months' practical experience in bibliography. That experience the amateur, if he is wise, will obtain in a public library, like the British Museum or the Bodleian. Nowhere else is he likely to see much of the earliest of printed books, which very seldom come into the market. Those of the first German press are so rare that practically they never reach the hands of the ordinary collector. Among them are the famous Psalters printed by Fust and Schoffer, the earliest of which is dated 1457; and the bible known as the Mazarine Bible. Two copies of this last were in the Perkins sale. I well remember the excitement on that occasion. The first copy put up was the best, being printed upon vellum. The bidding commenced at 1000 pounds, and very speedily rose to 2200 pounds, at which point there was a long pause; it then rose in hundreds with very little delay to 3400 pounds, at which it was knocked down to a bookseller.

The second copy was on paper, and there were those present who said it was better than the other, which had a suspicion attaching to it of having been "restored" with a facsimile leaf. The first bid was again 1000 pounds, which the buyer of the previous copy made guineas, and the bidding speedily went up to 2660 pounds, at which price the first bidder paused. A third bidder had stepped in at 1960 pounds, and now, amid breathless excitement, bid 10 pounds more. This he had to do twice before the book was knocked down to him at 2690 pounds.

A scene like this has really very little to do with book-collecting. The beginner must labour hard to distinguish different kinds of printing; he must be able to recognise at a glance even fragments from the press of Caxton. His eye must be accustomed to all the tricks of the trade and others, so that he may tell a facsimile in a moment, or detect a forgery.

But now let us return to the distinctive marks of early printed books. The first is, says M. Rouveyre, -

1. The absence of a separate title-page. It was not till 1476-1480 that the titles of books were printed on separate pages. The next mark is -
2. The absence of capital letters at the beginnings of divisions. For example, in an Aldine Iliad, the fifth book begins thus-it was intended that the open space, occupied by the small epsilon ([epsilon symbol]), should be filled up with a coloured and gilded initial letter by the illuminator. Copies thus decorated are not very common, but the Aldine "Homer" of Francis I., rescued by M. Didot from a rubbish heap in an English cellar, had its due illuminations. In the earliest books the guide to the illuminator, the small printed letter, does not appear, and he often puts in the wrong initial.
3. Irregularity and rudeness of type is a "note" of the primitive printing press, which very early disappeared. Nothing in the history of printing is so remarkable as the beauty of almost its first efforts. Other notes are -
4. The absence of figures at the top of the pages, and of signatures at the foot. The thickness and solidity of the paper, the absence of the printer's name, of the date, and of the name of the town where the press stood, and the abundance of crabbed abbreviations, are all marks, more or less trustworthy, of the antiquity of books.

It must not be supposed that all books published, let us say before 1500, are rare, or deserve the notice of the collector. More than 18,000 works, it has been calculated, left the press before the end of the fifteenth century. All of these cannot possibly be of interest, and many of them that are "rare," are rare precisely because they are uninteresting. They have not been preserved because they were thought not worth preserving. This is a great cause of rarity; but we must not hastily conclude that because a book found no favour in its own age, therefore it has no claim on our attention. A London bookseller tells me that he bought the "remainder" of Keats's "Endymion" for fourpence a copy! The first edition of "Endymion" is now rare and valued. In trying to mend the binding of an old "Odyssey" lately, I extracted from the vellum covers parts of two copies of a very scarce and curious French dictionary of slang, "Le Jargon, ou Langage de l'Argot Reforme." This treatise may have been valueless, almost, when it appeared, but now it is serviceable to the philologist, and to all who care to try to interpret the slang ballades of the poet Villon. An old pamphlet, an old satire, may hold the key to some historical problem, or throw light on the past of manners and customs. Still, of the earliest printed books, collectors prefer such rare and beautiful ones as the oldest printed Bibles: German, English,—as Taverner's and the Bishop's,—or Hebrew and Greek, or the first editions of the ancient classics, which may contain the readings of MSS. now lost or destroyed.

Talking of early Bibles, let us admire the luck and prudence of a certain Mr. Sandford. He always longed for the first Hebrew Bible, but would offer no fancy price, being convinced that the book would one day fall in his way. His foreboding was fulfilled, and he picked up his treasure for ten shillings in a shop in the Strand. The taste for incunabula, or very early printed books, slumbered in the latter half of the sixteenth, and all the seventeenth century.

It revived with the third jubilee of printing in 1740, and since then has refined itself, and only craves books very early, very important, or works from the press of Caxton, the St. Albans Schoolmaster, or other famous old artists. Enough has been said to show the beginner, always enthusiastic, that all old books are not precious. For further information, the "Biography and Typography of William Caxton," by Mr. Blades (Trubner, London, 1877), may be consulted with profit.

Following the categories into which M. Brunet classifies desirable books in his invaluable manual, we now come to books printed on vellum, and on peculiar papers. At the origin of printing, examples of many books, probably presentation copies, were printed on vellum. There is a vellum copy of the celebrated Florentine first edition of Homer; but it is truly sad to think that the twin volumes, Iliad and Odyssey, have been separated, and pine in distant libraries. Early printed books on vellum often have beautifully illuminated capitals. Dibdin mentions in "Bibliomania" (London, 1811), p. 90, that a M. Van Praet was compiling a catalogue of works printed on vellum, and had collected more than 2000 articles. When hard things are said about Henry VIII., let us remember that this monarch had a few copies of his book against Luther printed on vellum.

The Duke of Marlborough's library possessed twenty-five books on vellum, all printed before 1496. The chapter-house at Padua has a "Catullus" of 1472 on vellum; let Mr. Robinson Ellis think wistfully of that treasure. The notable Count M'Carthy of Toulouse had a wonderful library of books in membranis, including a book much coveted for its rarity, oddity, and the beauty of its illustrations, the "Hypnerotomachia" of Poliphilus (Venice, 1499). Vellum was the favourite "vanity" of Junot, Napoleon's general. For reasons connected with its manufacture, and best not inquired into, the Italian vellum enjoyed the greatest reputation for smooth and silky whiteness. Dibdin calls "our modern books on vellum little short of downright wretched." But the editor of this series could, I think, show examples that would have made Dibdin change his opinion.

Many comparatively expensive papers, large in format, are used in choice editions of books. Whatman papers, Dutch papers, Chinese papers, and even papier verge, have all their admirers. The amateur will soon learn to distinguish these materials. As to books printed on coloured paper—green, blue, yellow, rhubarb-coloured, and the like, they are an offence to the eyes and to the taste. Yet even these have their admirers and collectors, and the great Aldus himself occasionally used azure paper. Under the head of "large paper," perhaps "uncut copies" should be mentioned. Most owners of books have had the edges of the volumes gilded or marbled by the binders.

Thus part of the margin is lost, an offence to the eye of the bibliomaniac, while copies untouched by the binder's shears are rare, and therefore prized. The inconvenience of uncut copies is, that one cannot easily turn over the leaves. But, in the present state of the fashion, a really rare uncut Elzevir may be worth hundreds of pounds, while a cropped example scarcely fetches as many shillings. A set of Shakespeare's quartoes, uncut, would be worth more than a respectable landed estate in Connemara. For these reasons the amateur will do well to have new books of price bound "uncut." It is always easy to have the leaves pared away; but not even the fabled fountain at Argos, in which Hera yearly renewed her maidenhood, could restore margins once clipped away.

So much for books which are chiefly precious for the quantity and quality of the material on which they are printed. Even this rather foolish weakness of the amateur would not be useless if it made our publishers more careful to employ a sound clean hand-made paper, instead of drugged trash, for their more valuable new productions. Indeed, a taste for hand-made paper is coming in, and is part of the revolt against the passion for everything machine-made, which ruined art and handiwork in the years between 1840 and 1870.

The third of M. Brunet's categories of books of prose, includes livres de luxe, and illustrated literature. Every Christmas brings us livres de luxe in plenty, books which are no books, but have gilt and magenta covers, and great staring illustrations. These are regarded as drawing-room ornaments by people who never read. It is scarcely necessary to warn the collector against these gaudy baits of unregulated Christmas generosity. All ages have not produced quite such garish livres de luxe as ours. But, on the whole, a book brought out merely for the sake of display, is generally a book ill "got up," and not worth reading.

Moreover, it is generally a folio, or quarto, so large that he who tries to read it must support it on a kind of scaffolding. In the class of illustrated books two sorts are at present most in demand. The ancient woodcuts and engravings, often the work of artists like Holbein and Durer, can never lose their interest. Among old illustrated books, the most famous, and one of the rarest, is the "Hypnerotomachia Poliphili," "wherein all human matters are proved to be no more than a dream." This is an allegorical romance, published in 1499, for Francesco Colonna, by Aldus Manucius. Poliam Frater Franciscus Columna peramavit. "Brother Francesco Colonna dearly loved Polia," is the inscription and device of this romance. Poor Francesco, of the order of preachers, disguised in this strange work his passion for a lady of uncertain name. Here is a translation of the passage in which the lady describes the beginning of his affection. "I was standing, as is the manner of women young and fair, at the window, or rather on the balcony, of my palace.

My yellow hair, the charm of maidens, was floating round my shining shoulders. My locks were steeped in unguents that made them glitter like threads of gold, and they were slowly drying in the rays of the burning sun. A handmaid, happy in her task, was drawing a comb through my tresses, and surely these of Andromeda seemed not more lovely to Perseus, nor to Lucius the locks of Photis. On a sudden, Poliphilus beheld me, and could not withdraw from me his glances of fire, and even in that moment a ray of the sun of love was kindled in his heart." The fragment is itself a picture from the world of the Renaissance. We watch the blonde, learned lady, dreaming of Perseus, and Lucius, Greek lovers of old time, while the sun gilds her yellow hair, and the young monk, passing below, sees and loves, and "falls into the deep waters of desire."

The lover is no less learned than the lady, and there is a great deal of amorous archaeology in his account of his voyage to Cythera. As to the designs in wood, quaint in their vigorous effort to be classical, they have been attributed to Mantegna, to Bellini, and other artists. Jean Cousin is said to have executed the imitations, in the Paris editions of 1546, 1556, and 1561.

The "Hypnerotomachia" seems to deserve notice, because it is the very type of the books that are dear to collectors, as distinct from the books that, in any shape, are for ever valuable to the world. A cheap Tauchnitz copy of the Iliad and Odyssey, or a Globe Shakespeare, are, from the point of view of literature, worth a wilderness of "Hypnerotomachiae." But a clean copy of the "Hypnerotomachia," especially on VELLUM, is one of the jewels of bibliography. It has all the right qualities; it is very rare, it is very beautiful as a work of art, it is curious and even bizarre, it is the record of a strange time, and a strange passion; it is a relic, lastly, of its printer, the great and good Aldus Manutius.

Next to the old woodcuts and engravings, executed in times when artists were versatile and did not disdain even to draw a bookplate (as Durer did for Pirckheimer), the designs of the French "little masters," are at present in most demand. The book illustrations of the seventeenth century are curious enough, and invaluable as authorities on manners and costume. But the attitudes of the figures are too often stiff and ungainly; while the composition is frequently left to chance. England could show nothing much better than Ogilby's translations of Homer, illustrated with big florid engravings in sham antique style.

The years between 1730 and 1820, saw the French "little masters" in their perfection. The dress of the middle of the eighteenth century, of the age of Watteau, was precisely suited to the gay and graceful pencils of Gravelot, Moreau, Eisen, Boucher, Cochin, Marillier, and Choffard. To understand their merits, and the limits of their art, it is enough to glance through a series of the designs for Voltaire, Corneille, or Moliere. The drawings of society are almost invariably dainty and pleasing, the serious scenes of tragedy leave the spectator quite unmoved. Thus it is but natural that these artists should have shone most in the illustration of airy trifles like Dorat's "Baisers," or tales like Manon Lescaut, or in designing tailpieces for translations of the Greek idyllic poets, such as Moschus and Bion. In some of his illustrations of books, especially, perhaps, in the designs for "La Physiologie de Gout" (Jouaust, Paris, 1879), M. Lalauze has shown himself the worthy rival of Eisen and Cochin. Perhaps it is unnecessary to add that the beauty and value of all such engravings depends almost entirely on their "state." The earlier proofs are much more brilliant than those drawn later, and etchings on fine papers are justly preferred.

For example, M. Lalauze's engravings on "Whatman paper," have a beauty which could scarcely be guessed by people who have only seen specimens on "papier verge." Every collector of the old French vignettes, should possess himself of the "Guide de l'amateur," by M. Henry Cohen (Rouquette, Paris, 1880). Among English illustrated books, various tastes prefer the imaginative works of William Blake, the etchings of Cruikshank, and the woodcuts of Bewick. The whole of the book of this sketch is devoted, by Mr. Austin Dobson, to the topic of English illustrated books. Here it may be said, in passing, that an early copy of William Blake's "Songs of Innocence," written, illustrated, printed, coloured, and boarded by the author's own hand, is one of the most charming objects that a bibliophile can hope to possess.

The verses of Blake, in a framework of birds, and flowers, and plumes, all softly and magically tinted, seem like some book out of King Oberon's library in fairyland, rather than the productions of a mortal press. The pictures in Blake's "prophetic books," and even his illustrations to "Job," show an imagination more heavily weighted by the technical difficulties of drawing.

The next class of rare books is composed of works from the famous presses of the Aldi and the Elzevirs. Other presses have, perhaps, done work as good, but Estienne, the Giunta, and Plantin, are comparatively neglected, while the taste for the performances of Baskerville and Foulis is not very eager. A safe judgment about Aldines and Elzevirs is the gift of years and of long experience. In this place it is only possible to say a few words on a wide subject. The founder of the Aldine press, Aldus Pius Manutius, was born about 1450, and died at Venice in 1514. He was a man of careful and profound learning, and was deeply interested in Greek studies, then encouraged by the arrival in Italy of many educated Greeks and Cretans. Only four Greek authors had as yet been printed in Italy, when (1495) Aldus established his press at Venice.

Theocritus, Homer, AEsop, and Isocrates, probably in very limited editions, were in the hands of students. The purpose of Aldus was to put Greek and Latin works, beautifully printed in a convenient shape, within the reach of all the world. His reform was the introduction of books at once cheap, studiously correct, and convenient in actual use. It was in 1498 that he first adopted the small octavo size, and in his "Virgil" of 1501, he introduced the type called Aldine or Italic. The letters were united as in writing, and the type is said to have been cut by Francesco da Bologna, better known as Francia, in imitation of the hand of Petrarch. For full information about Aldus and his descendants and successors, the work of M. Firmin Didot, ("Alde Manuce et l'Hellenisme a Venise: Paris 1875)," and the Aldine annals of Renouard, must be consulted. These two works are necessary to the collector, who will otherwise be deceived by the misleading assertions of the booksellers. As a rule, the volumes published in the lifetime of Aldus Manutius are the most esteemed, and of these the Aristotle, the first Homer, the Virgil, and the Ovid, are perhaps most in demand. The earlier Aldines are consulted almost as studiously as MSS. by modern editors of the classics.

Just as the house of Aldus waned and expired, that of the great Dutch printers, the Elzevirs, began obscurely enough at Leyden in 1583. The Elzevirs were not, like Aldus, ripe scholars and men of devotion to learning. Aldus laboured for the love of noble studies; the Elzevirs were acute, and too often "smart" men of business. The founder of the family was Louis (born at Louvain, 1540, died 1617). But it was in the second and third generations that Bonaventura and Abraham Elzevir began to publish at Leyden, their editions in small duodecimo. Like Aldus, these Elzevirs aimed at producing books at once handy, cheap, correct, and beautiful in execution.

Their adventure was a complete success. The Elzevirs did not, like Aldus, surround themselves with the most learned scholars of their time. Their famous literary adviser, Heinsius, was full of literary jealousies, and kept students of his own calibre at a distance. The classical editions of the Elzevirs, beautiful, but too small in type for modern eyes, are anything but exquisitely correct. Their editions of the contemporary. French authors, now classics themselves, are lovely examples of skill in practical enterprise.

The Elzevirs treated the French authors much as American publishers treat Englishmen. They stole right and left, but no one complained much in these times of slack copyright; and, at all events, the piratic larcenous publications of the Dutch printers were pretty, and so far satisfactory. They themselves, in turn, were the victims of fraudulent and untradesmanlike imitations. It is for this, among other reasons, that the collector of Elzevirs must make M. Willems's book ("Les Elzevier," Brussels and Paris, 1880) his constant study. Differences so minute that they escape the unpractised eye, denote editions of most various value. In Elzevirs a line's breadth of margin is often worth a hundred pounds, and a misprint is quoted at no less a sum.

The fantastic caprice of bibliophiles has revelled in the bibliography of these Dutch editions. They are at present very scarce in England, where a change in fashion some years ago had made them common enough. No Elzevir is valuable unless it be clean and large in the margins. When these conditions are satisfied the question of rarity comes in, and Remy Belleau's Macaronic poem, or "Le Pastissier Francais," may rise to the price of four or five hundred pounds. A Rabelais, Moliere, or Corneille, of a "good" edition, is now more in request than the once adored "Imitatio Christi" (dateless), or the "Virgil"' of 1646, which is full of gross errors of the press, but is esteemed for red characters in the letter to Augustus, and another passage at page 92. The ordinary marks of the Elzevirs were the sphere, the old hermit, the Athena, the eagle, and the burning faggot. But all little old books marked with spheres are not Elzevirs, as many booksellers suppose.

Other printers also stole the designs for the tops of chapters, the Aegipan, the Siren, the head of Medusa, the crossed sceptres, and the rest. In some cases the Elzevirs published their books, especially when they were piracies, anonymously. When they published for the Jansenists, they allowed their clients to put fantastic pseudonyms on the title pages. But, except in four cases, they had only two pseudonyms used on the titles of books published by and for themselves. These disguises are "Jean Sambix" for Jean and Daniel Elzevir, at Leyden, and for the Elzevirs of Amsterdam, "Jacques le Jeune." The last of the great representatives of the house, Daniel, died at Amsterdam, 1680. Abraham, an unworthy scion, struggled on at Leyden till 1712. The family still prospers, but no longer prints, in Holland. It is common to add duodecimos of Foppens, Wolfgang, and other printers, to the collections of the Elzevirs. The books of Wolfgang have the sign of the fox robbing a wild bee's nest, with the motto Quaerendo.

Curious and singular books are the next in our classification. The category is too large. The books that be "curious" (not in the booksellers' sense of "prurient" and "disgusting,") are innumerable. All suppressed and condemned books, from "Les Fleurs du Mal" to Vanini's "Amphitheatrum," or the English translation of Bruno's "Spaccia della Bestia Trionfante," are more or less rare, and more or less curious. Wild books, like William Postel's "Three Marvellous Triumphs of Women," are "curious." Freakish books, like macaronic poetry, written in a medley of languages, are curious. Books from private presses are singular.

The old English poets and satirists turned out many a book curious to the last degree, and priced at a fantastic value. Such are "Jordan's Jewels of Ingenuity," "Micro-cynicon, six Snarling Satyres" (1599), and the "Treatize made of a Galaunt," printed by Wynkyn de Worde, and found pasted into the fly-leaf, on the oak-board binding of an imperfect volume of Pynson's "Statutes." All our early English poems and miscellanies are curious; and, as relics of delightful singers, are most charming possessions. Such are the "Songes and Sonnettes of Surrey" (1557), the "Paradyce of daynty Deuices" (1576), the "Small Handful of Fragrant Flowers," and "The Handful of Dainty Delights, gathered out of the lovely Garden of Sacred Scripture, fit for any worshipful Gentlewoman to smell unto," (1584). "The Teares of Ireland" (1642), are said, though one would not expect it, to be "extremely rare," and, therefore, precious. But there is no end to the list of such desirable rarities. If we add to them all books coveted as early editions, and, therefore, as relics of great writers, Bunyan, Shakespeare, Milton, Sterne, Walton, and the rest, we might easily fill a book with remarks on this topic alone.

The collection of such editions is the most respectable, the most useful, and, alas, the most expensive of the amateur's pursuits. It is curious enough that the early editions of Swift, Scott, and Byron, are little sought for, if not wholly neglected; while early copies of Shelley, Tennyson, and Keats, have a great price set on their heads. The quartoes of Shakespeare, like first editions of Racine, are out of the reach of any but very opulent purchasers, or unusually lucky, fortunate book-hunters. Before leaving the topic of books which derive their value from the taste and fantasy of collectors, it must be remarked that, in this matter, the fashion of the world changes. Dr. Dibdin lamented, seventy years ago, the waning respect paid to certain editions of the classics. He would find that things have become worse now, and modern German editions, on execrable paper, have supplanted his old favourites.

Fifty years ago, M. Brunet expressed his contempt for the designs of Boucher; now they are at the top of the fashion. The study of old booksellers' catalogues is full of instruction as to the changes of caprice. The collection of Dr. Rawlinson was sold in 1756. "The Vision of Pierce Plowman" (1561), and the "Creede of Pierce Plowman" (1553), brought between them no more than three shillings and sixpence. Eleven shillings were paid for the "Boke of Chivalrie" by Caxton. The "Boke of St. Albans," by Wynkyn de Worde, cost 1 pounds: 1s., and this was the highest sum paid for any one of two hundred rare pieces of early English literature.

In 1764, a copy of the "Hypnerotomachia" was sold for two shillings, "A Pettie Pallace of Pettie his Pleasures," (ah, what a thought for the amateur!) went for three shillings, while "Palmerin of England" (1602), attained no more than the paltry sum of fourteen shillings. When Osborne sold the Harley collection, the scarcest old English books fetched but three or four shillings. If the wandering Jew had been a collector in the last century he might have turned a pretty profit by selling his old English books in this age of ours. In old French, too, Ahasuerus would have done a good stroke of business, for the prices brought by old Villons, Romances of the Rose, "Les Marguerites de Marguerite," and so forth, at the M'Carthy sale, were truly pitiable. A hundred years hence the original editions of Thackeray, or of Miss Greenaway's Christmas books, or "Modern Painters," may be the ruling passion, and Aldines and Elzevirs, black letter and French vignettes may all be despised.

A book which is commonplace in our century is curious in the next, and disregarded in that which follows. Old books of a heretical character were treasures once, rare unholy possessions. Now we have seen so many heretics that the world is indifferent to the audacities of Bruno, and the veiled impieties of Vanini. The last of our categories of books much sought by the collector includes all volumes valued for their ancient bindings, for the mark and stamp of famous amateurs.

The French, who have supplied the world with so many eminent binders,—as Eve, Padeloup, Duseuil, Le Gascon, Derome, Simier, Bozerian, Thouvenin, Trautz-Bauzonnet, and Lortic—are the chief patrons of books in historical bindings. In England an historical binding, a book of Laud's, or James's, or Garrick's, or even of Queen Elizabeth's, does not seem to derive much added charm from its associations. But, in France, peculiar bindings are now the objects most in demand among collectors. The series of books thus rendered precious begins with those of Maioli and of Grolier (1479-1565), remarkable for their mottoes and the geometrical patterns on the covers. Then comes De Thou (who had three sets of arms), with his blazon, the bees stamped on the morocco.

The volumes of Marguerite of Angouleme are sprinkled with golden daisies. Diane de Poictiers had her crescents and her bow, and the initial of her royal lover was intertwined with her own. The three daughters of Louis XV. had each their favourite colour, and their books wear liveries of citron, red, and olive morocco. The Abbe Cotin, the original of Moliere's Trissotin, stamped his books with intertwined C's. Henri III. preferred religious emblems, and sepulchral mottoes—skulls, crossbones, tears, and the insignia of the Passion. Mort m'est vie is a favourite device of the effeminate and voluptuous prince. Moliere himself was a collector, il n'es pas de bouquin qui s'echappe de ses mains,—"never an old book escapes him," says the author of "La Guerre Comique," the last of the pamphlets which flew from side to side in the great literary squabble about "L'Ecole des Femmes." M. Soulie has found a rough catalogue of Moliere's library, but the books, except a little Elzevir, have disappeared. Madame de Maintenon was fond of bindings. Mr. Toovey possesses a copy of a devotional work in red morocco, tooled and gilt, which she presented to a friendly abbess. The books at Saint-Cyr were stamped with a crowned cross, besprent with fleurs-de-lys. The books of the later collectors—Longepierre, the translator of Bion and Moschus; D'Hoym the diplomatist; McCarthy, and La Valliere, are all valued at a rate which seems fair game for satire. Among the most interesting bibliophiles of the eighteenth century is Madame Du Barry.

In 1771, this notorious beauty could scarcely read or write. She had rooms, however, in the Chateau de Versailles, thanks to the kindness of a monarch who admired those native qualities which education may polish, but which it can never confer. At Versailles, Madame Du Barry heard of the literary genius of Madame de Pompadour.

The Pompadour was a person of taste. Her large library of some four thousand works of the lightest sort of light literature was bound by Biziaux. Mr. Toovey possesses the Brantome of this dame galante. Madame herself had published etchings by her own fair hands; and to hear of these things excited the emulation of Madame Du Barry. She might not be CLEVER, but she could have a library like another, if libraries were in fashion. One day Madame Du Barry astonished the Court by announcing that her collection of books would presently arrive at Versailles. Meantime she took counsel with a bookseller, who bought up examples of all the cheap "remainders," as they are called in the trade, that he could lay his hands upon. The whole assortment, about one thousand volumes in all, was hastily bound in rose morocco, elegantly gilt, and stamped with the arms of the noble house of Du Barry.

The bill which Madame Du Barry owed her enterprising agent is still in existence. The thousand volumes cost about three francs each; the binding (extremely cheap) came to nearly as much. The amusing thing is that the bookseller, in the catalogue which he sent with the improvised library, marked the books which Madame Du Barry possessed BEFORE her large order was so punctually executed. There were two "Memoires de Du Barry," an old newspaper, two or three plays, and "L'Historie Amoureuse de Pierre le Long." Louis XV. observed with pride that, though Madame Pompadour had possessed a larger library, that of Madame Du Barry was the better selected. Thanks to her new collection, the lady learned to read with fluency, but she never overcame the difficulties of spelling.

A lady collector who loved books not very well perhaps, but certainly not wisely, was the unhappy Marie Antoinette. The controversy in France about the private character of the Queen has been as acrimonious as the Scotch discussion about Mary Stuart. Evidence, good and bad, letters as apocryphal as the letters of the famous "casket," have been produced on both sides. A few years ago, under the empire, M. Louis Lacour found a manuscript catalogue of the books in the Queen's boudoir. They were all novels of the flimsiest sort,—"L'Amitie Dangereuse," "Les Suites d'un Moment d'Erreur," and even the stories of Louvet and of Retif de la Bretonne. These volumes all bore the letters "C. T." (Chateau de Trianon), and during the Revolution they were scattered among the various public libraries of Paris. The Queen's more important library was at the Tuileries, but at Versailles she had only three books, as the commissioners of the Convention found, when they made an inventory of the property of la femme Capet. Among the three was the "Gerusalemme Liberata," printed, with eighty exquisite designs by Cochin, at the expense of "Monsieur," afterwards Louis XVIII. Books with the arms of Marie Antoinette are very rare in private collections; in sales they are as much sought after as those of Madame Du Barry.

With these illustrations of the kind of interest that belongs to books of old collectors, we may close this chapter. The reader has before him a list, with examples, of the kinds of books at present most in vogue among amateurs. He must judge for himself whether he will follow the fashion, by aid either of a long purse or of patient research, or whether he will find out new paths for himself. A scholar is rarely a rich man. He cannot compete with plutocrats who buy by deputy. But, if he pursues the works he really needs, he may make a valuable collection. He cannot go far wrong while he brings together the books that he finds most congenial to his own taste and most useful to his own studies.

Here, then, in the words of the old "sentiment," I bid him farewell, and wish "success to his inclinations, provided they are virtuous." There is a set of collectors, alas! whose inclinations are not virtuous. The most famous of them, a Frenchman, observed that his own collection of bad books was unique. That of an English rival, he admitted, was respectable,—"mais milord se livre a des autres preoccupations!" He thought a collector's whole heart should be with his treasures.

En bouquinant se trouve grand soulas. Soubent m'en vay musant, a petis pas, Au long des quais, pour flairer maint bieux livre. Des Elzevier la Sphere me rend yure, Et la Sirene aussi m'esmeut. Grand cas Fais-je d'Estienne, Aide, ou Dolet. Mais las! Le vieux Caxton ne se rencontre pas, Plus qu' agneau d'or parmi jetons de cuivre, En bouquinant!

Pour tout plaisir que l'on goute icy-bas La Grace a Dieu. Mieux vaut, sans altercas, Chasser bouquin: Nul mal n'en peult s'ensuivre. Dr sus au livre: il est le grand appas. Clair est le ciel. Amis, qui veut me suivre En bouquinant?

## ILLUSTRATED BOOKS

Modern English book-illustration—to which the present chapter is restricted -has no long or doubtful history, since to find its first beginnings, it is needless to go farther back than the last quarter of the eighteenth century. Not that "illustrated" books of a certain class were by any means unknown before that period. On the contrary, for many years previously, literature had boasted its "sculptures" of be-wigged and be-laurelled "worthies," its "prospects" and "land-skips," its phenomenal monsters and its "curious antiques." But, despite the couplet in the "Dunciad" respecting books where ". .. the pictures for the page atone, And Quarles is saved by beauties not his own;" -

illustrations, in which the designer attempted the actual delineation of scenes or occurrences in the text, were certainly not common when Pope wrote, nor were they for some time afterwards either very numerous or very noteworthy. There are Hogarth's engravings to "Hudibras" and "Don Quixote;" there are the designs of his crony Frank Hayman to Theobald's "Shakespeare," to Milton, to Pope, to Cervantes; there are Pine's "Horace" and Sturt's "Prayer- Book" (in both of which text and ornament were alike engraved); there are the historical and topographical drawings of Sandby, Wale, and others; and yet—notwithstanding all these—it is with Bewick's cuts to Gay's "Fables" in 1779, and Stothard's plates to Harrison's "Novelist's Magazine" in 1780, that book-illustration by imaginative compositions really begins to flourish in England. Those little masterpieces of the Newcastle artist brought about a revival of wood-engraving which continues to this day; but engraving upon metal, as a means of decorating books, practically came to an end with the "Annuals" of thirty years ago. It will therefore be well to speak first of illustrations upon copper and steel.

Stothard, Blake, and Flaxman are the names that come freshest to memory in this connection. For a period of fifty years Stothard stands pre-eminent in illustrated literature. Measuring time by poets, he may be said to have lent something of his fancy and amenity to most of the writers from Cowper to Rogers. As a draughtsman he is undoubtedly weak: his figures are often limp and invertebrate, and his type of beauty insipid. Still, regarded as groups, the majority of his designs are exquisite, and he possessed one all-pervading and un-English quality—the quality of grace. This is his dominant note. Nothing can be more seductive than the suave flow of his line, his feeling for costume, his gentle and chastened humour. Many of his women and children are models of purity and innocence.

But he works at ease only within the limits of his special powers; he is happier in the pastoral and domestic than the heroic and supernatural, and his style is better fitted to the formal salutations of "Clarissa" and "Sir Charles Grandison," than the rough horse-play of "Peregrine Pickle." Where Rowlandson would have revelled, Stothard would be awkward and constrained; where Blake would give us a new sensation, Stothard would be poor and mechanical. Nevertheless the gifts he possessed were thoroughly recognised in his own day, and brought him, if not riches, at least competence and honour. It is said that more than three thousand of his drawings have been engraved, and they are scattered through a hundred publications. Those to the "Pilgrim's Progress" and the poems of Rogers are commonly spoken of as his best, though he never excelled some of the old-fashioned plates (with their pretty borders in the style of Gravelot and the Frenchmen) to Richardson's novels, and such forgotten "classics" as "Joe Thompson", "Jessamy," "Betsy Thoughtless," and one or two others in Harrison's very miscellaneous collection.

Stothard was fortunate in his engravers. Besides James Heath, his best interpreter, Schiavonetti, Sharp, Finden, the Cookes, Bartolozzi, most of the fashionable translators into copper were busily employed upon his inventions. Among the rest was an artist of powers far greater than his own, although scarcely so happy in turning them to profitable account. The genius of William Blake was not a marketable commodity in the same way as Stothard's talent. The one caught the trick of the time with his facile elegance; the other scorned to make any concessions, either in conception or execution, to the mere popularity of prettiness.

"Give pensions to the learned pig, Or the hare playing on a tabor; Anglus can never see perfection But in the journeyman's labour," -he wrote in one of those rough-hewn and bitter epigrams of his. Yet the work that was then so lukewarmly received—if, indeed, it can be said to have been received at all—is at present far more sought after than Stothard's, and the prices now given for the "Songs of Innocence and Experience," the "Inventions to the Book of Job," and even "The Grave," would have brought affluence to the struggling artist, who (as Cromek taunted him) was frequently "reduced so low as to be obliged to live on half a guinea a week." Not that this was entirely the fault of his contemporaries. Blake was a visionary, and an untuneable man; and, like others who work for the select public of all ages, he could not always escape the consequence that the select public of his own, however willing, were scarcely numerous enough to support him.

His most individual works are the "Songs of Innocence," 1789, and the "Songs of Experience," 1794. These, afterwards united in one volume, were unique in their method of production; indeed, they do not perhaps strictly come within the category of what is generally understood to be copperplate engraving.

The drawings were outlined and the songs written upon the metal with some liquid that resisted the action of acid, and the remainder of the surface of the plate was eaten away with aqua-fortis, leaving the design in bold relief, like a rude stereotype. This was then printed off in the predominant tone—blue, brown, or yellow, as the case might be—and delicately tinted by the artist in a prismatic and ethereal fashion peculiarly his own. Stitched and bound in boards by Mrs. Blake, a certain number of these leaflets—twenty-seven in the case of the first issue—made up a tiny octavo of a wholly exceptional kind. Words indeed fail to exactly describe the flower-like beauty—the fascination of these "fairy missals," in which, it has been finely said, "the thrilling music of the verse, and the gentle bedazzlement of the lines and colours so intermingle, that the mind hangs in a pleasant uncertainty as to whether it is a picture that is singing, or a song which has newly budded and blossomed into colour and form."

The accompanying woodcut, after one of the illustrations to the "Songs of Innocence," gives some indication of the general composition, but it can convey no hint of the gorgeous purple, and crimson, and orange of the original.

Of the "Illustrations to the Book of Job," 1826, there are excellent reduced facsimiles by the recently-discovered photo-intaglio process, in the new edition of Gilchrist's "Life." The originals were engraved by Blake himself in his strong decisive fashion, and they are his best work. A kind of deisidaimonia—a sacred awe— falls upon one in turning over these wonderful productions of the artist's declining years and failing hand.

"Leaving the old, both worlds at once they view, That stand upon the threshold of the new," sings Waller; and it is almost possible to believe for a moment that their creator was (as he said) "under the direction of messengers from Heaven." But his designs for Blair's "Grave," 1808, popularised by the burin of Schiavonetti, attracted greater attention at the time of publication; and, being less rare, they are even now perhaps better known than the others. The facsimile here given is from the latter book. The worn old man, the trustful woman, and the guileless child are sleeping peacefully; but the king with his sceptre, and the warrior with his hand on his sword-hilt, lie open-eyed, waiting the summons of the trumpet. One cannot help fancying that the artist's long vigils among the Abbey tombs, during his apprenticeship to James Basire, must have been present to his mind when he selected this impressive monumental subject.

To one of Blake's few friends—to the "dear Sculptor of Eternity," as he wrote to Flaxman from Felpham—the world is indebted for some notable book illustrations. Whether the greatest writers—the Homers, the Shakespeares, the Dantes—can ever be "illustrated" without loss may fairly be questioned. At all events, the showy dexterities of the Dores and Gilberts prove nothing to the contrary. But now and then there comes to the graphic interpretation of a great author an artist either so reverential, or so strongly sympathetic at some given point, that, in default of any relation more narrowly intimate, we at once accept his conceptions as the best attainable. In this class are Flaxman's outlines to Homer and AEschylus. Flaxman was not a Hellenist as men are Hellenists to- day.

Nevertheless, his Roman studies had saturated him with the spirit of antique beauty, and by his grand knowledge of the nude, his calm, his restraint, he is such an illustrator of Homer as is not likely to arise again. For who—with all our added knowledge of classical antiquity—who, of our modern artists, could hope to rival such thoroughly Greek compositions as the ball-play of Nausicaa in the "Odyssey," or that lovely group from AEschylus of the tender- hearted, womanly Oceanides, cowering like flowers beaten by the storm under the terrible anger of Zeus? In our day Flaxman's drawings would have been reproduced by some of the modern facsimile processes, and the gain would have been great. As it is, something is lost by their transference to copper, even though the translators be Piroli and Blake. Blake, in fact, did more than he is usually credited with, for (beside the acknowledged and later "Hesiod," 1817) he really engraved the whole of the "Odyssey," Piroli's plates having been lost on the voyage to England. The name of the Roman artist, nevertheless, appears on the title-page (1793). But Blake was too original to be a successful copyist of other men's work, and to appreciate the full value of Flaxman's drawings, they should be studied in the collections at University

College, the Royal Academy, and elsewhere. Flaxman and Blake had few imitators. But a host of clever designers, such as Cipriani, Angelica Kauffmann, Westall, Uwins, Smirke, Burney, Corbould, Dodd, and others, vied with the popular Stothard in "embellishing" the endless "Poets," "novelists," and "essayists" of our forefathers. Some of these, and most of the recognised artists of the period, lent their aid to that boldly- planned but unhappily-executed "Shakespeare" of Boydell,—"black and ghastly gallery of murky Opies, glum Northcotes, straddling Fuselis," as Thackeray calls it.

They are certainly not enlivening- -those cumbrous "atlas" folios of 1803-5, and they helped to ruin the worthy alderman. Even courtly Sir Joshua is clearly ill at ease among the pushing Hamiltons and Mortimers; and, were it not for the whimsical discovery that Westall's "Ghost of Caesar" strangely resembles Mr. Gladstone, there would be no resting-place for the modern student of these dismal masterpieces. The truth is, Reynolds excepted, there were no contemporary painters strong enough for the task, and the honours of the enterprise belong almost exclusively to Smirke's "Seven Ages" and one or two plates from the lighter comedies.

The great "Bible" of Macklin, a rival and even more incongruous publication, upon which some of the same designers were employed, has fallen into completer oblivion. A rather better fate attended another book of this class, which, although belonging to a later period, may be briefly referred to here. The "Milton" of John Martin has distinct individuality, and some of the needful qualities of imagination. Nevertheless, posterity has practically decided that scenic grandeur and sombre effects alone are not a sufficient pictorial equipment for the varied story of "Paradise Lost."

It is to Boydell of the Shakespeare gallery that we owe the "Liber Veritatis" of Claude, engraved by Richard Earlom; and indirectly, since rivalry of Claude prompted the attempt, the famous "Liber Studiorum" of Turner. Neither of these, however—which, like the "Rivers of France" and the "Picturesque Views in England and Wales" of the latter artist, are collections of engravings rather than illustrated books—belongs to the present purpose. But Turner's name may fitly serve to introduce those once familiar "Annuals" and "Keepsakes," that, beginning in 1823 with Ackermann's "Forget-me- Not," enjoyed a popularity of more than thirty years.

Their general characteristics have been pleasantly satirised in Thackeray's account of the elegant miscellany of Bacon the publisher, to which Mr. Arthur Pendennis contributed his pretty poem of "The Church Porch." His editress, it will be remembered, was the Lady Violet Lebas, and his colleagues the Honourable Percy Popjoy, Lord Dodo, and the gifted Bedwin Sands, whose "Eastern Ghazuls" lent so special a distinction to the volume in watered-silk binding. The talented authors, it is true, were in most cases under the disadvantage of having to write to the plates of the talented artists, a practice which even now is not extinct, though it is scarcely considered favourable to literary merit. And the real "Annuals" were no exception to the rule. As a matter of fact, their general literary merit was not obtrusive, although, of course, they sometimes contained work which afterwards became famous. They are now so completely forgotten and out of date, that one scarcely expects to find that Wordsworth, Coleridge, Macaulay, and Southey, were among the occasional contributors. Lamb's beautiful "Album verses" appeared in the "Bijou," Scott's "Bonnie Dundee" in the "Christmas Box," and Tennyson's "St. Agnes' Eve" in the "Keepsake."

But the plates were, after all, the leading attraction. These, prepared for the most part under the superintendence of the younger Heath, and executed on the steel which by this time had supplanted the old "coppers," were supplied by, or were "after," almost every contemporary artist of note. Stothard, now growing old and past his prime, Turner, Etty, Stanfield, Leslie, Roberts, Danby, Maclise, Lawrence, Cattermole, and numbers of others, found profitable labour in this fashionable field until 1856, when the last of the "Annuals" disappeared, driven from the market by the rapid development of wood engraving. About a million, it is roughly estimated, was squandered in producing them. In connection with the "Annuals" must be mentioned two illustrated books which were in all probability suggested by them—the "Poems" and "Italy" of Rogers. The designs to these are chiefly by Turner and Stothard, although there are a few by Prout and others. Stothard's have been already referred to; Turner's are almost universally held to be the most successful of his many vignettes. It has been truly said—in a recent excellent life of this artist —that it would be difficult to find in the whole of his works two really greater than the "Alps at Daybreak," and the "Datur Hora Quieti," in the former of these volumes. Almost equally beautiful are the "Valombre Falls" and "Tornaro's misty brow."

Of the "Italy" set Mr. Ruskin writes:- "They are entirely exquisite; poetical in the highest and purest sense, exemplary and delightful beyond all praise." To such words it is not possible to add much. But it is pretty clear that the poetical vitality of Rogers was secured by these well-timed illustrations, over which he is admitted by his nephew Mr. Sharpe to have spent about 7000 pounds, and far larger sums have been named by good authorities. The artist received from fifteen to twenty guineas for each of the drawings; the engravers (Goodall, Miller, Wallis, Smith, and others), sixty guineas a plate. The "Poems" and the "Italy," in the original issues of 1830 and 1834, are still precious to collectors, and are likely to remain so. Turner also illustrated Scott, Milton, Campbell, and Byron; but this series of designs has not received equal commendation from his greatest eulogist, who declares them to be "much more laboured, and more or less artificial and unequal." Among the numerous imitations directly induced by the Rogers books was the "Lyrics of the Heart," by Alaric Attila Watts, a forgotten versifier and sometime editor of "Annuals," but it did not meet with similar success.

Many illustrated works, originating in the perfection and opportunities of engraving on metal, are necessarily unnoticed in this rapid summary. As far, however, as book-illustration is concerned, copper and steel plate engraving may be held to have gone out of fashion with the "Annuals." It is still, indeed, to be found lingering in that mine of modern art-books—the "Art Journal;" and, not so very long ago, it made a sumptuous and fugitive reappearance in Dore's "Idylls of the King," Birket Foster's "Hood," and one or two other imposing volumes. But it was badly injured by modern wood-engraving; it has since been crippled for life by photography; and it is more than probable that the present rapid rise of modern etching will give it the coup de grace.

By the end of the seventeenth century the art of engraving on wood had fallen into disuse. Writing circa 1770, Horace Walpole goes so far as to say that it "never was executed in any perfection in England;" and, speaking afterwards of Papillon's "Traite de la Gravure," 1766, he takes occasion to doubt if that author would ever "persuade the world to return to wooden cuts." Nevertheless, with Bewick, a few years later, wood-engraving took a fresh departure so conspicuous that it amounts to a revival. In what this consisted it is clearly impossible to show here with any sufficiency of detail; but between the method of the old wood-cutters who reproduced the drawings of Durer, and the method of the Newcastle artist, there are two marked and well-defined differences. One of these is a difference in the preparation of the wood and the tool employed.

The old wood-cutters carved their designs with knives and chisels on strips of wood sawn lengthwise—that is to say, upon the PLANK; Bewick used a graver, and worked upon slices of box or pear cut across the grain,—that is to say upon the END of the wood. The other difference, of which Bewick is said to have been the inventor, is less easy to describe. It consisted in the employment of what is technically known as "white line." In all antecedent wood-cutting the cutter had simply cleared away those portions of the block left bare by the design, so that the design remained in relief to be printed from like type. Using the smooth box block as a uniform surface from which, if covered with printing ink, a uniformly black impression might be obtained, Bewick, by cutting white lines across it at greater or lesser intervals, produced gradations of shade, from the absolute black of the block to the lightest tints. The general result of this method was to give a greater depth of colouring and variety to the engraving, but its advantages may perhaps be best understood by a glance at the background of the "Woodcock" on the following page.

Bewick's first work of any importance was the Gay's "Fables" of 1779. In 1784 he did another series of "Select Fables." Neither of these books, however, can be compared with the "General History of Quadrupeds," 1790, and the "British Land and Water Birds," 1797 and 1804. The illustrations to the "Quadrupeds" are in many instances excellent, and large additions were made to them in subsequent issues. But in this collection Bewick laboured to a great extent under the disadvantage of representing animals with which he was familiar only through the medium of stuffed specimens or incorrect drawings. In the "British Birds," on the contrary, his facilities for study from the life were greater, and his success was consequently more complete. Indeed, it may be safely affirmed that of all the engravers of the present century, none have excelled Bewick for beauty of black and white, for skilful rendering of plumage and foliage, and for fidelity of detail and accessory. The "Woodcock" (here given), the "Partridge," the "Owl," the "Yellow-Hammer," the "Yellow-Bunting," the "Willow-Wren," are popular examples of these qualities. But there are a hundred others nearly as good.

Among sundry conventional decorations after the old German fashion in the first edition of the "Quadrupeds," there are a fair number of those famous tail-pieces which, to a good many people, constitute Bewick's chief claim to immortality. That it is not easy to imitate them is plain from the failure of Branston's attempts, and from the inferior character of those by John Thompson in Yarrell's "Fishes." The genius of Bewick was, in fact, entirely individual and particular. He had the humour of a Hogarth in little, as well as some of his special characteristics,—notably his faculty of telling a story by suggestive detail. An instance may be taken at random from vol. I. of the "Birds." A man, whose wig and hat have fallen off, lies asleep with open mouth under some bushes. He is manifestly drunk, and the date "4 June," on a neighbouring stone, gives us the reason and occasion of his catastrophe. He has been too loyally celebrating the birthday of his majesty King George III. Another of Bewick's gifts is his wonderful skill in foreshadowing a tragedy. Take as an example, this truly appalling incident from the "Quadrupeds."

The tottering child, whose nurse is seen in the background, has strayed into the meadow, and is pulling at the tail of a vicious-looking colt, with back-turned eye and lifted heel. Down the garden-steps the mother hurries headlong; but she can hardly be in time. And of all this—sufficient, one would say, for a fairly-sized canvas—the artist has managed to give a vivid impression in a block of three inches by two! Then, again, like Hogarth once more, he rejoices in multiplications of dilemma. What, for instance, can be more comically pathetic than the head-piece to the "Contents" in vol. I. of the "Birds"? The old horse has been seized with an invincible fit of stubbornness. The day is both windy and rainy. The rider has broken his stick and lost his hat; but he is too much encumbered with his cackling and excited stock to dare to dismount. Nothing can help him but a Deus ex machina,—of whom there is no sign.

Besides his humour, Bewick has a delightfully rustic side, of which Hogarth gives but little indication. From the starved ewe in the snow nibbling forlornly at a worn-out broom, to the cow which has broken through the rail to reach the running water, there are numberless designs which reveal that faithful lover of the field and hillside, who, as he said, "would rather be herding sheep on Mickle bank top" than remain in London to be made premier of England. He loved the country and the country-life; and he drew them as one who loved them. It is this rural quality which helps to give such a lasting freshness to his quaint and picturesque fancies; and it is this which will continue to preserve their popularity, even if they should cease to be valued for their wealth of whimsical invention.

In referring to these masterpieces of Bewick's, it must not be forgotten that he had the aid of some clever assistants. His younger brother John was not without talent, as is clear from his work for Somervile's "Chace," 1796, and that highly edifying book, the "Blossoms of Morality." Many of the tail-pieces to the "Water Birds" were designed by Robert Johnson, who also did most of the illustrations to Bewick's "Fables" of 1818, which were engraved by Temple and Harvey, two other pupils. Another pupil was Charlton Nesbit, an excellent engraver, who was employed upon the "Birds," and did good work in Ackermann's

"Religious Emblems" of 1808, and the second series of Northcote's "Fables." But by far the largest portion of the tail-pieces in the second volume of the "Birds" was engraved by Luke Clennell, a very skilful but unfortunate artist, who ultimately became insane. To him we owe the woodcuts, after Stothard's charming sketches, to the Rogers volume of 1810, an edition preceding those already mentioned as illustrated with steel- plates, and containing some of the artist's happiest pictures of children and amorini.

Many of these little groups would make admirable designs for gems, if indeed they are not already derived from them, since one at least is an obvious copy of a well-known sardonyx—("The Marriage of Cupid and Psyche.") This volume, generally known by the name of the "Firebrand" edition, is highly prized by collectors; and, as intelligent renderings of pen and ink, there is little better than these engravings of Clennell's. Finally, among others of Bewick's pupils, must be mentioned William Harvey, who survived to 1866. It has been already stated that he engraved part of the illustrations to Bewick's "Fables," but his best known block is the large one of Haydon's "Death of Dentatus." Soon after this he relinquished wood-engraving in favour of design, and for a long period was one of the most fertile and popular of book-illustrators.

His style, however, is unpleasantly mannered; and it is sufficient to make mention of his masterpiece, the "Arabian Nights" of Lane, the illustrations to which, produced under the supervision of the translator, are said to be so accurate as to give the appropriate turbans for every hour of the day. They show considerable freedom of invention and a large fund of Orientalism.

Harvey came to London in 1817; Clennell had preceded him by some years; and Nesbit lived there for a considerable time. What distinguishes these pupils of Bewick especially is, that they were artists as well as engravers, capable of producing the designs they engraved. The "London School" of engravers, on the contrary, were mostly engravers, who depended upon others for their designs. The foremost of these was Robert Branston, a skilful renderer of human figures and indoor scenes. He worked in rivalry with Bewick and Nesbit; but he excelled neither, while he fell far behind the former. John Thompson, one of the very best of modern English engravers on wood, was Branston's pupil.

His range was of the widest, and he succeeded as well in engraving fishes and birds for Yarrell and Walton's "Angler," as in illustrations to Moliere and "Hudibras." He was, besides, a clever draughtsman, though he worked chiefly from the designs of Thurston and others. One of the most successful of his illustrated books is the "Vicar of Wakefield," after Mulready, whose simplicity and homely feeling were well suited to Goldsmith's style. Another excellent engraver of this date is Samuel Williams. There is an edition of Thomson's "Seasons," with cuts both drawn and engraved by him, which is well worthy of attention, and (like Thompson and Branston) he was very skilful in reproducing the designs of Cruikshank. Some of his best work in this way is to be found in Clarke's "Three Courses and a Dessert," published by Vizetelly in 1830.

From this time forth, however, one hears less of the engraver and more of the artist. The establishment of the "Penny Magazine" in 1832, and the multifarious publications of Charles Knight, gave an extraordinary impetus to wood-engraving. Ten years later came "Punch," and the "Illustrated London News," which further increased its popularity. Artists of eminence began to draw on or for the block, as they had drawn, and were still drawing, for the "Annuals." In 1842-6 was issued the great "Abbotsford" edition of the "Waverley Novels," which, besides 120 plates, contained nearly 2000 wood- engravings; and with the "Book of British Ballads," 1843, edited by Mr. S. C. Hall, arose that long series of illustrated Christmas books, which gradually supplanted the "Annuals," and made familiar the names of Gilbert, Birket Foster, Harrison Weir, John Absolon, and a crowd of others. The poems of Longfellow, Montgomery, Burns, "Barry Cornwall," Poe, Miss Ingelow, were all successively "illustrated." Besides these, there were numerous selections, such as Willmott's "Poets of the Nineteenth Century," Wills's "Poets' Wit and Humour," and so forth. But the field here grows too wide to be dealt with in detail, and it is impossible to do more than mention a few of the books most prominent for merit or originality. Amongst these there is the "Shakespeare" of Sir John Gilbert. Regarded as an interpretative edition of the great dramatist, this is little more than a brilliant tour de force; but it is nevertheless infinitely superior to the earlier efforts of Kenny Meadows in 1843, and also to the fancy designs of Harvey in Knight's "Pictorial Shakespeare." The "Illustrated Tennyson" of 1858 is also a remarkable production.

The Laureate, almost more than any other, requires a variety of illustrators; and here, for his idylls, he had Mulready and Millais, and for his romances Rossetti and Holman Hunt. His "Princess" was afterwards illustrated by Maclise, and his "Enoch Arden" by Arthur Hughes; but neither of these can be said to be wholly adequate. The "Lalla Rookh" of John Tenniel, 1860, albeit somewhat stiff and cold, after this artist's fashion, is a superb collection of carefully studied oriental designs. With these may be classed the illustrations to Aytoun's "Lays of the Scottish Cavaliers," by Sir Noel Paton, which have the same finished qualities of composition and the same academic hardness. Several good editions of the "Pilgrim's Progress" have appeared,—notably those of C. H. Bennett, J. D. Watson, and G. H. Thomas.

Other books are Millais's "Parables of our Lord," Leighton's "Romola," Walker's "Philip" and "Denis Duval," the "Don Quixote," "Dante," "La Fontaine" and other works of Dore, Dalziel's "Arabian Nights," Leighton's "Lyra Germanica" and "Moral Emblems," and the "Spiritual Conceits" of W. Harry Rogers. These are some only of the number, which does not include books like Mrs. Hugh Blackburn's "British Birds," Wolf's "Wild Animals," Wise's "New Forest," Linton's "Lake Country," Wood's "Natural History," and many more. Nor does it take in the various illustrated periodicals which have multiplied so freely since, in 1859, "Once a Week" first began to attract and train such younger draughtsmen as Sandys, Lawless, Pinwell, Houghton, Morten, and Paul Grey, some of whose best work in this way has been revived in the edition of Thornbury's "Ballads and Songs," recently published by Chatto and Windus. Ten years later came the "Graphic," offering still wider opportunities to wood-cut art, and bringing with it a fresh school of artists. Herkomer, Fildes, Small, Green, Barnard, Barnes, Crane, Caldecott, Hopkins, and others,—quos nunc perscribere longum est—have contributed good work to this popular rival of the older, but still vigorous, "Illustrated." And now again, another promising serial, the "Magazine of Art," affords a supplementary field to modern refinements and younger energies.

Not a few of the artists named in the preceding paragraph have also earned distinction in separate branches of the pictorial art, and specially in that of humorous design,—a department which has always been so richly recruited in this country that it deserves more than a passing mention. From the days of Hogarth onwards there has been an almost unbroken series of humorous draughtsmen, who, both on wood and metal, play a distinguished part in our illustrated literature. Rowlandson, one of the earliest, was a caricaturist of inexhaustible facility, and an artist who scarcely did justice to his own powers. He illustrated several books, but he is chiefly remembered in this way by his plates to Combe's "Three Tours of Dr. Syntax." Gillray, his contemporary, whose bias was political rather than social, is said to have illustrated "The Deserted Village" in his youth; but he is not famous as a book-illustrator.

Another of the early men was Bunbury, whom "quality"-loving Mr. Walpole calls "the second Hogarth, and first imitator who ever fully equalled his original (!);" but whose prints to "Tristram Shandy," are nevertheless completely forgotten, while, if he be remembered at all, it is by the plate of "The Long Minuet," and the vulgar "Directions to Bad Horsemen." With the first years of the century, however, appears the great master of modern humorists, whose long life ended only a few years since, "the veteran George Cruikshank"—as his admirers were wont to style him. He indeed may justly be compared to Hogarth, since, in tragic power and intensity he occasionally comes nearer to him than any artist of our time.

It is manifestly impossible to mention here all the more important efforts of this indefatigable worker, from those far-away days when he caricatured "Boney" and championed Queen

Caroline, to that final frontispiece for "The Rose and the Lily"—"designed and etched (according to the inscription) by George Cruikshank, age 83;" but the plates to the "Points of Humour," to Grimm's "Goblins," to "Oliver Twist," "Jack Sheppard," Maxwell's "Irish Rebellion," and the "Table Book," are sufficiently favourable and varied specimens of his skill with the needle, while the woodcuts to "Three Courses and a Dessert," one of which is here given, are equally good examples of his work on the block. The "Triumph of Cupid," which begins the "Table Book," is an excellent instance of his lavish wealth of fancy, and it contains beside, one—nay more than one—of the many portraits of the artist. He is shown en robe de chambre, smoking (this was before his regenerate days!) in front of a blazing fire, with a pet spaniel on his knee.

In the cloud which curls from his lips is a motley procession of sailors, sweeps, jockeys, Greenwich pensioners, Jew clothesmen, flunkies, and others more illustrious, chained to the chariot wheels of Cupid, who, preceded by cherubic acolytes and banner-bearers, winds round the top of the picture towards an altar of Hymen on the table. When, by the aid of a pocket-glass, one has mastered these swarming figures, as well as those in the foreground, it gradually dawns upon one that all the furniture is strangely vitalised. Masks laugh round the border of the tablecloth, the markings of the mantelpiece resolve themselves into rows of madly- racing figures, the tongs leers in a degage and cavalier way at the artist, the shovel and poker grin in sympathy; there are faces in the smoke, in the fire, in the fireplace,—the very fender itself is a ring of fantastic creatures who jubilantly hem in the ashes. And it is not only in the grotesque and fanciful that Cruikshank excels; he is master of the strange, the supernatural, and the terrible. In range of character (the comparison is probably a hackneyed one), both by his gifts and his limitations, he resembles Dickens; and had he illustrated more of that writer's works the resemblance would probably have been more evident. In "Oliver Twist," for example, where Dickens is strong, Cruikshank is strong; where Dickens is weak, he is weak too. His Fagin, his Bill Sikes, his Bumble, and their following, are on a level with

Dickens's conceptions; his Monk and Rose Maylie are as poor as the originals. But as the defects of Dickens are overbalanced by his merits, so Cruikshank's strength is far in excess of his weakness. It is not to his melodramatic heroes or wasp-waisted heroines that we must look for his triumphs; it is to his delineations, from the moralist's point of view, of vulgarity and vice,—of the "rank life of towns," with all its squalid tragedy and comedy. Here he finds his strongest ground, and possibly, notwithstanding his powers as a comic artist and caricaturist, his loftiest claim to recollection.

Cruikshank was employed on two only of Dickens's books—"Oliver Twist" and the "Sketches by Boz." The great majority of them were illustrated by Hablot K. Browne, an artist who followed the ill-fated Seymour on the "Pickwick Papers." To "Phiz," as he is popularly called, we are indebted for our pictorial ideas of Sam Weller, Mrs. Gamp, Captain Cuttle, and most of the author's characters, down to the "Tale of Two Cities." "Phiz" also illustrated a great many of Lever's novels, for which his skill in hunting and other Lever-like scenes especially qualified him.

With the name of Richard Doyle we come to the first of a group of artists whose main work was, or is still, done for the time-honoured miscellany of Mr. Punch. So familiar an object is "Punch" upon our tables, that one is sometimes apt to forget how unfailing, and how good on the whole, is the work we take so complacently as a matter of course. And of this good work, in the earlier days, a large proportion was done by Mr. Doyle. He is still living, although he has long ceased to gladden those sprightly pages. But it was to "Punch" that he contributed his masterpiece, the "Manners and Customs of ye Englyshe," a series of outlines illustrating social life in 1849, and cleverly commented by a shadowy "Mr. Pips," a sort of fetch or double of the bustling and garrulous old Caroline diarist.

In these captivating pictures the life of thirty years ago is indeed, as the title-page has it, "drawn from ye quick." We see the Molesworths and Cantilupes of the day parading the Park; we watch Brougham fretting at a hearing in the Lords, or Peel holding forth to the Commons (where the Irish members are already obstructive); we squeeze in at the Haymarket to listen to Jenny Lind, or we run down the river to Greenwich Fair, and visit "Mr. Richardson, his show." Many years after, in the "Bird's Eye Views of Society," which appeared in the early numbers of the "Cornhill Magazine," Mr. Doyle returned to this attractive theme. But the later designs were more elaborate, and not equally fortunate. They bear the same relationship to Mr. Pips's pictorial chronicle, as the laboured "Temperance Fairy Tales" of Cruikshank's old age bear to the little-worked Grimm's "Goblins" of his youth. So hazardous is the attempt to repeat an old success!

Neverthcless, many of the initial letters to the "Bird's Eye Views" are in the artist's best and most frolicsome manner. "The Foreign Tour of Brown, Jones, and Robinson" is another of his happy thoughts for "Punch;" and some of his most popular designs are to be found in Thackeray's "Newcomes," where his satire and fancy seem thoroughly suited to his text. He has also illustrated Locker's well-known "London Lyrics," Ruskin's "King of the Golden River," and Hughes's "Scouring of the White Horse," from which last the initial at the beginning of this chapter has been borrowed. His latest important effort was the series of drawings called "In Fairy Land," to which Mr. William Allingham contributed the verses.

In speaking of the "Newcomes," one is reminded that its illustrious author was himself a "Punch" artist, and would probably have been a designer alone, had it not been decreed "that he should paint in colours which will never crack and never need restoration." Everyone knows the story of the rejected illustrator of "Pickwick," whom that and other rebuffs drove permanently to letters. To his death, however, he clung fondly to his pencil. In technique he never attained to certainty or strength, and his genius was too quick and creative—perhaps also too desultory—for finished work, while he was always indifferent to costume and accessory.

But many of his sketches for "Vanity Fair," for "Pendennis," for "The Virginians," for "The Rose and the Ring," the Christmas books, and the posthumously published "Orphan of Pimlico," have a vigour of impromptu, and a happy suggestiveness which is better than correct drawing. Often the realisation is almost photographic. Look, for example, at the portrait in "Pendennis" of the dilapidated Major as he crawls downstairs in the dawn after the ball at Gaunt House, and then listen to the inimitable context: "That admirable and devoted Major above all,—who had been for hours by Lady Clavering's side ministering to her and feeding her body with everything that was nice, and her ear with everything that was sweet and flattering—oh! what an object he was!

The rings round his eyes were of the colour of bistre; those orbs themselves were like the plovers' eggs whereof Lady Clavering and Blanche had each tasted; the wrinkles in his old face were furrowed in deep gashes; and a silver stubble, like an elderly morning dew, was glittering on his chin, and alongside the dyed whiskers, now limp and out of curl." A good deal of this—that fine touch in italics especially—could not possibly be rendered in black and white, and yet how much is indicated, and how thoroughly the whole is felt! One turns to the woodcut from the words, and back again to the words from the woodcut with ever-increasing gratification. Then again, Thackeray's little initial letters are charmingly arch and playful. They seem to throw a shy side-light upon the text, giving, as it were, an additional and confidential hint of the working of the author's mind. To those who, with the present writer, love every tiny scratch and quirk and flourish of the Master's hand, these small but priceless memorials are far beyond the frigid appraising of academics and schools of art.

After Doyle and Thackeray come a couple of well-known artists—John Leech and John Tenniel. The latter still lives (may he long live!) to delight and instruct us. Of the former, whose genial and manly "Pictures of Life and Character" are in every home where good- humoured raillery is prized and appreciated, it is scarcely necessary to speak. Who does not remember the splendid languid swells, the bright-eyed rosy girls ("with no nonsense about them!") in pork pie hats and crinolines, the superlative "Jeames's," the hairy "Mossoos," the music-grinding Italian desperadoes whom their kind creator hated so? And then the intrepidity of "Mr. Briggs," the Roman rule of "Paterfamilias," the vagaries of the "Rising Generation!" There are things in this gallery over which the severest misanthrope must chuckle—they are simply irresistible.

Let any one take, say that smallest sketch of the hapless mortal who has turned on the hot water in the bath and cannot turn it off again, and see if he is able to restrain his laughter. In this one gift of producing instant mirth Leech is almost alone. It would be easy to assail his manner and his skill, but for sheer fun, for the invention of downright humorous situation, he is unapproached, except by Cruikshank. He did a few illustrations to Dickens's Christmas books; but his best-known book-illustrations properly so called are to "Uncle Tom's Cabin," the "Comic Histories" of A'Beckett, the "Little Tour in Ireland," and certain sporting novels by the late Mr. Surtees. Tenniel now confines himself almost exclusively to the weekly cartoons with which his name is popularly associated. But years ago he used to invent the most daintily fanciful initial letters; and many of his admirers prefer the serio- grotesque designs of "Punch's Pocket-Book," "Alice in Wonderland," and "Through the Looking-Glass," to the always correctly-drawn but sometimes stiffly-conceived cartoons.

What, for example, could be more delightful than the picture, in "Alice in Wonderland," of the "Mad Tea Party?" Observe the hopelessly distraught expression of the March hare, and the eager incoherence of the hatter! A little further on the pair are trying to squeeze the dormouse into the teapot; and a few pages back the blue caterpillar is discovered smoking his hookah on the top of a mushroom.

He was exactly three inches long, says the veracious chronicle, but what a dignity!—what an oriental flexibility of gesture! Speaking of animals, it must not be forgotten that Tenniel is a master in this line. His "British Lion," in particular, is a most imposing quadruped, and so often in request that it is not necessary to go back to the famous cartoons on the Indian mutiny to seek for examples of that magnificent presence. As a specimen of the artist's treatment of the lesser felidae, the reader's attention is invited to this charming little kitten from "Through the Looking-Glass."

Mr. Tenniel is a link between Leech and the younger school of "Punch" artists, of whom Mr. George du Maurier, Mr. Linley Sambourne, and Mr. Charles Keene are the most illustrious. The first is nearly as popular as Leech, and is certainly a greater favourite with cultivated audiences. He is not so much a humorist as a satirist of the Thackeray type,—unsparing in his denunciation of shams, affectations, and flimsy pretences of all kinds.

A master of composition and accomplished draughtsman, he excels in the delineation of "society"—its bishops, its "professional beauties" and "aesthetes," its nouveaux riches, its distinguished foreigners,- -while now and then (but not too often) he lets us know that if he chose he could be equally happy in depicting the lowest classes.

There was a bar-room scene not long ago in "Punch" which gave the clearest evidence of this. Some of those for whom no good thing is good enough complain, it is said, that he lacks variety—that he is too constant to one type of feminine beauty. But any one who will be at the pains to study a group of conventional "society" faces from any of his "At Homes" or "Musical Parties" will speedily discover that they are really very subtly diversified and contrasted. For a case in point, take the decorously sympathetic group round the sensitive German musician, who is "veeping" over one of his own compositions. Or follow the titter running round that amused assembly to whom the tenor warbler is singing "Me-e-e-et me once again," with such passionate emphasis that the domestic cat mistakes it for a well-known area cry.

As for his ladies, it may perhaps be conceded that his type is a little persistent. Still it is a type so refined, so graceful, so attractive altogether, that in the jarring of less well-favoured realities it is an advantage to have it always before our eyes as a standard to which we can appeal. Mr. du Maurier is a fertile book-illustrator, whose hand is frequently seen in the "Cornhill," and elsewhere. Some of his best work of this kind is in Douglas Jerrold's "Story of a Feather," in Thackeray's "Ballads," and the large edition of the "Ingoldsby Legends," to which Leech, Tenniel, and Cruikshank also contributed.

One of his prettiest compositions is the group here reproduced from "Punch's Almanack" for 1877. The talent of his colleague, Mr. Linley Sambourne, may fairly be styled unique. It is difficult to compare it with anything in its way, except some of the happier efforts of the late Mr. Charles Bennett, to which, nevertheless, it is greatly superior in execution. To this clever artist's invention everything seems to present itself with a train of fantastic accessory so whimsically inexhaustible that it almost overpowers one with its prodigality. Each fresh examination of his designs discloses something overlooked or unexpected. Let the reader study for a moment the famous "Birds of a Feather" of 1875, or that ingenious skit of 1877 upon the rival Grosvenor Gallery and Academy, in which the late President of the latter is shown as the proudest of peacocks, the eyes of whose tail are portraits of Royal Academicians, and whose body-feathers are paint brushes and shillings of admission. Mr. Sambourne is excellent, too, at adaptations of popular pictures,—witness the more than happy parodies of Herrman's "A Bout d'Arguments," and "Une Bonne Histoire." His book-illustrations have been comparatively few, those to Burnand's laughable burlesque of "Sandford and Merton" being among the best.

Rumour asserts that he is at present engaged upon Kingsley's "Water Babies," a subject which might almost be supposed to have been created for his pencil. There are indications, it may be added, that Mr. Sambourne's talents are by no means limited to the domain in which for the present he chooses to exercise them, and it is not impossible that he may hereafter take high rank as a cartoonist. Mr. Charles Keene, a selection from whose sketches has recently been issued under the title of "Our People," is unrivalled in certain bourgeois, military, and provincial types. No one can draw a volunteer, a monthly nurse, a Scotchman, an "ancient mariner" of the watering-place species, with such absolutely humorous verisimilitude. Personages, too, in whose eyes—to use Mr. Swiveller's euphemism—"the sun has shone too strongly," find in Mr. Keene a merciless satirist of their "pleasant vices." Like Leech, he has also a remarkable power of indicating a landscape background with the fewest possible touches. His book-illustrations have been .mainly confined to magazines and novels. Those in "Once a Week" to a "Good Fight," the tale subsequently elaborated by Charles Reade into the "Cloister and the Hearth," present some good specimens of his earlier work. One of these, in which the dwarf of the story is seen climbing up a wall with a lantern at his back, will probably be remembered by many.

After the "Punch" school there are other lesser luminaries. Mr. W. S. Gilbert's drawings to his own inimitable "Bab Ballads" have a perverse drollery which is quite in keeping with that erratic text. Mr. F. Barnard, whose exceptional talents have not been sufficiently recognised, is a master of certain phases of strongly marked character, and, like Mr. Charles Green, has contributed some excellent sketches to the "Household Edition" of Dickens. Mr. Sullivan of "Fun," whose grotesque studies of the "British Tradesman" and "Workman" have recently been republished, has abounding vis comica, but he has hitherto done little in the way of illustrating books. For minute pictorial stocktaking and photographic retention of detail, Mr. Sullivan's artistic memory may almost be compared to the wonderful literary memory of Mr. Sala. Mr. John Proctor, who some years ago (in "Will o' the Wisp") seemed likely to rival Tenniel as a cartoonist, has not been very active in this way; while Mr. Matthew Morgan, the clever artist of the "Tomahawk," has transferred his services to the United States. Of Mr. Bowcher of "Judy," and various other professedly humorous designers, space permits no further mention.

There remains, however, one popular branch of book-illustration, which has attracted the talents of some of the most skilful and original of modern draughtsmen, *i.e.* the embellishment of children's books. From the days when Mulready drew the old "Butterfly's Ball" and "Peacock at Home" of our youth, to those of the delightfully Blake-like fancies of E. V. B., whose "Child's Play" has recently been re-published for the delectation of a new generation of admirers, this has always been a popular and profitable employment; but of late years it has been raised to the level of a fine art. Mr. H. S.

Marks, Mr. J. D. Watson, Mr. Walter Crane, have produced specimens of nursery literature which, for refinement of colouring and beauty of ornament, cannot easily be surpassed.

The equipments of the last named, especially, are of a very high order. He began as a landscapist on wood; he now chiefly devotes himself to the figure; and he seems to have the decorative art at his fingers' ends as a natural gift. Such work as "King Luckieboy's Party" was a revelation in the way of toy books, while the "Baby's Opera" and "Baby's Bouquet" are petits chefs d'oeuvre, of which the sagacious collector will do well to secure copies, not for his nursery, but his library. Nor can his "Mrs. Mundi at Home" be neglected by the curious in quaint and graceful invention. Another book—the "Under the Window" of Miss Kate Greenaway—comes within the same category. Since Stothard, no one has given us such a clear-eyed, soft-faced, happy-hearted childhood; or so poetically "apprehended" the coy reticences, the simplicities, and the small solemnities of little people.

Added to this, the old-world costume in which she usually elects to clothe her characters, lends an arch piquancy of contrast to their innocent rites and ceremonies. Her taste in tinting, too, is very sweet and spring-like; and there is a fresh, pure fragrance about all her pictures as of new-gathered nosegays; or, perhaps, looking to the fashions that she favours, it would be better to say "bow-pots." But the latest "good genius" of this branch of book-illustrating is Mr. Randolph Caldecott, a designer assuredly of the very first order. There is a spontaneity of fun, an unforced invention about everything he does, that is infinitely entertaining.

Other artists draw to amuse us; Mr. Caldecott seems to draw to amuse himself,—and this is his charm. One feels that he must have chuckled inwardly as he puffed the cheeks of his "Jovial Huntsmen;" or sketched that inimitably complacent dog in the "House that Jack Built;" or exhibited the exploits of the immortal "train- band captain" of "famous London town." This last is his masterpiece. Cowper himself must have rejoiced at it,—and Lady Austen. There are two sketches in this book—they occupy the concluding pages—which are especially fascinating. On one, John Gilpin, in a forlorn and flaccid condition, is helped into the house by the sympathising (and very attractive) Betty; on the other he has donned his slippers, refreshed his inner man with a cordial, and over the heaving shoulder of his "spouse," who lies dissolved upon his martial bosom, he is taking the spectators into his confidence with a wink worthy of the late Mr. Buckstone. Nothing more genuine, more heartily laughable, than this set of designs has appeared in our day. And Mr. Caldecott has few limitations. Not only does he draw human nature admirably, but he draws animals and landscapes equally well, so one may praise him without reserve. Though not children's books, mention should here be made of his "Bracebridge Hall," and "Old Christmas," the illustrations to which are the nearest approach to that beau-ideal, perfect sympathy between the artist and the author, with which the writer is acquainted. The cut on page 173 is from the former of these works.

Many of the books above mentioned are printed in colours by various processes, and they are not always engraved on wood. But—to close the account of modern wood-engraving—some brief reference must be made to what is styled the "new American School," as exhibited for the most part in "Scribner's" and other Transatlantic magazines. Authorities, it is reported, shake their heads over these performances. "C'est magnifique, mais ce nest pas la gravure," they whisper. Into the matter in dispute, it is perhaps presumptuous for an "atechnic" to adventure himself. But to the outsider it would certainly seem as if the chief ground of complaint is that the new comers do not play the game according to the old rules, and that this (alleged) irregular mode of procedure tends to lessen the status of the engraver as an artist. False or true, this, it may fairly be advanced, has nothing whatever to do with the matter, as far, at least, as the public are concerned.

For them the question is, simply and solely—What is the result obtained? The new school, availing themselves largely of the assistance of photography, are able to dispense, in a great measure, with the old tedious method of drawing on the block, and to leave the artist to choose what medium he prefers for his design—be it oil, water-colour, or black and white—concerning themselves only to reproduce its characteristics on the wood. This is, of course, a deviation from the method of Bewick. But would Bewick have adhered to his method in these days? Even in his last hours he was seeking for new processes. What we want is to get nearest to the artist himself with the least amount of interpretation or intermediation on the part of the engraver. Is engraving on copper to be reproduced, we want a facsimile if possible, and not a rendering into something which is supposed to be the orthodox utterance of wood-engraving. Take, for example, the copy of Schiavonetti's engraving of Blake's Death's Door in "Scribner's Magazine" for June 1880, or the cut from the same source at page 131 of this book. These are faithful line for line transcriptions, as far as wood can give them, of the original copper-plates; and, this being the case, it is not to be wondered at that the public, who, for a few pence can have practical facsimiles of Blake, of Cruikshank, or of Whistler, are loud in their appreciation of the "new American School." Nor are its successes confined to reproduction in facsimile. Those who look at the exquisite illustrations, in the same periodical, to the "Tile Club at Play," to Roe's "Success with Small Fruits," and Harris's "Insects Injurious to Vegetation,"—to say nothing of the selected specimens in the recently issued "Portfolios"—will see that the latest comers can hold their own on all fields with any school that has gone before.

Besides copperplate and wood, there are many processes which have been and are still employed for book-illustrations, although the brief limits of this chapter make any account of them impossible. Lithography was at one time very popular, and, in books like Roberts's "Holy Land," exceedingly effective. The "Etching Club" issued a number of books circa 1841-52; and most of the work of "Phiz" and Cruikshank was done with the needle.

It is probable that, as we have already seen, the impetus given to modern etching by Messrs. Hamerton, Seymour Haden, and Whistler, will lead to a specific revival of etching as a means of book-illustration. Already beautiful etchings have for some time appeared in "L'Art," the "Portfolio," and the "Etcher;" and at least one book of poems has been entirely illustrated in this way,—the poems of Mr. W. Bell Scott. For reproducing old engravings, maps, drawings, and the like, it is not too much to say that we shall never get anything much closer than the facsimiles of M. Amand-Durand and the Typographic Etching and Autotype Companies. But further improvements will probably have to be made before these can compete commercially with wood-engraving as practised by the "new American School."

"Of making many books," 'twais said, "There is no end;" and who thereon The ever-running ink doth shed But probes the words of Solomon: Wherefore we now, for colophon, From London's city drear and dark, In the year Eighteen Eight-One, Reprint them at the press of Clark.

# Bibliography


Arrow, Kenneth J.: *Social Choice and Individual Values*, New York, Wiley, 1951.

Campbell, J.Y., Lo, A.W.: *The Econometrics of Financial Markets*, Princeton University Press, 1996.

Chaudhuri, Pramit: *The Indian Economy: Poverty and Development*, New York, St. Martin's Press, 1979.

Dhingra, C.: *The Indian Economy: Resources, Planning, Development, and Problems*, Delhi, Sultan Chand, 1983.

Greer, Douglas F.: *Industrial Organization and Public Policy*, MacMillan Publishing Company, 1992.

Ishwar, C.: *The Indian Economy: Resources, Planning, Development, and Problems*, Delhi, Sultan Chand, 1983.

Little, I.M.D.: *India: Macroeconomics and Political Economy, 1964-1991*, Washington, World Bank, 1994.

Mongia, J.N.: *India's Economic Development Strategies, 1951-2000 A.D.*. New Delhi, Allied, 1986.

Pranab, K.: *The Political Economy of Development in India*, Delhi, Oxford University Press, 1984.

Sargent, Thomas J.: *Dynamic Macroeconomic Theory*, Harvard University Press, 1987.

Tirole, Jean: *The Theory of Industrial Organization*, MIT Press, 1988.

Williamson, Jeffrey G.: *American Inequality: A Macroeconomic History*, New York, Academic Press, 1980.

Xavier Sala-i-Martin: *Economic Growth*. McGraw-Hill, 1995.

# Index

## I



## L



## M



## N



## O

□□□